D1557921

American Literary Regionalism in a Global Age

American Literary
Regionalism
in a Global Age

PHILIP JOSEPH

LOUISIANA STATE UNIVERSITY PRESS

BATON ROUGE

Published by Louisiana State University Press
Copyright © 2007 by Louisiana State University Press
All rights reserved
Manufactured in the United States of America
First printing

Designer: Laura Roubique Gleason
Typeface: Whitman
Typesetter: The Composing Room of Michigan, Inc.
Printer and binder: Edwards Brothers, Inc.

Library of Congress Cataloging-in-Publication Data

Joseph, Philip, 1967–
    American literary regionalism in a global age / Philip Joseph.
        p. cm.
    Includes bibliographical references and index.
    ISBN-13: 978-0-8071-3188-6 (cloth : alk. paper)
    ISBN-10: 0-8071-3188-1 (cloth : alk. paper)
    1. Regionalism in literature.   2. American fiction—19th century—History and
criticism.   3. American fiction—20th century—History and criticism.   4. Community
in literature.   5. Literature and society—United States—History—19th century.
6. Literature and society—United States—History—20th century.   I. Title.
    PS374.R4J67 2007
    813.008′032—dc22

                                                                        2006030163

For Gillian

CONTENTS

PREFACE

SINCE THIS IS A STUDY NOT ONLY ABOUT AMERICAN REGIONALISM but also about literature and its relation to community, it may come as no surprise that Benedict Anderson's *Imagined Communities* has played a large part in my thinking. With respect to Anderson's influence, my book has plenty of company in literary studies, where *Imagined Communities* has been thriving for more than a decade. Anderson places literature (specifically novels) and reading at the center of his analysis, treating them as indispensable components of nation-building. According to his introduction, the nation is a community in which "the members . . . will never know most of their fellow-members, meet them, or even hear of them, yet in the minds of each lives the image of their communion." He asserts that few technologies are as integral to this sense of abstract communion as the novel—a view that may explain the appeal of *Imagined Communities* to literary scholars. If reading novels has taught modern subjects to think about their connections to unknown fellow nationals, then studying these artifacts in retrospect has to be a significant endeavor. For many literary scholars, *nation* became a compelling category specifically because it provided strong justification for the study of literature.

Such reasoning motivated me, at least, when I began writing this book. What drew me to the study of regionalism originally was that it offered an intriguing instance of literature's contribution to nation-building. Here was a body of literature that focused ostensibly on the local, face-to-face community. Yet, as many scholars have pointed out, this focus obscured the work that regionalism did in creating one or several national reading publics, with shared points of origin and a shared group history.

Although nation-building was my approach when I began this project, the focus has shifted over time. American literary regionalism, I continue to believe, played its part in establishing public communities of national readers, but those publics have themselves been continuously preoccupied with the very real and very modern question of *local* belonging. In other words, it no longer seems sufficient to treat the civil community at the heart of regional-ism suspiciously, as an instrument for constituting the nation. What matters about regionalism is not simply that it made readers aware of their national-ity, but that it made them think about their nationality as a question concern-ing local solidarity and commitment. Throughout the nineteenth and twenti-eth centuries, American citizens have taken their communities at the local level very seriously. Regionalist writing has made of those communities—the power that they possess or lack and the nature of life within them—an area of primary thematic interest. Regionalism's focus on the local community is thus much more than a nostalgic failure to come to terms with the nationalist work that the literature is really doing.

My interest in regionalism's local communities can be accounted for in several ways. First, my experience living in Buffalo, Durham, New York, and finally Denver over the past ten years has continued to demonstrate the pas-sionate investments that many people make in their neighborhood associa-tions, reading groups, religious congregations, recreational leagues, lecture series, and activist groups. It surprised me to learn, after finishing an earlier version of this work, that a vibrant conversation about such local communities was under way in disciplines other than literary studies. Political theorists and sociologists were examining civil society, that social realm between nation and family, as an integral part of a participatory democracy. Moreover, they were writing about the local community as a cornerstone of a healthy civic life. The "civil society debate" was raging in the social sciences, with scholars looking to local groups not only as ballast to offset modern alienation but as sources of political power, with the capacity to influence government and corporations. This debate had an obvious relation to literary regionalism. Like civil society advocates, regionalist writers took the local community as a discursive topos, exploring how this form of association would respond to the challenges of modern life. These writers addressed their readership through the mediation of print; but they assumed, among their readers, a shared concern for those persistent communities of proximity and presence at the center of our civil society.

American literary regionalism appears to me now, therefore, as part of the same modern conversation on local community to which civil society advo-cates contribute. The regionalist writers I examine were writing in the late nineteenth and early twentieth centuries. But because they share a set of mod-ern conditions and communal concerns that continue to preoccupy us today, their writing has the potential to influence our own discussions of community.

Such a potential for textual travel from one context to another has led me to rethink my approach to literary history. Instead of focusing on how literature reflected and helped shape the public world in which it first appeared, I inquire into the viability of regionalism in the public worlds of today and tomorrow. My claim is that the works in question have a persistent timeliness about them and that we ought to foster their presence in contemporary contexts. The questions that guide me, accordingly, revolve around the temporal reach of American regionalism rather than its situatedness: to what extent, I ask, does regionalism speak to contemporary readers living in a globalized world? And to what extent does it speak to them in a specifically literary way?

Although this project has followed me to different places, its origin was decisively in Buffalo. For providing valuable feedback and guidance at many different stages of writing, I want to thank, first of all, Ken Dauber, Stacy Hubbard, Carrie Tirado Bramen, Neil Schmitz, and Deidre Lynch, each of whom has shaped my thinking about regionalism and literary scholarship in memorable ways. All five read an early version of this work with great critical care, providing essential comments in writing and in conversation. I am especially grateful to Nancy Glazener, who continues to invest generously and insightfully in my work and who suggested the civil society debate as a relevant research area.

A number of others have been essential to the project as readers and interlocutors: Jake York and John Plotz have read the study almost in its entirety and made me think much more sharply about it. Adam Lerner made substantial contributions to chapter 1, which also benefited from readings by Kent Casper, Susie Linville, Ross Posnock, Phil Weiser, and all the members of the University of Colorado—Denver English Department Colloquium. The second chapter began as a seminar paper in Carrie Bramen's American 1890s course and became a journal article in *Studies in American Fiction* 26.2 (Autumn 1998): 147–70 before being revised during several stages of manuscript preparation. I am grateful to the anonymous reader for *Studies in American Fiction*, who helped to make the treatment much better than it was, as well as to Kim Miller, Sam Stoloff, Patrick Wilkinson, and Joewon Yoon for their helpful comments on an early version. An anonymous reviewer for *MELUS* provided helpful and encouraging comments on a shorter version of chapter 3, which appeared in *MELUS* 27.4 (Winter 2002): 3–32. Chapter 6 appeared in somewhat different form as "The Verdict from the Porch: Zora Neale Hurston and Reparative Justice," in *American Literature* 74.3 (September 2002): 455–83. For valuable contributions to that article, I am indebted to Wai Chee Dimock, Jonathan Grossman, Frances Kerr, Sean McCann, and the anonymous readers for *American Literature*. Material from all three articles is reprinted here by permission of *Studies in American Fiction*, *MELUS*, and *American Literature*.

Moving the project from typescript to print has been more involved and complicated than I ever imagined. Brian Lloyd, Julie Crawford, and John-Michael Rivera led me through the early stages of that process. At the Louisiana State University Press, Candis LaPrade and John Easterly have been wonderfully responsive editors and sage navigators. Lois Crum copyedited the manuscript with great precision and care. I am deeply grateful, as well, to the anonymous reader for LSU Press, whose comments improved the book and indicated an especially thoughtful assessment of it.

The English Department at the University of Colorado–Denver and, earlier, the History and Literature Program at Harvard University have offered nurturing environments in which to complete and revise the project. I owe special thanks to Dan Itzkovitz and Natasha Lifton for welcoming me into their family for two nights a week in Cambridge; the junior faculty at the University of Colorado–Denver for encouraging me in this project and then making me forget about it on Thursday nights; and Brad Mudge for allowing me time to focus on getting the manuscript into print. A grant from the Mark Diamond Fund at SUNY-Buffalo provided resources for beginning the project. I feel grateful always to Barry O'Connell, whose mentoring helped get me started in my career.

I have received a wealth of support and replenishment from students, friends, and family, a company too numerous to thank individually. The group that has been closest to me for the duration of the project, however, is my immediate family. For their emotional generosity, their limitless love and support, and the pleasure of their too-infrequent company, I thank, insufficiently, my parents, Micki and Gary Joseph, and my brother, Dan Joseph. My sons, Julius and Desmond, brought new sweetness and adventures into my private world just as I was finishing the manuscript.

All those mentioned above have changed the project in subtle and sometimes significant ways. The hardest debt to acknowledge, however, is the largest one. Gillian Silverman has helped me work through ideas, discussed books with me, edited my writing as if it were her own, and played with me when I was morbidly preoccupied. She has always been my most trusted reader and my best inspiration.

American Literary Regionalism in a Global Age

1

INTRODUCTION

Regionalism and the Literary Encounter
with Local Community

SINCE THE RISE OF THE WORLD WIDE WEB OVER THE LAST DECADE, U.S. and Canadian university administrators have been touting the benefits of distance learning, and York University history professor David Noble is justifiably angry about it. In a series of articles assembled in a recently published book, Noble maintains that the possibility for great profits from expanded educational networks and the resultant partnerships between media-savvy corporations and universities threatens to commodify "the educational function of the university" and "the activity of instruction itself."[1]

Noble concedes that the new technologies may enable a greater number of students to get their diplomas and to obtain perhaps a modicum of vocational training. But what of the pedagogical costs of the virtual university: the deterioration of the student-teacher relationship, the standardization of "an essentially unscripted and undetermined process," the creation of a two-tier system in which a select group of privileged students continue to benefit from dynamic interaction with professors while the masses settle for an exclusively electronic communication? As Noble explains, "Education is a process that necessarily entails an interpersonal (not merely interactive) relationship between people—student and teacher (and student and student). . . . The actual content of the educational experience is defined by this relationship between people and the chief determinant of quality education is the establishment and enrichment of this relationship."[2] According to Noble, the learning process, which demands dynamic and nuanced communication between individuals, would be deeply compromised if virtual interaction simply replaced face-to-face classroom and campus communities.

Noble's critical stance toward an unexamined use of technological prosthesis, his insistence on securing a communal interaction mediated primarily by human speech and perception, places him at the tail end of a nineteenth- and twentieth-century conversation on local communities and their necessary place within expanding national and global networks. The participation of ed-

1

ucators in this ongoing conversation on local community is nothing new. What we now call distance learning had a previous incarnation in the correspondence education movement, which reached its peak popularity in the 1920s before being undermined by a wave of skepticism resembling Noble's.[3]

Outside the realm of education, the electronic infrastructure has its nineteenth-century analogues in the spread of telegraph and telephone lines, the increased reach and speed of the postal service, and the print distribution networks that allowed book and magazine publishers in the United States to reach ever wider audiences.[4] In all of these cases, technological mediation deepened the sense of abstract, interpersonal relations. Some voices glorified the new technology because it transcended the apparent limitations of time and space, while critics of "progress" pointed to the impoverished understanding, compromised forms of knowledge, and loss of intimate communal relations that the expanded networks seemed to entail.

Underlying the criticism and unease over an excessive reliance on technological communication has always been a belief that conditions of presence make an important difference in human relations. Sociologist Erving Goffman regarded this belief as a central premise of social organization: "When individuals are in one another's presence, a multitude of words, gestures, acts, and minor events become available, whether desired or not, through which one who is present can intentionally or unintentionally symbolize his character and his attitudes."[5] Sharing concrete space with others changes our relations to them, bringing the body fully to bear on social interaction. Mediated by technology, encounters between individuals will inevitably exclude certain senses (touch and smell, for instance), behaviors (the handshake or hug), and threats (physical aggression, unsolicited touching, or illness). In the immediate presence of others, we rely on the body as our only instrument to send and receive messages. In addition, we devise a set of shifting rules on interaction in order to ensure that the risks of gathering together have been appropriately managed.[6] These conditions have led artists and critics to regard local communities, organized on the basis of frequent face-to-face encounters between members, as specific in kind and worthy of attention. "The Great Community," wrote John Dewey, "can never possess all the qualities which mark a local community. . . . There is no substitute for the vitality and depth of close and direct intercourse and attachment."[7] For Dewey and many others before and after him, religious congregations, neighborhood and township associations, union chapters, reading groups, and community theater all fulfill a legitimate need to meet other people with whom we share a set of significant activities, values, and/or beliefs, on bodily terms.[8]

This book examines the place of American literary regionalism in this on-going conversation on local community. By regionalism, I am referring specifically to two self-conscious movements in American literary history, both of which focused on rural hamlets and urban neighborhoods with marginal access to the centers of economic and political power. One of these movements reached its peak in the 1880s and early 1890s, and the other one during the 1920s and 1930s. In both cases, contributing writers understood their own work as crucial to the national discussion of locality. At the heart of their fiction were communities defined by the proximity and familiarity of their members and the durability of their commitments to one another amid modernity's expanded networks. Accordingly, I treat literary regionalism's centrality in the conversation on local community as its most important attribute.

Rather than recovering a wide and representative sampling of writers from this literary tradition, however, I limit myself to those most capable of making a lasting modern contribution. Regionalism is essential in illustrating, through narrative fiction, the predicaments posed by broad communication networks and the continued importance of local forms of social organization. It also, however, presents us with many models of local community that are incompatible with a globalized world, a world where people and ideas circulate widely and populations often have little say in the regulation of state and market. Many regionalist texts feed the fantasy of a hermetic community, sealed off against the corrosive effects of modernity. Part of the challenge, therefore, is to distinguish between versions of regionalism that speak nostalgically to modern readers and those that might enter actively into a more progressive public dialogue. How do specific writers unsettle and redirect what is often a reactionary conversation about local community? How do they reconcile values like home, neighborhood, and locality with democratic ideals like freedom of movement, individual self-determination, collective empowerment, and open-ended debate? Approached selectively, literary regionalism can help us to address the challenges raised by virtual communication and to imagine democratic forms of local community in response to them.

Regionalism and the Civil Society Debate

By recognizing and responding to the modern yearning for local community, regionalism overlaps in compelling ways with our contemporary discussion of American civil society. The concept of civil society has a long history, beginning in the seventeenth century and extending into the twenty-first in a dizzying variety of forms. It emerged at the moment when God and king were displaced as the primary sources of social order, when people began to view the members of a society themselves as its ordering agents. *Civil society* was the name given to this internally generated mode of social organization.[9] From the beginning of its conceptual history, political theorists offered divergent accounts of what human attributes a civil society, conceived in these terms, could rely on and what it should look like in its ideal form. What was consistent was a question that nearly all who invoked the term addressed: How could the need for social order and a shared public vision of the Good be squared with the autonomy of individual private actors?[10]

In the nineteenth century, responses to this question began to focus on the social realm between the family and the state, where individuals could associate with one another voluntarily.[11] This realm had become increasingly important given the limitations of family and state: while the family unit restricted social choice (most familial relations were matters of kinship and birth), the state was both remote in its governing operations and backed by access to legal violence.[12] Civil society occupied an important in-between space, borrowing characteristics from both sides and offering subjects alternative forms of social membership.

What concerns me here is the resuscitation of the nineteenth-century civil society concept over the past decade and a half. Following the fall of the Berlin Wall, eastern Europeans began to invoke the concept to measure their burgeoning democracies against the totalitarian past. The mark of a democracy for many in eastern Europe was a civil society composed of relatively independent social groups, free of state surveillance and domination. Responding to this renewed interest in civil society, a range of American social scientists and political theorists began using the term to denote previous periods in American history when voluntary membership in social groups was particularly high.[13] The tendency among these critics has been to view a vigorous civil society as an alternative not so much to a vast and coercive state apparatus, but to a body politic that has retreated unhappily into detached privacy and given up on political participation.[14] Civil society advocates have continually reminded us of the need for stronger ties to local communities, which provide citizens with both a concrete sense of belonging and an instrument for shaping corporate and government decision making. For many such advocates, a major goal of public policy must be to sustain local communities as bulwarks against social isolation and political disempowerment.

Participating in the civil society debate means, inevitably, taking a position on the liberal individual subject; for this subject, depending on one's vision, is either the entity that must be protected by a civic community or an obstacle to a fully realized social order. Michael Sandel, in presenting his argument about the decline of American civil society, has argued that real change hinges on a diminished faith in the individual subject. Under liberalism, he argues, the fundamental unit in public life is the unencumbered self, whose obligations and duties derive strictly from choice rather than from inheritance and circumstance.[15] Restoring civic communities and reinvigorating public life require replacing this unencumbered self with one whose loyalties and solidarities are given rather than chosen. For Sandel, the idea of the originally encumbered subject licenses citizens, as members of one or another community, to bring the full force of their morality into politics, since properly socialized citizens cannot simply remove their notion of the good society upon entering the public sphere, as if that notion were a piece of clothing. Likewise, the concept of the originally encumbered subject licenses government to restrict individual choices, as individuals are never originally free to choose their own values and beliefs in the first place.[16] To return to the question that civil society theorists have repeatedly posed: For Sandel, the social integration of individuals—as participants in local communities and contributors to public life—must take precedence over their rights as freely choosing, autonomous actors.

Through my analysis of literary regionalism, I implicitly question the claim that a healthy civil society, consisting of strong local communities and widespread political engagement, must rest on the conceptual foundation of the encumbered subject.[17] As regionalism has demonstrated in at least some of its varieties, the rejection of voluntarism—or, to put it differently, the rigid distinction between active engagement in collective life and the individual's right to choose between versions of the good life, as if the two cannot be fought for together—has worrisome consequences. Sandel may be right that our loyalties and solidarities are not all originally chosen. Still, most of us live within situations that render our approach to the good life indeterminate, whatever that approach may look like in its original articulation. That is to say, we are confronted by a variety of life paths and systems of value, most of which have no necessary claim on the determination of our decisions. Modern subjects often find themselves encumbered, paradoxically, by a spectrum of possibilities. Given this particular kind of encumbrance, there is an urgency about granting the individual a voluntarist authority. In an age that inevitably complicates the process of social affiliation, original ties can become binding only through the mediation of a deliberating arbiter. Recognizing and protecting the rights of this arbiter may well lower the stakes of political activity by limiting the nature of political participation, restricting the degree to which moral and religious positions may be brought into the realm of government.[18] But the cost of a less-than-perfect system of self-government is well worth the benefit of a communal life that values the subject's unpredictable destiny and self-determination.

For the civil society proponents with whom this book is aligned, the objective is only partly to create powerful local communities with an engaged citizenry. It is also to ensure that such communities allow for individual mobility and choice and that they accommodate citizens who live in an interconnected, nomadic world. As E. J. Dionne Jr. has written, "the quest for new forms of civil society can be seen as a rational response to social change—not a rebellion against the modern world but a new attempt to deal with modernity's discontents and dislocations. It is an attempt to build the social, communal, ethnic, and neighborhood associations that suit these times." Giving expression to a similar desire and conception, the art critic Lucy Lippard calls herself "an emotional nomad and a radical . . . playing the relatively conservative values of permanence and rootedness off against restlessness and a constructed 'multicenteredness.'"[19] While I would characterize the values that she invokes as "duration" and "togetherness" rather than "permanence" and "rootedness," I am drawn as well to the possibility of negotiating between such values on the one hand and modern realities like migration and multiple group affiliation on the other. The local community need not preclude "multicenteredness." A defining limit (perhaps based on a set of religious practices, political goals, educational aims, or environmental concerns) will always differentiate a community, but that border can easily be imagined in an adaptive form, one that allows for revised collective agreements and for the movement of people and ideas into and out of the community.

Literary Endurance and the Presence of Regionalism

One of my claims, then, is that regionalist fiction can make visible and apparent some of the forms of local community upon which a strong modern civil society depends. In the process, regionalism can function correctively in relation to versions of the civil society argument that seem unsuited to a globalized world. Approached selectively, regionalism reminds us, for example, that we can borrow from the communitarian critique of apathetic citizenship and abstract belonging without resigning ourselves to the communitarian view of the encumbered subject-citizen. In this instance and in a variety of other ways as well, regionalism has a continued place in our discursive life. Writers who participated in regionalism's flourishing and who responded with sharp critical judgment to conceptions of local community circulating in their time can have a vital impact on our own public discussion.

This emphasis on the current cultural effects of the regionalist text gives this book a specific kind of historicist slant, one that turns on the expressive power of literature over time. Much of the influential recent literary and historical criticism on American regionalism inquires, first and foremost, into how regionalist texts functioned during the period of their original production and reception. Such criticism provides important contextual explanations for regionalism's emergence and popularity in an attempt to trace current assumptions about place and identity to their cultural origins. Because many of these critics see regionalism as crucial to nineteenth- and early-twentieth-century nation-building, their primary concern is to contribute to a genealogy of American nationhood.[20] The objects they study offer evidence of literature's active engagement in a *previous* context, related through a chain of causation to our own.[21] While I also explore the particular uses to which regionalism was put over the course of its history, I begin by treating this group of texts less as distant evidence and more as a body of writing capable of an active, transformative role in the lives of contemporary and future readers. I am interested in how regionalism continues to live over time as a specific kind of pedagogy, how it might impact contemporary readers and enter into current debates. My aim is to recognize the specific value that regionalist writers have as active interlocutors in the contemporary context and to look back at the tradition with that value in mind. Just as readers alter texts, so too can texts, when accorded their power, shape public dialogue across vast temporal fields. If regionalism can help us to understand how we got to where we are, it can also help us to influence where we are going.

Encouraging regionalism to function as a durable discursive agent, however, requires approaching the tradition cautiously. Despite its potential for introducing vital democratic perspectives into the conversation on local community, the tradition has often embraced communal cohesion more than individual mobility, cultural preservation more than exchange with an outside world. One of my central contentions is that regionalism speaks most pertinently to us when it recognizes a dynamic, mutually informing relationship between members of a locality on the one hand and the institutions and cultures of a globalized world on the other.[22] Thus the versions of regionalism foregrounded in this book envision local communities in dialogue with the outside world, capable both of shaping governmental decisions and of benefiting from the knowledge and experiences of external peoples. Where regionalism has denied such an open and dynamic relationship, it has tended toward disempowering the citizens of local communities, refusing them control over the forces that figure most powerfully in their own lives. Moreover, it has promoted local communities that are cut off from external sources of plurality and dissent—the very sources that might lead a community to rethink, rather than blindly reproduce, its habitual mores and practices. Michael Walzer has written that "[t]he exact character of our associational life is something that has to be argued about."[23] Yet in some versions of regionalism, the priority is not a vital debate over the character of one or another community, but the smooth transmission of a community's culture from generation to generation, undisturbed by external values and knowledge. Such versions of regionalism leave us little to discuss, treating "the character of our associational life" as something to be preserved intact, a more or less finished product shaped by local geography or inherited culture, or both.[24] These versions seem to yearn for the end of the very conversation in which they take part. They imply that the character of authentic communities can only be replicated, not debated or called into question.

Responding to this emphasis on cultural preservation and purity, several recent critics from different positions on the political spectrum have sought to expose regionalism—and the value it places on locality—for its refusal to accept historical change. From the Marxist left, Roberto Dainotto argues that regionalist literature posits a preindustrial pastoral place as a resolution to the conflicts of modernity and that, in doing so, it conceals "the historical forces, struggles, and tensions that made a culture what it is."[25] Regionalism uses the epistemological category of place to naturalize culture—that is, to render it impervious to historical processes taking place elsewhere in the world. "To put it bluntly," Dainotto writes, "regionalism is the figure of an otherness that is, essentially, otherness *from,* and against history" (9). He defines the otherness as an offspring of the same desire for "cultural homogeneity" (20) that informs romantic nationalism: "regionalism is merely taking the place and role that once was given to nationalism: they speak the same language, they foster the same desires, menacing and *unheimlich,* of purity and authenticity" (173).

While Dainotto gives a cogent account of the misuses of "place" in regionalism, in reducing the discourse to pastoralism and organic community, he fails to offer any alternative approach to life at the local level. "[C]an any interest of class continue to exist if the sense of locality prevails?" he asks. To open oneself to history is to renounce not only "place," it would seem, but sustained local attachments, mediated by specific beliefs and practices, altogether. Who, other than an intellectual, would wish to face "history" under such abstract circumstances and at such concrete cost?[26] Dainotto urges readers to embrace a class struggle that seems incompatible—rather than contin- uous—with the commitments and values distinguishing particular groups within that struggle at any given time. There is only one worldwide struggle for Dainotto, and its success rests on an unambiguous negation of the local community.

Whereas Dainotto pits regionalism against class solidarity, Philip Fisher contrasts regionalism with the broad and loosely fitted cultural frameworks that characterize and, in Fisher's account, give democratic value to American nationality. In Fisher's *Still the New World*, the driving force behind American "democratic social space" is technological innovation, the endless cycle of cre- ation and destruction that introduces new worlds, one after another, in suc- cession: steamboat travel replaces horse and buggy, trains replace steam, and cars and planes follow. Each time a new and reproducible technology alters the national landscape, citizens are turned effectively into immigrants once again. Under these conditions, the common national idea must remain, in Fisher's terminology, highly "abstract" and "minimal," removed from local realities and specific histories, able to accommodate the individual's need for continuous change and adaptation. Fisher's repeated reference to innovations in trans- portation as representative of technological newness in general is no coinci- dence. For Fisher understands the overarching and unbinding national ab- straction in relation not only to temporal change, but to spatial mobility as well. As technology spreads, establishing a source of thin mediation that ex- tends to all present and potential citizens, Americans readily transplant them- selves just as they adapt to new phases of national history. The outcome is a national self-understanding unattached to concrete places and times. As Fisher sees it, regionalism therefore represents a *pathological* reaction to the "culture of creative destruction" and its penchant for starting over. "[I]n Amer- ica," Fisher writes, "regionalism's real alternative is mobility, change over time, both changes that we make and changes that occur around us in the economic frame within which we conduct our lives."[27] Whereas American nationality promotes turnover and adaptation, regionalism clings conservatively to sta- bility and the transmission of values, habits, and forms of expression from one generation to the next. Whereas Americanism encourages movement across mass society, regionalism embraces discrete, traditional cultures to which sub- jects are exclusively committed. In short, regionalism is code here for spatial and temporal rootedness and, accordingly, for the rejection of modernity.

Fisher's account raises what seem to me obvious questions about the dem- ocratic benefits of a rudderless pursuit of technological innovation. Are we to suppose that democracy would necessarily be served by maximizing the speed with which new technology replaces old? Such changes clearly privilege those who can afford to pay for them and make them familiar. What Fisher's account cries out for is a public supervision of "creative destruction," an engaged civic sphere, working with the state, to check and reform the market. Yet he disqualifies as reactionary the very body of literature that might contribute to achieving this goal. Regionalism can make such a contribution because it does not simply celebrate the local community; in the hands of writers like Hamlin Garland and Abraham Cahan, for instance, it regards the local community as a potential instrument of political, economic, even aesthetic empowerment for those who are most vulnerable to market forces.

If Fisher's critique of regionalism neglects this literature's potential contribution to an engaged civic sphere, it also treats the values of solidarity and belonging—values that regionalism so often embraces—as dispensable ones. Recognizing these values in our conversations about "democratic space" seems crucial to avoiding the kind of pathological rootedness that Fisher rightly stigmatizes.[28] As Benjamin Barber warns, "it is a basic law of modern politics that where democratic communities cannot be found to do the work of solidarity and identity which human existence seems to require, undemocratic communities that do so will appear." Barber reminds us here that a potential consequence of an impoverished discussion of local belonging is a return to a reactionary, tradition-bound localism.[29] Enriching that discussion as a literary critic means neither abandoning a body of literature that consistently values local solidarity, nor simply applauding it for doing so. It means rather choosing carefully the depictions of local solidarity and belonging that we would like to import into our own conversations.

Fisher and Dainotto are right, then, to be skeptical toward regionalism. As both writers insist, the history of regionalism has been suffused with longing for primeval communities, determined not by worldly subjects in dialogue with each other but by local traditions putatively rooted in land and in blood. Literary regionalism often appears to be at the center of a public conversation on locality that has become all but closed to the modern realities of transcultural movement and multicentered subjectivity. But contrary to what Fisher and Dainotto suggest, such instances do not exhaust the category's history, nor should they discredit the attention regionalism has always paid to the local community. In the texts that this book foregrounds, writers situate local communities in the same modern temporal frame that they themselves and their readers occupy. The subjects within these fictive communities insist on shaping modern history, not exempting themselves from it; and they often possess the same capacity for imaginative movement and shifting opinion central to the activities of reading, writing, and aesthetic production. Now as then, the literary voices that give expression to such communities need to be heard, not simply collapsed into a single category defined by its antimodernism.

I distinguish such voices from some of the major reactionary currents in American regionalism's history. Focusing on the two periods of regionalism's greatest flourishing, the 1890s and the 1920s and 1930s, I give primary place to writers who attempted to revitalize the discussion of local community by situating a given community and its subjects squarely in an interconnected nation and world. The writers at the core of each chapter—Hamlin Garland, Abraham Cahan, Willa Cather, and Zora Neale Hurston—chafed against the conventions for depicting local communities that were promoted by the major magazines and book presses of their times. In the 1890s, much "local color" regionalism tended to reinforce the drive toward national "incorporation" and postwar reunion, which benefited from the appearance that local communities were disengaged from national politics and, at the same time, easily available for touristic visitation; in the 1920s and 1930s, many "new regionalists" sought to curb the impact of tourism on local cultural difference, promoting insular and unchanging folk communities as the predominant form of national social organization. The writers that I feature express a sophisticated skepticism toward such tendencies. That skepticism, alongside an accelerated history of expanding markets and innovation in communication technology, equips their work to influence an enduring modern conversation on local community. Studied in a discriminating manner, regionalism survives over time as something more than an artifact or a body of evidence. It makes its claim as shaper and guide in the highly fraught interpretation of the local community as a crucial building block of a strong civic life.

Making Room for Literature

I have proposed that literary regionalism can contribute to our public discussion of civil society and that it can lead to the enrichment of modern local communities. Thus far, however, my concern has *not* been to distinguish the literary from other modes of writing, since other modes—philosophical, sociological, or legal, for instance—aspire to the same durability and diachronic influence. I have offered, simply, a method for sorting out the models of local communities best suited to enduring in a global world and impacting our own conversation. The question that arises at this point is whether literature ought to enter our conversation on locality as a specific kind of writing, given its particular attributes and aspirations. Having argued for a tradition with the capacity to shape a public conversation over time, I inquire here into the specific nature of its agency. How might regionalism as *literature* contribute to the conversation on local community?

Two primary assumptions inform this question: first, while literature is in dialogue with other historical discourses, it is also responsive, at any given time, to aspirations that differentiate it; second, while literature has appeared in vastly different guises over time, it has also exhibited *some* degree of constancy in the functions that it serves. How literature functions, in other words, depends on historical contingencies, but history itself is defined by continuities as well as discontinuities, and the continuities give rise to significant repetitions and patterns within literary history. Wary of participating in canon-building projects, recent scholars have often avoided privileging any of these patterns as normative, seeking instead to leave the question of literary value wide open in our time. Yet a brief look at the collections of recent essays addressing regionalist literature outside the United States shows quite clearly that the question has once again become relevant to critics, no matter their political positions or affinity for noncanonical literature.

For instance, in *The Places of History: Regionalism Revisited in Latin America*, Doris Sommer equates literature with the plenitude of its historical context when she writes that "[l]iterariness, like historicity, is what fits badly into paradigms." Sommer's word for the distinguishing feature is "historicity," by which she seems to mean a tendency toward immersion in a material world that does not conform to the most determinative rational abstractions. Rather than a direct, ideological opposition to the reigning "paradigms," literature suffuses itself in the disordered and contradictory living matter surrounding it. It enters our world as a historical object laden with doubt and irreverence. In contrast, K. D. M. Snell's introduction to a collection entitled *The Regional Novel in Britain and Ireland, 1800–1990* treats literary regionalism, as opposed to "conventional historical evidence," as counterfactual; the function of regional fiction, she argues, is partly to furnish a "didactic model of how things ought to be."[30] For Sommer the important attribute is literature's abundant historicity, for Snell its capacity to imagine new historical worlds. But in either case, regionalism, with greater or lesser success, gives expression to an exemplary form of literary distinctiveness.

The fact that two scholars studying two different areas of the world should both at this moment concern themselves with defining literary value comes as no surprise.[31] State funding for higher education has been dwindling, and neither administrators nor students seem particularly clear about the value of literature in contemporary society. Why should students pay such close attention to literary texts when their lives often have little to do with specifically literary interpretation? With virtual experience becoming increasingly more visual and print communication more abbreviated and utilitarian, what role do literary texts have in a twenty-first-century education? In this kind of precarious climate, literary critics have been forced to ponder the importance of studying their chosen cultural objects. The intradisciplinary question of what texts should be studied in courses and included in anthologies needs to be understood now in the context of how critics should go about defending the discipline and how they can retain conviction about literary study when so many others within the university devalue it.

The new context for critics becomes more apparent when we compare the brief comments by Sommer and Snell to Barbara Herrnstein Smith's *Contingencies of Value* (1988), which persuasively challenges traditional notions of literary value that at one time were preeminent in the field. In the interest of undermining the epistemological grounds of orthodox canon formation and maintenance, Herrnstein Smith exposes the "radically contingent" way in which value has always been assigned. Value does not inhere in a text, nor can determinations of value be arrived at objectively; rather they depend on "the continuous process of our interactions with our environments or what could also be described as the continuous interplay among multiply configurable systems."[32] In other words, the functions that literature performs inevitably change according to the specific contexts in which it gets produced and received. While such an approach may seem fundamentally correct, it does leave a certain practical void; for without any patterning or privileging of its functions, literature appears to play no function particularly well at all. Establishing foundational norms for assigning value will result in the marginalization of certain texts and ways of reading, but failing to do so has its costs. Without any such norms at all, literature has no agreed-upon functions and no ground to stand on when its social contributions are explicitly or implicitly called into question.

Herrnstein Smith may not be able to anticipate the current situation of literary studies in the university, but she is certainly aware of the above dilemma. She lays the groundwork for addressing it in the first chapter of her book, when she speaks of certain "patterns and principles" that pertain to the assignation of literary value:

If we recognize that literary value is "relative" in the sense of *contingent* (that is, a changing function of multiple variables) rather than *subjective* (that is, personally whimsical, locked into the consciousness of individual subjects and/or without interest or value for other people), then we may begin to investigate the dynamics of that relativity. Such an investigation would, I believe, reveal that the variables in question are limited and regular—that is, that they occur within ranges and that they exhibit patterns and principles—and that in *that* sense, we may speak of "constancies" of literary value.[33]

While such constancies open up a variety of theoretical questions and angles, however, Herrnstein Smith chooses not to pursue them in proposing a theoretical model for assessing value. As she writes further on, "The type of investigation I have in mind here would not seek to establish normative 'criteria,' to devise presumptively objective evaluative procedures, or to discover grounds for the 'justification' of critical judgments or practices" (28). And given her pragmatist commitments, in conjunction with the pressing institutional project of opening literary studies to multiple textual traditions and critical paradigms, her priority seems perfectly legitimate. For contemporary critics interested in maintaining that openness while at the same time moving toward a modicum of consensus about literature's most crucial functions for our own time, however, the reluctance to make more of literary "constancies" seems outdated. If it is good at some moments to allow for many different approaches toward value, it is good also, particularly at this moment, to agree on one or several fundamental premises. Herrnstein Smith speaks at one point of "uniformities and constancies" that might be considered "contingently objective," good for an entire community under certain specific conditions (182). Building on this possibility of the "contingently objective," then, what I propose is a provisional and highly minimal standard for choosing literary objects and imputing value to them. I call this standard "provisional" because it derives whatever authority it has not from any characteristic intrinsic to literature but from a particular definition that has repeatedly and productively been assigned to it over time. In other words, I focus on *one* of the public functions that literature as a specific discourse has previously aspired to play and which it might, given the contingencies of the contemporary context, continue to play. By calling this standard "minimal," I mean to underscore the plurality of literary history and the importance of an inclusive framework for differentiating it as a type of discourse.

The task of first articulating a minimal, provisional standard for judging literature and then applying it to specific texts is especially pertinent to this study, because regionalism has historically been undervalued as a literary category. I wish to show that certain regionalist texts deserve a special recognition—not only for providing durable modern forms of local community but, in addition, for fulfilling a discursive function that critics, proponents, and even practitioners of regionalism have all too often reserved for so-called major literature. As many have noted, regionalism's history in the magazines of the Gilded Age, and later in the academy, points emphatically to its diminishment. In determining what counted as fully literary, what as marginally literary, and what as not literary at all, writers and critics have frequently placed regionalism in the middle category and thereby denied its potential for making any substantial contribution to public discussions of national significance. At the end of the nineteenth century, the logic behind such devaluation tended to rest on two related assumptions: that mastery of short fiction (the novella, the short story, the travel sketch) required less talent than mastery of the novel, and that certain areas of the country—due to a population's lack of education, its dialect, and its historical isolation—were better suited to the shorter forms and the lesser talents than other areas.[34] In a particularly telling example of how these assumptions were deployed in tandem, Brander Matthews contrasts James Fenimore Cooper with "that little army of industrious miners now engaged in working every vein of local color and character."[35] Clearly Matthews wishes to make a distinction between the "bolder sweep" of Cooper and the "miniature portraits" that fill the pages of magazines in 1889 (796). "For the free movement of his figures and for the proper expansion of his story," he explains in an obvious contrast to the little army of miners, "Cooper needed a broad region and a widening vista" (798). Such comments convey quite clearly that the production of regional literature as a form, its placement in a generic category, and the perception of its value have all frequently turned on the maintenance of overlapping geographical and literary hierarchies.

Over the years, regionalists themselves contributed to this undervaluing, even as they attempted to elevate their own work. During the 1920s and 1930s, Carey McWilliams rejected 1890s local color as "merely a polite movement to gratify Eastern curiosity, to make the Eastern reader think that what he had always thought about the West was true." In place of this view, McWilliams embraced the "new regionalism" of his own time, which challenged the old assumption that some places, namely cities on the East Coast, were broader and more representative in scope than others. As Henry Smith wrote, "There is no resentment of the dominance of New York, but a growing conviction that Manhattan provincialism has little claim to stand for American life as a whole."[36] For McWilliams and Smith, the limitations of 1890s local color derived not from the relative insignificance of the places depicted, but from the capitulation of writers to the biases of one group of readers, which had imposed its standardized taste on the literary public. The local color of the 1890s catered to the fantasies of a homogenized literary public rather than to the concrete local reality pursued by the "new regionalists."[37]

The effort to reclaim regionalism as a valuable object of study has led more recently to its association with several kinds of political projects. Feminist critics have contended that regionalism provided women writers with spaces in which to realize nurturing, matriarchal communities, marked by independent female role models and positioned against the dominant world of competitive individualism and aggressive acquisition.[38] Such criticism has tended to celebrate the tradition for its opposition to the patriarchal values that prevailed in urban and commercial centers. Challenges to the feminist embrace of regionalism have come in large part from critics influenced by a theoretical focus on nationhood. The local communities featured within regionalism were, according to accounts by Richard Brodhead and Amy Kaplan, symbolic sites of national origin, crucial to the construction of a shared narrative and to the operation of a national tourist economy.[39] Sensing that such an approach again devalued the form by stripping it of its counterhegemonic potential, a second wave of nation-based and feminist criticism has revived the critical interest in regionalism's alternative politics, but this time with a crucial difference. To qualify as alternative, a text cannot simply separate the local culture from urban and commercial centers of national power, for such separation too easily exposes regionalism to the charge of complicity in official nation-building; rather the text must depict regional subjects explicitly resisting the colonial exploitation typical of American nation-building. Thus, Nancy Glazener has argued convincingly that regionalism in some of its guises was adaptable to a populist national agenda that challenged the subordination of agricultural regions, while more recently Judith Fetterley and Marjorie Pryse have pointed to literary depictions of "regions that derive their identity less from their political subordination to nation-states and more from their rejection of imperialism."[40]

When the primary critical objective is to secure for regionalism a specifically literary value, however, the most recent feminist and nation-based criticism falls short in several ways. It tends, first of all, to privilege the evidentiary status of regionalist writing, recognizing literature's potential to shape a previous context but ushering it into our own world primarily as historical evidence.[41] The critical history itself takes on the status of primary agent or interlocutor, much as a lawyer draws on documents that once helped to determine the outcome of events in pleading for a pivotal narrative interpretation.[42] What gets compromised in the process is the power of the literary text itself to influence readers, and shape perspectives, outside of its immediate context.

Given the need to agree on a public function for literature, however, recent criticism on regionalism poses a second problem, pertaining not simply to the temporal extent of literary agency but to the kind of agency that literature exerts. What all of the nation-based and feminist critics on regionalism share is an assumption that literature, despite its claims to the contrary, does exactly what all other significant discourses do: in the terminology of one recent critic of regionalism, it performs "cultural work."[43] In other words, it participates in a historical context composed of a variety of cultures, each of them defined by a political project or, more accurately, a set of interrelated projects. As a method that implicitly values literature for its political usefulness—a method, therefore, with normative consequences if not intentions—the culturalist approach places literature in a precarious position, because other argumentative discourses (the editorial article, the pamphlet, the legal opinion, the political speech) tend to be more direct and therefore more effective means of inspiring politically meaningful action.[44] Importing regionalism in this form into current conversations on local community would render it redundant and ill equipped to make its own distinctive contribution to conversations of public importance. The point is not that a metaphysical border separates literary texts from argument, so that the former can never function as the latter: these texts clearly can express and reinforce the political positions of their writers and readers. Yet literature has repeatedly aspired to be something different, and given its tenuous place in the contemporary public sphere, critics need to consider the relative success it has had in living up to one or several of its distinguishing aspirations.

Choosing one such aspiration that makes sense in the world that we currently inhabit is what concerns me here and throughout this study. With this goal in mind, I underscore an emphasis in literary discourse on *open-ended critique*.[45] Literature ought to be valued, I am saying, not because it arrives at judgments about the world and defends them over long stretches of textual time, but because it recognizes the limitations of one's judgments and rethinks them accordingly. Self-placement—the process by which a subject defines herself in relation to something other—may always be provisional, but literature repeatedly commits itself to performing this provisionality, offering rational assessments of motivation and action only to unsettle those assessments through the introduction of another character or another authorial viewpoint. The process must of course come to an end; the fiction in question has its limits, just as public discourse itself will not venture off anachronistically into perspectives unavailable at the time. But over the course of the fictional text, readers encounter a subject (the authorial consciousness) less situated in a sustained position, more likely to generate and prolong its suspension, than other subjects engaged in publicizing themselves.

Friedrich Schiller calls this condition "determinability," in reference to the fact that the subject's discursive position is potentially determined by *all* available agents but actually determined by none of them.[46] This epistemological orientation recalls, in addition, Doris Sommer's brief allusion to the text's suffusion in empirical history, its skepticism toward the cognitive frameworks that people employ to control their worlds. As Terry Eagleton explains, aesthetic theory and practice have always recognized the resistance of lived experience to the apprehension of reason: "From Baumgarten to phenomenology, it is a question of reason deviating, doubling back on itself, taking a *detour* through sensation, experience, 'naivety' as Husserl calls it . . . so that it will not have to suffer the embarrassment of arriving at its *telos* empty-handed, big with wisdom but deaf, dumb and blind into the bargain." While Eagleton places weight on the telos that culminates the literary process, Wai Chee Dimock has recently foregrounded the detour that, in her account, never returns decisively to generalization. She defines literature in relation to the worldly "residues" that contradict and therefore trouble its judgments and verdicts. In literature, as opposed to law and philosophy, such verdicts are always "wayward and unsatisfactory," leaving "the sense of shortfall, that burdens the endings of these [literary] texts."[47] What all of these writers agree on is that literary texts should teach us not only how to question the prevalent assumptions of a culture but how to remain skeptical toward our own points of view, open to unfamiliar objects and ideas that require revision of previous judgments.[48]

The texts that these critics implicitly value rest on a specific relation toward alterity, a repeated gesturing toward the other allowing it to trouble and reconstitute the self. As Derek Attridge explains, "The coming into being of the wholly new requires some relinquishment of intellectual control, and *the other* is a possible name for that to which control is ceded. . . . [W]hen I experience alterity, I experience not the other as such (how could I?) but the remolding of the self that brings the other into being as, necessarily, no longer entirely other."[49] The creative obligation for Attridge, in other words, is not simply respect for and acknowledgment of otherness but a dynamic engagement with it that leads ultimately to a new self, defined by its provisional apprehension of some object or idea that had previously been unknown to it. As the phrase "no longer *entirely* other" should suggest, this process does not exhaust the object or idea in question. Rather it recognizes that object or idea's independent existence outside an altered self, which will in turn again be creatively unsettled by a reconsideration of the same object or idea or an entirely novel engagement with otherness. It is not difficult to see why this habit of mind would be a crucial resource, to be recognized and protected, in an increasingly globalized, interconnected world. Practiced in good faith, the relation to alterity that Attridge describes leads to greater understanding between alien populations; it leads to individuals and communities that avail themselves of knowledge and experience outside of their current boundaries; and it leads to democratic judgments, informed by consideration of multiple viewpoints. While literary texts do not always reflect and promote this way of thinking, they are exceptional in identifying with it more consistently than other types of writing do. In doing so, they offer critics an exceptional opportunity to affirm, in accordance with current contingencies, the value of open and dynamic encounters with alterity.

By investing in this way in the ethics of literary creation, critics promote not simply the transformative process undergone by the literary artist, but the potential publicness of the process—that is, its effect on an audience of readers. Attridge reiterates that "innovative mental acts produce lasting alterations in the subjectivity that achieves them," but he goes on to explain that "[i]f this new articulation becomes public, with the disarticulation of settled modes of thought that made it possible (and thus that it made possible), it may alter cognitive frameworks across a wider domain."[50] Herein lies the public promise of literary creation in the contemporary world: the unsettled judgment that characterizes authorial subjectivity constitutes the text's alterity and produces, in theory, a similar (although certainly not identical) experience in the reader. The text is marked by the ethical process that Attridge has described. Writers seek out objects and thoughts that trouble the worlds in which they live and the moral worlds that they have created. While that process does not ensure that the reader will enter into the ongoing dance with alterity, it does render the text a *potential* record of, and stimulus to, the process. Such an understanding of writing and reading would encourage the recovery of passages or texts that meet a certain standard of self-critique and revision. It would also discourage critical commentaries that truncate the recorded subjective process by illuminating only the positionality or situatedness of the writer. How does the authorial subject move, reposition himself, question the assumptions that at one time over the course of our reading seemed valid? Failing to distinguish this subject, critics risk promoting a discursive field in which subjects are all equally entrenched in their political projects, all equally instrumentalist in their relation to norms and values.

In much of the theory that informs cultural studies, the assumption is that all socially significant subjects occupy analogous positions within an historical context, insofar as all of them do their "cultural work" with the same *degree of partisanship*. According to this logic, a literary text is no different in its public function from a legal argument or a newspaper editorial because the purpose of all three, no matter how conscious or overt, is to further some particular political objective. "It is the notion of literary texts as doing work," Jane Tompkins writes, "expressing and shaping the social context that produced them, that I wish to substitute finally for the critical perspective that sees them as attempts to achieve a timeless, universal ideal of truth."[51] But in the process of stripping away literature's privilege as an entirely disinterested form of writing, critics who continue to work this vein deprive literature of a promising discursive difference it can make in the modern world. The literary text can create space in the world for an expressive subject who is not yet committed, not yet finished engaging with unfamiliar knowledge and alternative viewpoints. The critic George Levine makes exactly this point when he writes: "There must be a distinction between aspiration to some impossible ideal disinterested stance, and the effort to resist, in certain situations, the political thrust of one's own interests in order—in those situations—to keep open to new knowledge of alternative possibilities and to avoid the consequences of simple partisanship. There is something utterly nihilistic, not to say counterproductive, about the extension of the truism that everything is political into a practical obliteration of grades of interest in all circumstances."[52] Again, the argument is not that all literature should be distinguished from speech that reiterates a political position and works toward the achievement of a collective end, but rather that in much literary discourse there is an "effort to resist" such location and to maintain "a vital sense of the other," as Levine phrases it (17). This effort invites us to make a valuable distinction—not to privilege the subject who practices reflexivity and self-revision, but to recognize and at times encourage her difference from someone who is staunchly committed. The literary text becomes a particular kind of space, where the need to commit to values and goals is temporarily suspended.[53]

Moreover, collapsing the distinction between literary and political discourse means attenuating not only literary practice but political practice as well. By marking not only continuities between aesthetic and political forms of action but also differences, we give to politics a clearer sense of the methods and discourses best suited to achieving its ends. This is a criticism that the political left within cultural studies has made of its own emergent discipline. Too often in theory that claims to be political, the habits of mind associated with playful reading and aesthetic pleasure come to supplant and, in Meaghan

Morris's words, "discredit" direct affirmation of concrete political goals. As Morris explains, such theory fails to "leav[e] much place for an unequivocally pained, unambivalently discontented, or *aggressive* theorizing subject. It isn't just negligence. There is an active process going on . . . of discrediting . . . the voices of grumpy feminists and cranky leftists. To discredit such voices is, as I understand it, one of the immediate political functions of the current boom in cultural studies (as distinct from the intentionality of projects invested by it)."[54] In Morris's view, speaking out unambivalently comes to seem unsophisticated when politics can be practiced just as easily by making art and receiving it. Treating aesthetic activity as if it were equivalent to political action, we risk creating blurry spaces of artistic and political expression, unfriendly to the self-in-suspension on the one hand and to Morris's "grumpy feminists and cranky leftists" on the other.

Throughout the following chapters, this understanding of literary discourse informs my approach to regionalist writing and defines its particular place in the conversation on locality. The texts around which this study has been constructed offer us conceptions of local community not only novel in their own time but also responsive to some of the demands that modernity continues to place on us. If the writers of these texts contribute to our discussion as regionalists, as literary writers their contribution is more specific than this. What interests me in all of the succeeding chapters is the convergence of the literary, as a habit of mind committed to open-ended critique, and the face-to-face local community.

In the work of Hamlin Garland and Abraham Cahan, the featured subjects of chapters 2 and 3 respectively, this convergence leads to consideration of the local community as an entity with power and significance in the globalized world. Garland treats the rural community as an active critical player in national debates over regionalist representation—a force in the writer's deliberation about how to depict local subjects and in the public conversation about local community more generally. Much like Garland, Cahan focuses attention on the historicity of his communities, chafing against the assumption of many Americans that Jews were a minor historical people stuck in the Middle Ages. Holding himself to high standards of literary authorship, Cahan undermines the prevailing view of Jews as an insignificant population, while remaining undecided about the exact nature of Jewish participation in American civil society.

For Willa Cather and Zora Neale Hurston, who are featured in the latter chapters of the book, the coming together of the literary and the local community places important obligations not only on the artist figure, but on the community as well. Cather and Hurston speak to each other because they share an uneasiness toward communities that burden their members with impassable racial and geographical boundaries. Remaining in place together for sustained periods can generate valuable forms of collective experience, but such arrangements quickly lose their appeal when they demand the sacrifice of physical and imaginative movement. Both writers stage the process of self-revision underlying their own creative practice and then deliberate over how it might be incorporated into collective life. What they contemplate, in other words, is the possibility that the ethical grounds of their fiction might also serve as the minimal foundations of their local communities.

The earlier chapters, then, emphasize the literary representative's obligation to the local community; in the latter chapters, the local community adapts to the literary. The communal sphere retains its face-to-face concreteness, offering inhabitants a sense of presence, familiarity, and belonging. At the same time, it takes on some of the primary features of the literary public sphere: an openness in relation to the outside world, an enthusiasm for divergent opinion, an acceptance of ethical or epistemological positions as provisional, and—underlying all of the above—a recognition of the unencumbered subject as the starting point for modern conceptions of citizenship. I treat this kind of transfer between literature and community as crucial to the continued promise of regionalist writing. I search for moments when like transfers take place, and I understand them as leading not to an end point of the conversation in question—not to a fully realized form of local community—but to a few basic principles for maintaining the local community within expansive networks of communication. Informed by such principles, regionalist literature can help us to realize more porous and historically adaptive communities. Such communities, in turn, ensure that the conversation on locality goes on in dynamic and unpredictable ways.

2

THE ARTIST MEETS THE RURAL COMMUNITY

Hamlin Garland, Sarah Orne Jewett, and the Writing of 1890s Regionalism

LIKE SO MANY REGIONALIST NARRATIVES FROM THE END OF THE NINE-teenth century, Sarah Orne Jewett's *The Country of the Pointed Firs* (1896) de-picts an encounter between a metropolitan traveler and a sedentary commu-nity at the fringes of national life.[1] Part of what makes *Country* distinctive is that Jewett not only provides a compelling instance of this paradigmatic form; she also positions that form in a literary trajectory that goes back at least as far as Chaucer. More than other regionalist writers of her time, Jewett reminds us in *Country* of her own fiction's relation to the Anglophone travel writing that preceded it. In their introduction to *The Cambridge Companion to Travel Writ-ing*, Peter Hulme and Tim Youngs note that "the centrality of the pilgrimage to Christianity produces much medieval travel writing as well as the framing de-vice for Chaucer's *Canterbury Tales*. In many respects pilgrims were ancestors of modern tourists." Jewett saw the traveling narrator, and the other visiting characters in *Country*, in similar terms: On a journey to Shell-Heap Island, home of a recluse named Joanna, the narrator recognizes the footprints of pre-vious visitors as those of "pilgrims" and Joanna's grave as one of "the shrines of solitude the world over."[2] As if the point might be lost on her reader, Jewett has her narrator speak later of the "straggling processions walking in single file" to the Bowden reunion, "like old illustrations of the Pilgrim's Progress" (*CPF*, 98).

If the pilgrim's narrative is a distant relative to late-nineteenth-century re-gionalism, a closer kin can be found in the literature of exploration (or narra-tive of fact) that emerged in the sixteenth century and crystallized into form at the beginning of the nineteenth. "[B]y 1800," writes Roy Bridges, a scholar of travel writing, "a typical pattern had emerged. Proceeding from a base in civ-ilization to an unknown region, the traveler must describe experiences and ob-servations day to day on the basis of a log or a journal. This format left some scope for the depiction of the picturesque or exotic but the emphasis was more on science and precision."[3] The same description could apply to the story that Captain Littlepage tells the narrator of *Country* about exploration in the area of the North Pole—a story that Littlepage himself has heard while traveling in the arctic region. We learn that Gaffett, the person who tells Littlepage the story while the two men are living together on a missionary station, believed that his listener might be able to "interest the scientific men in his discovery. . . . He was always talking about the Ge'graphical Society" (*CPF*, 24, 27). As Jewett must have known, such stories as Gaffett's were the specific domain of the Royal Geographical Society, which "emerged in this period [1830–1880] as the greatest promoter of travel and exploration. . . . because it linked . . . the search for the exotic or picturesque with hard-nosed science and even harder-nosed diplomatic and economic concerns."[4]

Jewett thus places her own regionalist writing and that of her peers in an identifiable literary history. Yet she takes pains at the same time to differentiate her work, in particular from the literature of exploration embodied by Gaffett's tale. At the center of Gaffett's story is a community of "fog-shaped" inhabitants, who share a propensity for running away from their visitors: "Gaffett said that he and another man came near one o' the fog-shaped men that was going along slow with the look of a pack on his back, among the rocks, an' they chased him; but, Lord! he flittered away out o' sight like a leaf the wind takes with it, or a piece of cobweb" (*CPF*, 25). Unlike Gaffett's story, where the traveler never gets close enough to the ethnic group to give it any kind of real definition, *Country* tells of a visitor's successful integration into a marginal community. Many of the Dunnet characters whom the narrator encounters share the flightiness of the "fog-shaped men": William, brother of the narrator's host, was, we are told, "always odd about seein' folks, just's he is now. I run to meet 'em from a child, an' William, he'd take an' run away" (41). Likewise, at first, "[Elijah Tilley] seemed to be one of those evasive and uncomfortable persons who are so suspicious of you that they make you almost suspicious of yourself" (114). But even characters like William and Elijah Tilley become relatively familiar to the narrator over time.[5] In regionalism of the 1890s, an urban character's full acceptance by a peripheral community is by no means a given. What is a given—and, as Jewett understands, part of what distinguishes the episode of American regionalism in the long history of travel writing—is the *potential* membership of the traveling party. That is to say, unlike Gaffett, regionalism's mobile visitors are similar enough to the fringe community to make citizenship both a subject for narrative suspense and a question for aesthetic deliberation.

Furthermore, in the American literary sphere of the 1890s, this issue of the traveler's membership becomes not simply a social and political question—not simply, that is, a question about whether the traveling figure will belong and the conditions for that belonging—but an issue of knowledge and truthful representation as well. Jewett makes this point quite clearly by problematizing both the truth value of Gaffett's story and the reliability of Littlepage as a provider of knowledge. Just after meeting Littlepage for the first time and hearing him quote from Milton, the narrator notes, "Mrs. Todd had told me one day that Captain Littlepage had overset his mind with too much reading." Littlepage considers *Paradise Lost* to be the greatest poem because it is "all lofty, all lofty," while Shakespeare "copied life but you have to put up with a great deal of low talk" (*CPF*, 17). Littlepage's bias against "low talk" places him in opposition to the narrator, who thrives on the dialect of the folks that she visits. It also calls into question Littlepage's ability both to observe foreign populations and to transmit knowledge about them. Although he himself did not witness the events described by Gaffett, his preference for "lofty" books over "low talk" highlights a habit of mind characteristic of the old-time explorer who never cares to close the gap between himself and a foreign population. The presence of such a gap may, in fact, lead the narrator to equivocate on the truth value of Gaffett's story after hearing Littlepage tell it. She reflects that the tale "had such an air of truth that I could not argue with Captain Littlepage" (28). Although she finds the tale credible enough to desist from arguing, she can only refer to an "air of truth" rather than to the story's accuracy. And if, at this point, both the narrator and the reader of *Country* are inclined to doubt the accuracy of the story, they are encouraged further in this direction by the comments of Mrs. Todd, the narrator's host, in an exchange with the narrator: "The stories are very interesting," notes the narrator. "Yes," replies Mrs. Todd, "you always catch yourself a-thinkin' what if they was all true" (103). Again, Littlepage may succeed in lending these tales a veneer of authenticity, but as anthropological documents they are suspect. Uncertainty about the truth behind the fiction haunts Gaffett's narrative of exploration, despite Littlepage's authoritative telling. This is because Gaffett, the traveling informant, never overcomes the distance that defines his relation to "the fog-shaped men." The alienness of the population—in combination with Gaffett's tendency to chase his objects rather than acquaint himself to them gradually—has preempted the experience of local belonging so crucial to the narrator's visit to Dunnet Landing. Littlepage may tell a believable story, but the ethnic population remains in an epistemological "fog."

Gaffett's story highlights the connection in 1890s regionalism between two issues that appear at first unrelated, one concerning the local belonging of a metropolitan character, the other the representation of a local community. For Jewett, reliable representation rests on the population's accessibility as both a community to enter and an object for knowledge. The burden of the narration is to show that good visitation manners on both sides—tact on the part of the narrator and welcoming hospitality on the part of the community—are enough to ensure the narrator's temporary inclusion and representational accuracy. Once the community recognizes the narrator as a friendly visitor, they embrace her in fellowship and make their local difference fully available to her. Inclusion in the community is thus for Jewett a necessary condition for the traveling character to provide an accurate representation.

This model, according to which a traveler's acceptance by a local population is the basis for the legitimate representation of that population, does not, however, adequately explain what happens in all regionalist texts of the 1890s.[6] In this chapter I juxtapose *Country* with Hamlin Garland's "Up the Coolly" (1891) in order to dramatize an important divergence within 1890s regionalism. Like *Country* and so many other regionalist texts, "Up the Coolly" features an encounter between a traveler from the city and a sedentary regional community. Moreover, like *Country*, it focuses our attention on the traveler's proximity to his subjects and on the possibility of his inclusion. In Garland's story, however, ethnic difference remains a significant obstacle, one that cannot be overcome by the hospitality of a community or by a visitor's respectfulness. That is, in "Up the Coolly," the regional community continues to present itself, even at the end of the story and despite its native Americanness, as a place that harbors "fog-shaped men." What interests me here is less the persistence of this ethnic difference than the way Garland accounts for it. Garland traces the excessive particularity of his local community to the impotence visited on the region by politicians and speculators, government and market structures. The lack of any influence over decision making leads to the formation of foreign— that is to say, nonassimilable—identities. Put quite simply, Garland recognizes the voicelessness of the local community as the fundamental problem dividing the nation into discrete ethnic enclaves.

This problem of voicelessness directly affects Garland's approach not only to the communal membership of the traveling character but also to the legitimacy of the stories that character tells. For Howard McLane, the visitor and protagonist in "Up the Coolly," is, like the writing narrator in *Country*, both urban and artistic by profession (an actor and playwright). If, in Jewett, inclusion in the community is a primary condition for reliable representation, the inverse can be said of "Up the Coolly." In Garland's text, Howard McLane must first concern himself with the public representation of the local community— and, more specifically, with how that representation might appear to local subjects—in order to achieve his local citizenship. The traveling artist's member-

ship in the local community rests, therefore, on his agonizing struggle to redress the problem of its voicelessness.

Through the blindnesses and perceptions of his artistic character (Howard
McLane), Garland considers the extent to which aesthetic experience of the
region has been shaped by the same conditions that suppress regional voices
and interfere with national unity. Artists, alongside other public figures, can
participate in silencing criticism stemming from the rural regions, and the
consequences of this silencing are aesthetic as well as political. That is to say,
Garland understands the voicelessness of the local community as not only a
political problem of national sentiment but a literary-cultural problem of uni-
vocality as well. Alongside his main character, Garland reflects on his own
artistic practices, questioning the homogenizing tendencies of contempora-
neous regionalism and its complicity in perpetuating a system as crippling to
artistic discourse as it is to the local community and the nation. Rigorously examining contemporary realist representation from a local perspective, he attempts to achieve both a complex, multivocal form and the beginning of the
urban artist's membership in local community.

The Country of the Pointed Firs and the Ethics of Visitation

In *Country,* Jewett attempted to distance herself and her contemporary readers from the period in American history prior to the Civil War, when regional
and unionist loyalties repeatedly came into conflict. To do so, she needed to
restore faith in both a decentralized union, defined by its capacity to encompass a plurality of cultures, and in local communities that remained open and
available to alliances with fellow nationals. Seen in this context, Jewett's narrator in *Country* functions as a kind of model representative for the diversified
nation, a well-traveled resident of the city who, in identifying with the inhabitants of Dunnet Landing and becoming one of them for a period of time,
achieves the authority to represent local distinctiveness to Americans outside
the locality. Jewett lets us know early on that the narrator has traveled a good
deal and that her wide body of experience has made her more capable of valuing Dunnet for its particularity: "There was something about the coast town
of Dunnet which made it seem more attractive than other maritime villages of
eastern Maine" (*CPF,* 1). What makes Dunnet so delightful to the narrator is
precisely its resistance to traveling figures who might attempt to update it. The
"unchanged shores of the pointed firs" (2) invite the narrator's love because
they promise more experiential contrast than the shores of assimilated maritime villages. Dunnet will allow the narrator to realize her own elastic capac-

ity for social adaptation and the representation of local difference. Thus, rather than trying to make the residents over in her cosmopolitan image, she sets herself the task of adapting to Dunnet culture for the period of her sojourn. Although at the beginning of the period, she feels as if she "did not really belong to Dunnet Landing" (15), after the Bowden reunion at the end she regrets momentarily that she must "return to the world in which [she] feared to find [herself] a foreigner" (129). Foreignness carries more than one meaning in Jewett's text.[7] The most apparent one here, however, is that the narrator's potential sense of foreignness in "the world" reflects a successful immersion and temporary transformation over the course of her stay in Dunnet.

Part of what makes for this successful immersion is the narrator's own talents as a visitor. *Country* is filled with episodes in which the narrator, often with Mrs. Todd, journeys to the home of a new acquaintance. Much like the narrator, regional residents like Mrs. Todd take pleasure and pride in traveling to the homes of others.[8] Midway through *Country,* the narrator meets Mrs. Fosdick, who comes to stay at Mrs. Todd's house and who, as the daughter and wife of sea captains, has considerable experience in going abroad to visit. Just after Mrs. Fosdick's arrival, the narrator notes that she "had often been told that [Mrs. Fosdick] was the 'best hand in the world to make a visit,'—as if to visit were the highest of vocations" (*CPF,* 58). By contrast, we hear about bad visitors like Gaffett, who chases after the inhabitants of the polar community, and Parson Dimmick, who journeys to the hermit Joanna and rather than "read[ing] somethin' kind of fatherly," shows himself "cold an' unfeelin' [in] the way he inquired" (75). Collectively, all of these instances reveal an ethics of domestic visitation at play in the region. Those who visit well enter the home of another with the intent not to seize or judge or convert, but to sympathize and understand. Mrs. Fosdick, the narrator tells us, was "full of a good traveler's curiosity and enlightenment" (59)—the first quality, we might infer, acting as a condition for the latter. Good visitors know that understanding takes time and effort and that to achieve it, they must travel to the other not simply in body, but in mind and heart as well.

Through the many scenes of visiting inside the region, the narrator demonstrates to her readership and to her hosts that she is a skilled hand at entering an unfamiliar regional home and learning about its inhabitants. In order for her to display this talent, Dunnet must appear to be an ethnically distinct population, a group whose manners, modes of speaking, anecdotes, and collective rituals strike the narrator as noticeably different from her own. Dunnet's embrace of Norman ethnicity is, in other words, crucial to the affirmation of the narrator's capacious sentiment as a visitor. Recognizing the importance of

Dunnet's ethnicity to the narrative as a whole, recent critics on *Country* have focused attention on the Bowden reunion scene, in which the narrator celebrates the family's Norman lines of descent, the racial purity of their blood, and their territorial rootedness.[9] Jewett gathers the Bowden tribe in order to reaffirm a common genealogical origin and the importance of reproducing that origin in unadulterated form. I would add to this account of the reunion scene that maintaining the purity of Bowden blood and the continuity of local tradition is both a matter of tribal loyalty *and* a means of displaying the versatility of the national character within carefully defined white racial limits. By rooting their culture to the distinctive landscape of Maine and to the Norman past, and by guarding against marriages that might dilute the influences of place and blood, the Bowdens exempt themselves from the processes of modern assimilation affecting other villages. They hold out against the power of industry and the patterns of migrations that seem to be turning the world's populations into a single mongrelized mob.[10] If, in doing so, they provide the narrator with a temporary antidote to the social impurities of the city, they also allow her to exhibit her social mobility and her appreciation of certain kinds of cultural difference, as she adapts herself to a local Anglo community.

What Jewett offers us is a model of nationality, in which the construction of cultural difference participates not only in purifying but also in diversifying the national character. The problem that this model poses, however, is that cultural distinctiveness can all too easily become ethnic and sectional exclusivity. The narrator can demonstrate her appreciation of difference only with populations that allow themselves to be appreciated. Jewett's narrator will not visit just any ethnic population, and the range of her movement, I want to suggest, depends as much on the capacity of her hosts for affective reciprocity with fellow whites as it does on the degree of their ethnic purity. As the ideal national counterparts to the narrator, Dunnet inhabitants represent a particular shade of regional and ethnic loyalty, one that does not seem to conflict with the project of consensus-building between white Americans.[11] The Bowden reunion scene turns, in fact, on Jewett's attempt to render these two features of her local community—ethnic purity and national affect—compatible. Thus, at the beginning of the reunion, Mrs. Todd generously includes those who "aren't kin by blood" but "by marriage" (*CPF*, 96), and as a consequence of like-minded generosity, the narrator, whose ethnic origins are never revealed, feels "like an adopted Bowden" (99).

This is to say that the ethics of visitation in this region applies not only to the visitor, but to the visited as well. If the narrator must demonstrate to the community that she can enter the regional home with the appropriate mix of patience, curiosity, and sympathetic feeling, the residents have an equal obligation to welcome the traveler and open themselves to her. Model hosts include Mrs. Blackett, the mother of Mrs. Todd, whose "hospitality was something exquisite; she had the gift which so many women lack, of being able to make themselves and their houses belong entirely to a guest's pleasure,—that charming surrender for the moment of themselves and whatever belongs to them, so that they make a part of one's own life that can never be forgotten" (*CPF*, 46). Such hospitality is not limited to the women of Dunnet Landing. Elijah Tilley, who at first appeared to the narrator as "evasive" (114) and impossible to apprehend, later responds to the narrator's gentle manner of visiting by opening up to her. In a passage that again recalls Gaffett's story, the narrator explains that after sharing a friendly exchange and a respectful silence with the old fisherman, she "found that [she] had suddenly left the forbidding coast and come into the smooth little harbor of friendship" (118). Unlike the fog-shaped inhabitants of Gaffett's story, Dunnet residents enjoy the company of strangers, provided the strangers are recognizable as fellow nationals and tactful, curious visitors. Once these conditions have been met, they make their own cultural difference accessible and effectively authorize the narrator to transmit the knowledge that she has gained.

The ethics of visitation that I have described provides a context for understanding Dunnet Landing's earlier history as a player in the global shipping economy. As the presence of characters like Captain Littlepage and Mrs. Fosdick indicates, Dunnet was previously part of a network of exchange that encompassed Europe, the South Seas, and Greenland, among other areas. The sea becomes a complicated figure in *Country* precisely because it was once a medium for global exchange, as opposed to a regional mode of transportation and a border destination for national travel. Captain Littlepage and Mrs. Fosdick lament the loss of shipping and cosmopolitan influence, raising the possibility that the local community in its present, self-contained form is not the only one that Jewett is considering here.[12] But if intimate visitation is as important to this text as it appears to be, the demise of shipping is more of a benefit than the above two characters are able to recognize. "Ought to see them painted savages I've seen when I was young out in the South Sea Islands!" exclaims Mrs. Fosdick. "That was the time for travel, 'way back in the old whalin' days!'" (*CPF*, 64). Mrs. Fosdick's enthusiasm for the kind of exotic travel that Melville wrote about in his narratives of exploration would seem to indicate that travel has taken a turn for the worse in the contemporary period. From the privileged perspective of the narrator, however, the sensationalist experience provided by "painted savages" during the "whalin' days," and described here in comically exaggerated terms by Mrs. Fosdick, is precisely the problem. It fails to deliver both real participation in a community and the basis for a reliable transmission of knowledge. Mrs. Fosdick's enthusiasm notwithstanding, meaningful travel can only happen once history has displaced the region as a global gateway, resituating it in a network of local and national visitation.[13]

In the contemporary world of Dunnet, the narrator insinuates herself into this network and becomes, for the regional insiders, an unexceptional visitor to be treated like any other. Unlike Mrs. Todd and Mrs. Fosdick in her present incarnation, she travels from the metropolis with a pen, and with the intention of learning something about a relatively unfamiliar population. But although she understands her trip as a temporary sojourn on the coast and, more importantly, as the basis for public representation, those facts have no bearing on the way she is received by her many hosts. If anything, her dual status as a sympathetic outsider and a fellow national raises the bar of hospitality, making it even more crucial that she be offered the full benefits of communal membership.

Jewett does provide us with a character who seems incapable of meeting this standard of hospitality. Santin Bowden, the militaristic leader of the family procession, exhibits erratic behavior and violent tendencies, both of which are linked by Jewett to the excessively ethnic influence of his bloodline. Santin's untempered ancestral influence conflicts with the ethics of visitation and presents the possibility of an ethnic difference inaccessible to the narrator. From Mrs. Todd we learn first that Santin "ain't a sound man, an' [the Union Army] wouldn't have him" (CPF, 101). Later in the same conversation, Mrs. Todd explains that "our family came of very high folks in France, and one of 'em was a great general in some of o' the old wars. I sometimes think that Santin's ability has come 'way down from then.'Taint nothin' he's ever acquired; 'twas born in him" (102). This conversation, in which Santin's strangeness points to a personal history determined *entirely* by inheritance and to a total absence of "acquired" characteristics, segues into a discussion of Mari' Harris, another Dunnet resident who belongs to the class of "strange folks" (103). Susan Gillman and Sandra Zagarell have both commented that Jewett's nativism emerges in her comparison of Mari' Harris to a "Chinee."[14] But it is crucial to the reunion episode that Santin also gets associated with the Chinese immigrant. Mrs. Todd and the other conversationalists worry that an overly zealous family loyalty is akin to foreign behavior, for it suggests that the ancestral community—rather than some combination of ancestry and sympathy for fellow nationals—determines Santin's attachments. That Santin was rejected by the Union Army makes sense in this context, for his limited potential to form alliances with those outside his immediate ethnic family casts doubt on his reliability as a national subject and soldier. As Mrs. Todd informs us just after rendering Santin the product of what is "born in him," he's "got his papers so he knows how to aim a cannon right for William's fish-house five miles out on Green Island, or up there on Burnt Island where the signal is" (102). The point is not that Santin Bowden is *intentionally* destructive to the broader community's interest, but that his unmodified form of Norman ethnic identity may preclude identification and affiliation with those who belong to the extended white national family.

Jewett's negotiation between a scene that celebrates Anglo-Norman ethnic difference unequivocally and one that tempers its role in the constitution of self and national community culminates in the narrator's account of her own departure from the reunion: "I fancied that old feuds had been overlooked, and the old saying that blood is thicker than water had again proved itself true, though from the variety of names one argued a certain adulteration of the Bowden traits and belongings. Clannishness is an instinct of the heart,—it is more than a birthright, or a custom; and lesser rights were forgotten in the claim to a common inheritance" (*CPF*, 110). On the one hand, "blood is thicker than water" and "[c]lannishness is an instinct," much more than a custom that can be acquired. On the other hand, Bowdenness allows for a "certain adulteration of . . . traits and belongings," and clannishness is a kind of sentiment of the "heart," a feeling of attachment rather than a "birthright." What, if anything, does blood determine? In a contradiction that is typical of the reunion scene, we might infer that the Bowdens' thick blood confers to its inheritors the potential to suppress Bowdenness in the right contexts, the capacity to diminish the shaping influence of the condition into which they are born. Whether they are Bowdens from birth or, instead, through their affiliations with other white Americans is entirely unclear. Yet this very ambiguity distinguishes the Anglo-Norman from the "Chinee," whose racial inheritance authors his life and relations. In the regionalism of *Country*, local Norman Americans must not only absent themselves from modern processes of mixing and massification; they must also distance themselves from the excessive particularity of other ethnic groups. Those, like Santin Bowden, who fail to pursue affective bonding with fellow nationals such as the narrator risk the loss of their family claim.

While the marginalization of Santin Bowden underscores Dunnet's hospitality toward outsiders like the narrator, it points simultaneously to Dunnet's limitations as a civic community. Santin's militaristic expression of ethnic difference emerges as an aberration, an individual pathology that the narrator need not address in order to be accepted as a member of the regional community. From the perspective of a Mrs. Todd or a Mrs. Blackett or anyone else at the Bowden reunion, Santin's militarism has no relation at all to decisions being made outside the region. Therefore it has no relation to the narrator's position as a national mediator, with the capacity for making the local community's needs, interests, and ideas understood in a national public arena. Santin's militarism exists, rather, in a historical vacuum, disconnected from the contemporary world. As a traveler with a public voice, the narrator can enter this community without worrying about any exceptional civic obligations; for the only ones that accrue to her are the ones that pertain to any insider engaged in visiting. Inclusion in the community does not require that the narrator reckon with the possibility that the subjects whom she represents might not approve of her depiction. This is because Jewett's regional community appears unaware of its contemporary situation in a national network, with centers of power located outside the region. As we learn in the opening chapter, this community is defined, in part, by its "childish certainty of being the center of civilization" (*CPF*, 2). Looked at with this passage in mind, the Bowden reunion is conspicuous for its lack of interest in publicity. Despite the presence of a writer with national public access, the Bowdens' focus is not their potential future representation in the national sphere but the remembrance of their historical origins.

Migration and the Estrangement of America

In *Country*, Jewett gives us one account of the way in which a destination community received its visitors from outside the region. It goes without saying that relations between such visitors and communities were in no way stable during the 1890s. They were constantly being constructed outside the text, as vacationers came into contact with the residents of local villages. Likewise, they were being formulated and interpreted within the text, as writers dramatized encounters between characters from divergent backgrounds. If in *Country* the narrator can write off Santin Bowden's local militarism as a harmless and somewhat comic spectacle, in Garland's "Up the Coolly" ethnic estrangement becomes an unavoidable reality, thwarting the traveler's desire for temporary citizenship in the local community and for an insider's perspective.

Garland's approach to ethnic estrangement emerges out of the conditions in which he published. His early career, leading up to the writing of "Up the Coolly," began amid the rallies, lectures, and journalism that were publicizing the voices of discontent during the rise of the populist movement.[15] The young Garland both benefited from radical venues that had already been established and contributed to the short-lived process of increasing their number. In his hands, regional writing could appear in a variety of guises, depending on who, at a given time, was exerting the most influence on him and what options were available to him as a publishing writer.[16] At times, his desire to be published by the major monthly magazines, and his unique position as a transplant in Boston from the rural Midwest, led to generic local color sketches, described by one reviewer as "quaint, old-fashioned and very sweet."[17] But with the backing of an editor like the *Arena's* Benjamin O. Flower, who invited and frequently published radical opinion, Garland worked to make his fiction more compatible with his writings on agrarian discontent. A follower of Henry George's

single-tax program, Garland believed that the government needed to free land from the control of speculators and monopolists, who often sat on unused plots and drove up prices. Single-taxers argued for a tax policy that distinguished between land and the fruits of labor. Farmers would pay the government for the privilege of occupying land and, in return, reap all the rewards of production. By contrast, the current system was a form of paternalism, for it denied the mass of individuals the opportunity to compete with the landed aristocracy and the captains of industry. The single tax leveled out the playing field without nationalizing property and limiting the rights of the individual.[18]

In the rural region as Garland describes it, migration to the city often seems like the only avenue of escape from a life of drudgery and indebtedness. Thus, Bradley Talcott, the protagonist of Garland's 1892 novel *A Spoil of Office*, reflects on his own part in a pervasive demographic trend: "Everywhere was a scramble for office—everywhere a pouring into the city from the farms and villages. . . . Did it not all spring from the barrenness and vacuity of rural life?" For Harvard philosopher Josiah Royce, writing at the beginning of the twentieth century, the trend that a character like Bradley Talcott represented was disconcerting. "It is not on the whole well," Royce explained, "when the affairs of a community remain too largely under the influence of those who mainly feel either the wanderer's or the new resident's interest in the region where they are now dwelling." Royce directed his comments, in part, against urban aspirants like Garland himself, who were rejecting the terms of their local settlement and not only migrating, but disrupting life in their new communities by publicizing the reason for their migration. Royce's insistence on provincialism belies a concern over the management of an expanding and incorporating nation, attempting to include and at the same time control diverse populations. The movement from the country to the city raised the specter of an inefficient and interrupted command at the centers of wealth and power. By disseminating an ethics of rootedness, government officials and other administrators of region could organize and contain local populations without restricting them legally to a given territory.[19]

From the agrarian perspective with which Garland was quite familiar, staying at home might, in an ideal world, have benefited the individual farmer, the local community, and the nation as a whole. Under current conditions, however, the choice to remain in place led mainly to rural dissatisfaction. Land speculators had placed farmers in a state of perpetual indebtedness, chaining them to a plot of land that they had no chance of ever owning. Moreover, farmers had no say over the mortgage rates, land prices, crop values, and currency fluctuations that governed their economic lives. With rural laborers denied any opportunity to affect the conditions under which they worked, they had become indentured to the land rather than empowered to determine its future. Like "the plodding Swedes and Danes" in feudal Europe, as Garland wrote in his autobiography, rural subjects who remained at home had "no share in the soil from which they sprung."[20] By denying these subjects the chance to own their own land and to influence the nation's agricultural policy, speculators and government officials were forcing rural children to become either slaves in effect or immigrants in their own country. For Garland, the *primary* site of American denaturalization, therefore, was not the city, where Royce and Jewett most probably would have located it, but the regional districts, where the sentimental attachment between citizen and soil was being systematically ruptured.

Garland presents this moment of rupture most clearly in "Up the Coolly," a story about an East Coast actor and playwright, Howard McLane, who returns to his native Midwest after ten years in New York. Fairly early in the story, we learn that the McLane family has fallen from a previous condition of harmony, characterized by the pastoral immersion of the two brothers—Howard and Grant—in the natural landscape around them: "It was the place where [Howard] was born. The mystery of his life began there. In the branches of those poplar and hickory trees he had swung and sung in the rushing breeze, fearless as a squirrel. Here was the brook where, like a larger kildee, he with Grant had waded after crawfish, or had stolen upon some wary trout, roughcut pole in hand."[21] The early postbellum stage of Western settlement hints at the promise of Jeffersonian agrarianism, each farmer in possession of his own land, families bonded together by the healthful influences of nature. But the union between the brothers, and between the brothers and the land, never fully materializes. After the death of their father, Howard leaves home, perhaps sensing the imminent collapse of the agrarian dream, and the family fails to pay back its mortgage. Most importantly, the loss of the family homeland leads to its repossession by a German family that does not speak English. As the McLane family is displaced and replaced by the aberrant conditions of the Midwest, the entire region becomes peopled by aliens. In the arborescent terms that often depict cultural identity as a natural product of geography, Americans do not grow from midwestern soil.[22] Not only do the Germans remain linguistic outsiders, but the effects of this cultural infertility extend to English-speakers like Grant, who is anything but enamored of his country's history and territory. In response to Howard's attempts to help out on the farm, Grant informs him that if he "had to come here and do it all the while, [he] wouldn't look so white and soft in the hands. . . . Singular we think the country's going to hell" ("UC," 61–62). Forced to farm against his will, Grant despises the land that has, in his view, blackened and enslaved him.

The great travesty for Garland is that both Grant and the German family have enormous potential to become fully naturalized citizens. If active citizenship requires economic and political conditions that permit the natural landscape to function as an inspirational agent, it demands, in addition, subjects whose ancestry makes them capable of such inspiration. In "Among the Corn Rows," another story from the *Main-Travelled Roads* collection, Garland signifies the capacity for a Scandinavian woman's territorial assimilation by pointing to "the high cheek-bones of her race" and "their exquisite fairness of color."[23] He addresses the question of ancestry more explicitly in *Crumbling Idols*. Musing over his prediction that the West will produce "the original utterance of the coming American democracy," he writes that he "might adduce arguments based on the difference in races" and that he "might speculate upon the influence of the Irish and Jews and Italians upon New York and Boston, and point out the quicker assimilation of the Teutonic races in the West."[24] In these passages, Garland treats those races typically associated with the city as biologically indisposed to Americanization. Not surprisingly, an urban ethnic figure surfaces in "Up the Coolly" as a means of defining one of the two major characters, both of whom have become, in their own ways, aliens. Responding to Grant's criticisms of his fine clothing, Howard decisively rejects his brother's lifestyle and limitations by declaring himself a patron of "Breckstein, on Fifth Avenue" ("UC," 61). Breckstein, like the "Jew salesman" referred to in *A Spoil of Office*, is not only a perpetual alien to American soil but an agent of denaturalization, in effect the urban counterpart of the land system.[25] Howard's ability to negotiate in German with the new owners of the land and his ultimate failure to buy back the farm testify to his urbanization and his overexposure to foreigners.

If migration to the city presents the problem of too much racial and cultural mixing in "Up the Coolly," remaining on the farm threatens to render its victims incapable of *all* unions across lines of descent. At one point during Howard's return trip, a cousin, Rose, comes to visit and explains her own failure to marry: "Most all the boys have gone West. That's the reason there's so many old maids" ("UC," 71). When Howard suggests that some young people must come around to court her, she responds, "Oh, a young Dutchman or Norwegian once in a while. Nobody that counts. . . . and when you consider that we're getting more particular each year, the outlook is—well, it's dreadful!" (72). While Howard makes the mistake of doing business with Germans in their own language, Rose fails to acknowledge the great capacity of Teutonic immigrants for assimilation. Taken to its extreme, Rose's "particularity" will lead to a defiant abstention from the process of forging and perpetuating nationally useful unions, and to the degeneration of American-born Westerners. Rather than allowing her own genealogical stream to converge with and be rescued by a tributary, Rose prefers to maintain her stream's separateness and to let it dry up—in effect, to terminate the life of her people. In a world suffering from a shortage of space, the various Anglo-Saxon national groups become competitors rather than partners in the cultivation of American soil, each group coveting its own plot of impoverished land and living independently from others. Such competition results ultimately in artificial divisions of territory and, as signified by Rose's fallowness, in the failure of cultural, agricultural, and biological regeneration.

Rose's "particularity" comments most powerfully on the nature of Grant's alienation. For we learn early on that the two brothers descend from Puritan ancestry on the one side and Scottish on the other, and that Grant "had more of the Scotch in his face than Howard" ("UC," 54). The physical contrast between the two brothers is especially evident at the end of the story: "The two men stood there, face to face, hands clasped, the one fair-skinned, full-lipped, handsome in his neat suit; the other tragic, sombre in his softened mood, his large, long, rugged Scotch face bronzed with sun and scarred with wrinkles that had histories, like sabre-cuts on a veteran, the record of his battles" (87). Here, Grant's biological difference becomes legible in combination with the scars and wrinkles that farm life has inscribed on his face, as if his life experience brings out the Scottishness of his features. Just as the current distribution of land and power fail to make Americans out of Germans, so too this uneven distribution reverses the course of American assimilation and produces Scottish ethnics out of naturalized citizens.

As Peter Onuf has argued, for those who believed in the redemptiveness of the West, the mythical power of the region often resided in its capacity to erase sectional identities that stood in the way of unionization.[26] Garland challenges this myth through the character of Grant, giving us a West that produces, rather than erases, sectional opposition to the nation-state. Grant's own name testifies to the belief of his father in the legitimacy of Northern victory and the cause of reunion. Despite the father's attempts to perpetuate his unionist sympathies, however, the son rejects them decisively. When Howard returns to the West with a bundle of presents, Grant responds to his gift—a copy of "General Grant's autobiography for his namesake" ("UC," 70)—by pushing it aside and reading his newspaper. This gesture sheds light on the Scottishness of his features. By calling attention to Grant's ancestry and racial characteristics, Garland locates him in a tradition of anti-union defiance that had its supposed origin in Scotland and its American manifestations in the South.[27] Under current conditions, angry sectionalism could rear its head wherever the state conspired with the speculator.

While the speculator may be one source of Grant's ethnic sectionalism, Grant and his fellow farmers must contend, just as crucially, with their impotence as political speakers, with having no one in power to whom they can speak. When family and friends assemble at the McLane house for the ostensible purpose of giving Howard a surprise party, the talk among the farmers turns quickly to politics. "'The worst of it is,' said Grant, without seeing Howard, 'a man can't get out of it during his lifetime, and I don't know that he'll have any chance in the next—the speculator'll be there ahead of us'" ("UC," 75). The conversation continues, with other farmers expressing their own discontent. This is a community with the potential to become a political association. Yet the overall impression that Garland creates is that discussions such as this one feel futile to the participants. "A man like me is helpless," says Grant in summation. And after another farmer states explicitly that Grant can do "nothin'" about conditions, the conversation ends with "[t]he men listen[ing] in silence" (76). Because talk cannot lead to the public export of expression, a period of silence becomes the inevitable end of the discussion, signaling awareness on the part of community members that their speech is ineffectual. Grant and the other farmers share tendencies with "the irrepressible bluejay" that Howard notices on a dreary day in the climactic scene of the story. Like the blue jay, these farmers will continue "scream[ing] amid it all, with the same insolent spirit" (81). But like the blue jay, they seem to be screaming into a void.

Grant's desire for political voice, combined with his failure to transcend his own ethnic and regional limits, invites a comparison to Jewett's Anglo ethnic, Santin Bowden. Just as Santin is ill equipped to attain a position among other Union soldiers, so Grant seems less than capable of reconciling with his brother. By forfeiting individual agency to genealogy and geology, so that social relations become *wholly* determined by these factors, both Grant and Santin fail to differentiate themselves sufficiently from foreign subjects. But in *Country*, Jewett accounts for Santin Bowden's flawed identity by attributing it only to his own strangeness, as if Nordic blood surfaced a bit too powerfully in this one genetic accident. By contrast, "Up the Coolly" suggests that the rural community's disenfranchisement threatens to turn not only Grant but other farmers as well into compromised citizens, incapable of extending fellow feeling across local lines. In the Middle Border of this story, the estrangement of the two brothers from each other and from the land that once united them appears to follow from historical circumstances. Under the national conditions in which Garland writes, strangeness has become something of a norm. The unionist sentiments of white farmers like Grant and the rootedness of cultural producers like Howard hinge on a system that enables local power.

Troubling Beauty in Regional Art

In suggesting that the rural community's lack of public power obstructed sympathetic relations not only between disparate populations but also between a farmer and an actor, Garland was raising implicit questions about the status of his own representation as well. Grant's reluctance to welcome Howard back into the regional family derives, at least in part, from his mistrust of his brother's profession. It is not simply that Howard is "soft in the hands" ("UC," 61) from lack of manual labor. More importantly, his perceptions of the Midwest have been colored by his life in the city and his career on the stage. The city and the stage, of course, go hand in hand. Howard absorbs the rural Midwest through an urban theatrical lens unavailable to his brother and antagonistic to his interests. Howard's future representations may very well end up reflecting the needs and realities of his East Coast audiences rather than those of the region he visits. By making his protagonist a narrative artist and associating that artist with the mistrust of a regional character, Garland foregrounds his own unresolved struggle over the problem of a regional aesthetic: if conditions of asymmetry interfered with sympathy across regions, he wondered, how might they affect the production of aesthetic knowledge?

Garland's own early career had repeatedly impressed upon him the degree of constraint under which a publishing writer worked. With the single-tax program as a political orientation, he had set out as a fiction writer hoping to reveal both the injustices of the land system and the fraudulence of the pastoral myths that obscured it. In doing so, however, he confronted the predictable criticism that his stories lacked artfulness. The artist had an obligation to improve on life and to avoid communicating its sordid aspects as a photographer might do. To editors like the *Century*'s Richard Watson Gilder, with whom Garland had an extended correspondence, realism in its early years had the contradictory burden of reproducing life and clearly distinguishing itself from the very thing that it reproduced;[28] if a writer could make the mistake of writing fanciful fictions, he could err as well by seeming overly mimetic.[29]

In an attempt to negotiate between art as artifice and art as "the real thing," Garland at times divided his literary representation of the West into opposing categories, so that the West could appear uncontaminated in both its "beauty" and its "significance." As he notes in an essay entitled "Local Color in Art," collected in *Crumbling Idols*, "beauty is the world-old aristocrat who has taken for mate this mighty young plebeian Significance." On the one side were the natural attributes of the region, its "seas of ripe grasses, tangled and flashing with dew, out of which the bobolinks and larks sprang," as described in Garland's early story "A Prairie Heroine"; on the other side were the knotted hands of farmers, the weary horses, and the houses devastated by storms. Not surprisingly, women function as metonyms for both the original beauty of the region and its fall into significance at the hands of speculators. Of Lucretia Burns, the farmer's wife in "A Prairie Heroine," Garland writes that the "the woman might have sung like a bird if men were only as kind to her as Nature. . . . The goodness and glory of God was in the very air, the bitterness and oppression of man in every line of her face."[30] In sorting out the figure of Lucretia into a natural potential for beauty and an all but ruined condition, Garland struggles to avoid both the aestheticizing of poverty in his work and the impoverishment of aesthetics.

What Garland implicitly proposes in the above passage is that unpleasant social realities and art can coexist provided that the two are segregated. The suffering West must appear in all its sordidness, while the glorious West and its reproduction must not be compromised by the social circumstances that dictate human lives. The same attempt at a neat categorical division informs Howard McLane's first perception of the Midwest upon his return:

> The town caught and held his eyes first. How poor and dull and sleepy and squalid it seemed. . . . unrelieved by a tree or a touch of beauty. . . . the same [as when he left]—only worse and more squalid—was the town.
>
> The same, only more beautiful still, was the majestic amphitheater of green wooded hills that circled the horizon, and toward which he lifted his eyes. He thrilled at the sight. ("UC," 46)

In this opening scene, however, Garland does not simply invite his reader to participate in Howard's sorting of the region into "beautiful" and "significant" parts. The fact that this division occurs at the beginning of the narrative, prior to Howard's reeducation in farm living, suggests a different perspective from the one implied in the passage on Lucretia Burns. There is little doubt that Howard's naive aesthetic lens needs to be adjusted in order for him to have a chance at achieving local citizenship. In "Up the Coolly," Garland treats his own form—his own technique of organizing the rural region aesthetically—as a topic of narrative deliberation, and one that is central to the outcome of Howard's return to the Midwest.

It is no wonder that Garland would trouble his interpretation of realism at this stage of his career and at the moment of American populism's greatest intensity.[31] His attempts to separate the region into categories and to avoid a two-sided contamination can be made to function all too easily as an instrument of rural containment. The text seems to reflect and reinforce a desire to keep rural subjects circumscribed in their places, walled off by virtue of an inevitable and sordid victimhood in the category of the significant. Garland's early effort to control the depiction of dialect, the spoken language of his rural characters, foregrounds a related problem. In reference to dialect, he writes to Richard Watson Gilder at one point that "[i]t is *usually* spoken by one whom the child reading feels is illiterate and not to be copied. I believe in general that *dialect* does not corrupt a child so much as 'high falutin language.' The child says to itself, 'This man talks funny—The writer knows he talks funny. I mustn't talk as he does.'"[32] What makes the language of his illiterate characters less threatening to impressionable readers than the "high-falutin" language of genteel characters (or so Garland argues) is the relative ease with which he can make the former discourse look "funny" or deviant. The writer can protect against the vulgarization of his product and his consumer by framing the language of illiterate characters as unacceptable dialect, thus stripping it of its potential to alter so-called respectable speech.

Responding to like treatments of "low" speech and "low" characters, Amy Kaplan argues in *The Social Construction of American Realism* that the central anxiety informing realism has to do with a history moving so quickly that it eludes representation. Realist writers, according to Kaplan, needed to contain those social forces with the potential to disrupt the image of a stable, reliably consistent world. Excessive description in realist texts comments on a culture-wide desire "to pin down the objects of an unfamiliar world to make it real."[33] Pinning down a familiar social reality required not simply the construction of a stable social world but the suppression, or containment, of those "alien"

classes that might alter it. Whatever their successes, realists struggled to cap-
ture and preserve the world as they knew it by managing and controlling class
pressures from below. As the major magazines increased the scope of their representation to include rural communities and urban neighborhoods, skillful
management of the lower classes became crucial to the consumption not only
of realism but also of regionalism, as a subset of realism. Extending Kaplan's
argument, we might say that many regionalist writers confronted the question
of whether and to what extent local subjects should be acknowledged as agents
of change, capable of disruptive speech and action. To grant them this potential was inevitably to jeopardize the privileged space of literature and to desta-
bilize the act of literary consumption.

We have already seen that in Jewett's *Country*, the local community includes the narrator without questioning her intentions as a regional representative. The narrator's authority as mediator between locality and literary public goes essentially unchallenged. This type of relation between a mediating
authority within realism and the lower-class subjects of a representation
emerges even more vividly in the work of Jacob Riis, who was exposing the sordid secrets of the urban underworld much in the same way that Garland was
exposing the Middle Border.[34] In *How the Other Half Lives* (1890), Riis proposes
that the slum can be kept from spreading uptown and contaminating his readers through a program of improvement and supervision. His own camera becomes a model supervisor of slum subjects, kind in its sympathetic treatment
of their plight and strict in its expectations of good behavior and complicity.
As others have commented, by modern documentary standards Riis focuses a
curious amount of attention on the posing that occurs before his pictures are
taken.[35] Thus, a street urchin smiles as he pretends to sleep; gang members en-
act a robbery "in character" for the sake of the camera; and a homeless man,
learning the value of work, agrees to pose for a picture in exchange for a few
coins. By contrast, the Chinese find themselves on the bottom of a racial hierarchy because of their "stealth and secretiveness," in effect their resistance to
the photographer.[36] For Riis and his viewers, complicity on the part of the slum
subjects signals the very possibility of art and aesthetic enjoyment. By demonstrating that his subjects, properly controlled, will give themselves over completely to the photographer's representation, Riis suggests that his pictures retain their transcendent artfulness in spite of their sordid subject matter.
Conversely, the artfulness of the pictures, their improvement of real slum conditions according to the vision of the artist, reassures readers that the figures
behind the images have placed themselves faithfully in the photographer's
hands. In Riis's work, aesthetic pleasure depends on the dominance of a single

aesthetic conception belonging to the photographer. The depiction of "the other half" requires its visible transformation into seamless, unchallenged artifice. The text must display not simply the slum, but the slum fully adapted to the photographer's studio.

Just as Riis shows slum characters that conform to familiar types before his camera, leaving undisturbed the aesthetic experience of his audience, so too Garland can at times call attention to the management of his farmers within the category of "the significant" and to his exclusive control over Western beauty. Yet in "Up the Coolly," the rural subjects that he depicts do not always seem to *belong* at the passive end of an aesthetic hierarchy, subdued by the conditions of their lives into dependence on an outside representative. "Why should his brother sit there in wet and grimy clothing, mending a broken trace, while he enjoyed all the light and civilization of the age?" Howard McLane asks himself ("UC," 85). What seems a reified distinction between the significant and the beautiful begins to appear more fluid at this point in the story, for Garland is pointing not only to the underlying perversion of human life on the farm but to the restless discontent, the unrealized aspiration for knowledge and authority, that continues to plague rural characters like Grant. Howard's question implies that rural subjects might be imagined not merely as the raw material of protest but as artistic producers in their own right, capable of interpreting the beauty around them and of transforming their own pain into something aesthetically pleasing. The question surfaces, in fact, just after Howard witnesses a performance by a talented fiddle player:

> And then William played again. His fingers, now grown more supple, brought out clearer, firmer tones. As he played, silence fell on these people. The magic of music sobered every face. . . . It seemed to Howard as if the spirit of tragedy had entered this house. Music had always been William's unconscious expression of his unsatisfied desires. He was never melancholy except when he played. Then his eyes grew sombre, his drooping face full of shadows. . . . He seemed to find in these melodies, and especially in a wild, sweet, low-keyed negro song, some expression for his indefinable melancholy. He played on, forgetful of everybody, his long beard sweeping the violin, his toil-worn hands marvellously obedient to his will. (77)

Throughout his work on agrarian life, Garland focuses on hands as a sign of the contorted lives of tenant farmers. In a passage from *A Son of the Middle Border*, for instance, he writes of "the hard, crooked fingers" and the "heavy knuckles" that he encounters on his first trip West.[37] In the passage from "Up the Coolly," William McTurg's display of expertise and emotional power is tied to the state of his hands, which are transformed during artistic production. Through the hands, Garland lets us know that William improves as he plays—"[h]is fingers, now grown more supple"—and that he achieves a certain mastery over his instrument and his own body ("his toil-worn hands . . . obedient to his will"). William does not transcend his experience on the farm. In fact, the music's melancholy, combined with the striving for refinement it conveys ("clearer, firmer tones"), points—as in the case of the African American spiritual—to the distance in the performer's mind between life as it is and life as it could have been. What emerges quite clearly in this passage, however, is a subject who gains a measure of expressive control over the circumstances of his life. These conditions no longer determine the self entirely. Rather the articulate self gives an aesthetic order to its experiences and longings.

In "Up the Coolly," then, Garland offers an image of a rural subject who, rather than being made beautiful as an object, claims the authority and the composure to make something artful out of his own experience. The image refers us to the discursive agency of the lower-class subject—not, as in Riis, to that subject's recognition of an external artist better equipped to uplift and express him. But in "Up the Coolly," Garland's experimentation with a model of documentary realism other than the one applied by Riis and at times by himself goes even further. For the problem with defining the region's beauty against its residents is not simply that those residents will be deprived the discursive agency that they, in fact, can claim. It is also that American art, in being deprived of the benefit of that agency, will cease to be as worthy as it might have been.

Garland's views on the potential devaluation of American art can be traced to his theory on space. Speaking in terms of rights and laws, Garland argues in "A New Declaration of Rights" that unnatural laws have violated "the right of each man to space. . . . The need of space is as undeniable as the fact of weight and coherency of our bodies, and to allow any part of a social group, short of the entire membership of that group, to have absolute monopoly of space is a social crime, and human reason revolts against it as against the most vital infringement of the rights of man."[38] Space becomes a metaphor in this essay for freedom more generally. While some Americans can claim no space of their own, others sit on vast tracts of uninhabited land or coveted urban real estate. The image that emerges is of a national social body artificially constricted in some of its most vital parts. In the realm of art, this constriction results in an uneven distribution of consumers. Despite the desire and the capacity for art among rural subjects, the constraints within which they live lead not only to their own attenuated artistic lives but to the attenuation of the nation's cultural production, which suffers from an anemic reception by a small and un-representative percentage of the population. Garland makes this point clearly in "The Land Question and Its Relation to Art and Literature": "because of the toil and worry and poverty everywhere the common inheritance of the rising generation . . . the artist's best pictures hang on his studio walls, the novelist's best thought is unsold, the dramatist's best play is refused by the manager, and the actor is forced to play the buffoon."[39] In this analysis, the effects of the un-natural economic system return to haunt the American leisure classes in the form of an unnourishing and unnaturally narrow artistic production.

Garland often distinguishes himself as a regionalist, but not by a claim that regionalism democratizes a previously elitist literature, introducing readers to their less visible and less fortunate countrymen. Such claims were made im-plicitly by the form itself, which—like the political parties of the Gilded Age—could include subjects who had never before figured in the public realm and at the same time afford them only the most nominal representation. Garland's uniqueness lies rather in his suspicion that a truly democratic literature, freed from past convention and reflective of a wide spectrum of contemporary opin-ion, depends itself on deep structural changes in history. Regionalism could achieve its potential as a democratic form only under market conditions brought about by radical social change. In his own terms, "the beautiful" could only emerge in art when the characters who made up "the significant" were no longer contained within the category by current political and economic con-ditions. True beauty hinged not on the suppression of farmers and their lead-ers, but on a national transformation initiated and undergone by them. It de-pended ultimately, in other words, on the collapse of the two categories in history. "The fictionist of to-day sees a more beautiful and peaceful future so-cial life, and, in consequence, a more beautiful and peaceful literary life," he wrote in *Crumbling Idols*.[40] In such statements, Garland envisioned a future time when rural characters like Grant McLane, with unhindered access to Western nature and to the world of art, would realize themselves fully as cul-tural producers and consumers, so that culture, in turn, would be fully in-formed by rural voices.

Carried to its extreme, such a conviction might have led Garland to give up on "the beautiful" for the moment and to make fiction-writing an unambigu-ous extension of political activism. After all, art, to be worthy of the name, needed first to be enabled by a political and economic restructuring. In his novel *A Spoil of Office*, which takes the populist movement as its primary sub-ject, Ida Wilbur, the novel's radical orator, declares that "the heart and centre of this movement is a demand for justice, not for ourselves alone, but for the toiling poor wherever found. If this movement is higher and deeper and broader than the Grange was, it is because its sympathies are broader." In "The Land Question" essay, and implicitly in many of his stories, Garland pondered the possibility of a populist alliance that included the fiction writer as well.[41] Yet for Garland, such an alliance did not necessarily mean consecrating his own literary work to the political cause that he endorsed, so that his literature would appear identical to his journalism and lectures. Rather, in "Up the Coolly," Garland attempts to distinguish his work from pure activism on the one side and from the claim of a transcendent beauty, immured against the critical voices of rural subjects, on the other.

The region that appeared in print or on the wall had, first of all, to be cropped and reorganized in order for it to be pleasing. As an artist, Garland could not afford to avoid such redactions, nor could he ignore the aesthetic preferences of his audiences. What he could do was to turn a critical eye to the task of redacting and to the incompleteness of the representation. "Up the Coolly" reveals a writer seeking to make his own object artful, but to do so while encouraging a critical contemplation of that object from the perspectives of those who were depicted. Rural characters are presented as legitimate art critics, duly skeptical toward the process of aesthetic transformation. The idea was to force readers, intent on an uninterrupted experience of beauty, to imagine the artistic process through the lens of the critical regional subject. If characters (like William) who were severely inhibited by the land system could participate in making beautiful things, those who made beautiful things for a living could include such characters as potential interlocutors in a dialogue over aesthetic method and form.

Compared with the informed artist described above, Howard McLane often seems like a deluded aesthete, who turns the region into aesthetic experience by force of habit and allows his own enthusiasm for beauty to blot out any critical consideration of his process. After hearing one farmer compare his "'cattle-raisin' and butter-making'" to the lives of slaves, Howard has little problem transforming this speech into art and deriving his own pleasure from it: "These brutally bald words made Howard thrill with emotion like some great tragic poem." But Garland takes the wind out of Howard's experience in the following sentence by noting that "[a] silence fell on the group" ("UC," 76). Howard's reading is clearly not the general reading, and his experience of exalted emotion corresponds awkwardly to the silence that defines the group. Such awkward correspondences punctuate the entire scene in which William plays the fiddle. In response to the music, Howard's "eyes filled with a tender light. He came closer to them all than he had been able to do before." Yet again, in order to have his tender experience, he must suppress the information that Garland provides in the very next sentence: "Grant had gone out into the kitchen" (77). The entire narrative seems to hinge at times on whether Howard will ultimately recognize the suppression of others that underlies his responses, or whether he will remain much like the horses in his brother's barn, who, despite the bad odors and dead rats therein, "stood, looking up with their calm and beautiful eyes, in which the whole scene was idealized" (84).

In the conception of aesthetics that emerges in "Up the Coolly," the mature artist refuses to grant beauty its autonomy from local voices. These voices continue to remind him of the representational casualties that attach to beauty's production, haunting it after it has been produced. Informed beauty involves not simply forgetting or cordoning off such casualties, then, but a kind of deliberate play between forgetting and retrieving them. As a potential practitioner of such an art, Howard McLane must struggle with the fact that rural subjects may place themselves into an aesthetic frame that they consider inadequate for its omissions and distortions. In a scene reminiscent of the posing that takes place in Riis's exposé, Howard witnesses a performance that his family puts on for him: "A casual observer would have said, 'What a pleasant bucolic—this little surprise-party of welcome!' But Howard with his native ear and eye had no such pleasing illusion. . . . He knew that, like the smile of the slave, this cheerfulness was self-defence; deep down was another unsatisfied ego" ("UC," 75). Like Riis, Garland stages a kind of minstrel show, in which "low" characters comply with ideas of them held by outsiders. What we get in Garland's minstrelsy, and what is missing in Riis's, however, is this "deep down" other self, which exists in a kind of tense relation with the performance. Garland's characters transform themselves into the set pieces of a "pleasant bucolic," but they do so without relinquishing the bitterness and despair that characterize their daily lives. They participate only partially in the aesthetic uplift that leaves them stuck on the farm with only the compliments of the "casual observer" to show for it. Beauty appears in the region here, but it appears in a qualified form, mediated by the all-too-audible voices questioning its completeness. Whereas in Riis the remaking of the lower-class character into an aesthetic object fit for consumption erases the viewpoint of the character, here the local character is doubled, part art object and part viewer of the representation. By giving us the two selves in tandem, Garland asks us to engage in a deliberative process in which local subjects, as discursive agents, become sources of critique. In Riis, the purity of the photographer's conception signals the ease with which the independent voices of the lower classes can be made to disappear in the encounter with the artist. In Garland, the presence of the "deep-down" other self reminds readers to register these active voices and to speculate on what they might want others to notice, before indulging in beauty. Through the figure of this "deep-down" self that survives and regards its own artistic presentation, Garland teaches his readers that the validity of regional beauty depends on affording local subjects a place in the conversation on regional aesthetics.

Reconciliation through Realism

"Up the Coolly" ends with the two brothers gripping each other by the hand, even as Grant is refusing Howard's offer to buy back the family farm. As an urban cosmopolitan in Garland's fictional landscape, Howard has at best a limited chance to win the full reconciliation that he desires. The land system has driven him to the metropolis, exposed him to a variety of foreign tongues, and placed him into close relation with unassimilable figures such as the Jewish store owner Breckstein. Moreover, it has turned Grant into a defiantly situated subject, scornful of alliances with subjects (like Howard and the German settlers) who, from Garland's perspective, have the potential for national citizenship. In "Up the Coolly," Garland tells a family history, in which uneven political and economic conditions uproot citizens, damaging the strength of a regional community. At the same time, however, in the portrayal of the brothers shaking hands, he seems to wonder whether at least some of the damage to the regional community might be corrected.

Throughout the story, Garland's central concern is the type of contribution that the artist can make in bringing about this correction. Given the conditions of form, function, and audience under which he worked, what could he hope to achieve for regional subjects, and to what extent was his claim to regional belonging justified? In responding to such questions, one of the aesthetic strategies that he considers, the one that Howard McLane assumes to be the right one when he arrives in the Midwest, is the division of the region into parts of natural beauty and social reality. Such an approach allowed him to convey the burdens imposed upon tenant farmers in all their harshness, while depicting the "groves of oak," "swift streams," and "curiously carved cliffs" ("UC," 45) in all their splendor. Garland often sensed, however, that any such division gave readers the impression, first of all, that regional subjects had been entirely crushed by conditions and, second, that the experience of regional beauty could legitimately bypass consideration of their judgment. In "Up the Coolly," the aesthetic judgments of farmers must be taken into consideration if the mobile artistic traveler is to win inclusion in the community. After noticing the unplowed land in the area, Howard comments to a gathering of farmers that "[i]t makes the hills more beautiful to have them covered with smooth grass and cattle." In a telling statement about the artist's precarious place in the region, Garland writes that Howard was met by "dead silence to this touching upon the idea of beauty" (74). Throughout the end of the story, the silence of the community points simultaneously to its sense of powerlessness and to its exclusion of the artist-figure in pursuit of a transcendent beauty.

A second possibility for achieving reconciliation rested on a belief that the artist *as artist* could do little to represent the interests of a local community and to gain its trust. As Garland's comments in the essay "The Land Question" suggest, he was keenly aware that the markets that determined artistic production were specific to geography and class. The same conditions that gnarled the hands of farmers and left them perpetually indebted to speculators diminished their influence on the nation's cultural production. Faced with limitations that seemed to demand a betrayal of self and regional home, the best approach was perhaps to abandon the quest for beauty and to redefine artistic practice strictly as a vehicle for social justice. If beauty in history preceded beauty in art, did it not follow that the writer who wrote as an activist invested his energies most appropriately? As part of an alliance of laborers contesting the project of nationalization as it was presently being pursued, artists might abandon concern for the artistry of their own objects and devote themselves instead to the ushering in of a new nation. Seen in this light, the final image of the story suggests a singular commitment to a common political goal. Reconciliation between the two brothers rests perhaps on the artist's identification of beauty as an end to be realized only in the future, not under present conditions.

Yet Garland was not entirely satisfied with this version of reconciliation either. He had chosen to be a writer, and the choice did not make sense if the achievement of literary art, distinctive in its artfulness, was an impossibility in the present climate. Through the character of Howard McLane, Garland considered whether it might be reasonable to think of himself as both a member of the above alliance and a writer who made not merely a difference, but an artistic difference. In pursuing this negotiation, he experimented with turning his dualistic framework of "the beautiful" and "the significant" into a dialectic one. The worn-out hands and bared knuckles that might have stood in as synecdoches for rural characters in some of his earlier fiction no longer adequately represent their owners. Hands become transformed as a rural subject like William McTurg gains a measure of expressive control over his own experience. William becomes a maker of art, not simply a passive object inside of it. In the music scene described previously, he turns life on the farm into a source of artistic production, rather than allowing it to remain only the instrument of art's negation.

William's method functions not only as affirmation of the small-scale farmer's artistic capacity but as implicit criticism of Howard's aesthetic method and form. For while William recognizes and incorporates material circumstances into his expression, Howard pursues an exalted art, out of touch with the pain and drudgery of labor. He can achieve his exalted art only by ignoring both William's artistic expressions and the responses to his own experiences of aesthetic transport by Middle Border subjects. Over the course of the story, he undergoes a kind of aesthetic reeducation. While he continues to translate the circumstances of rural life into a more idealized form, he also comes to recognize the work that has been done—the voices suppressed—in order to achieve that translation. This type of approach to aesthetic production distinguishes Garland's work from that of other artists of the period, literary and otherwise, who were documenting the lives of the lower classes. By pointing readers to the "deep down" ("UC," 75) self that could trouble the artist's vision, Garland was proposing that legitimate beauty could emerge only as the product of a multivocal dialogue. Only through such dialogue might beauty appear in a mature form, realistic in the best of ways and acceptable to the subjects it translated.

Thus, the handshake between the two brothers offers the possibility of yet another version of reconciliation—one that involves neither the segregation of beauty and significance nor the abandonment of beauty altogether. According to this version, Howard McLane returns to New York committed to a form both distinguishable as art and alert to the critical responses of the underrepresented. Realism here means first the making of art out of experience and then the return of art to some part of experience that local subjects themselves might like to see depicted. Garland was attempting to imagine an aesthetic method and form that might justify an artist's claim to regional belonging. At the same time, the reconciliation of artist and farmer through the transformation of art was not a matter of charity for Garland—not a gesture of largesse on the part of the artist. Just as inclusion of local perspectives might allow for the artist's reintegration into the community, so too it might lead to more complex and enduring forms of representation—to the "artist's best picture," "the novelist's best thought," and "the dramatist's best play."[42] By treating figures like Grant McLane as artistic critics and giving voice to them accordingly, Garland was tending to his own artistic achievement.

3

NEW WORLD RELATIONS

Abraham Cahan and the Puzzle of Jewish American Affiliation

ABRAHAM CAHAN WAS THE FOUNDER OF THE *JEWISH DAILY FORWARD*
and for much of his lifetime one of the foremost spokesmen in the Yiddish-
speaking world. By the end of the 1890s, however, Cahan had all but abandoned the Yiddish press. In 1895 he published his first story in English, and in
1897 he gave up the editorship of the *Forward* in order to pursue his literary
and journalistic career almost exclusively in English.[1] But in 1902 Cahan returned to the *Forward* and dedicated himself once again to Yiddish writing. Although his career in the American press was shorter than that of many other
local colorists, his movement between different public spheres makes it exceptional. Always writing with the knowledge that he need not be as accom-
modating to editors and readers as others were, Cahan appears perpetually dis-
satisfied with the reading communities to which he contributed. Like Garland,
he had both options as a publishing writer and the intellectual benefit of participating in multiple discursive networks. As a result, he tended to look critically at the assumptions that were being imposed upon him, both by his American public and by the Russian-Jewish intelligentsia. His ability to think
critically and dialogically about the question of local belonging, as it pertained
to Jewish Americans, makes him central to the formation of a viable regionalist tradition.

In the recent past, Cahan's move into English-language fiction has often
been treated as a literary "fall" from Yiddish—a capitulation to the conventions
of local color for the purpose of gaining credibility in a "major" literature and
a "major" language.[2] I begin by contesting that view. Much like Garland, Cahan could turn the aesthetic habits of the American reading public into a subject of narrative deliberation. Moreover, he staged encounters between unreliable spectators from the centers of wealth and power and characters from the
Jewish margins in order to challenge the way these localized Jewish characters
were being perceived in the public domain. Cahan may indeed have been seeking recognition as a major writer. But the assumptions of many readers that

Jews were a minor historical people—cut off by history and geography and incapable of making a difference in the modern world—undermined not only his collective pride, but his own aesthetic ambitions. Art about Jewish communities would be taken seriously only when Jews themselves were recognized as significant historical actors.

If Cahan's desire to attain major status led him to challenge (sometimes gently, sometimes more explicitly) the habits and expectations of his English-language audience, a similar aspiration for literary esteem brought him into conflict with the leaders of the Yiddish socialist press. When he gave up the editorship of the *Forward* in 1897, Cahan had already distanced himself from the partisan polemics that prevailed among Yiddish journalists. As Hutchins Hapgood explained the move to English, Cahan had become alienated by "socialism in its narrow sense" and, in response, had "turned, disgusted, to English newspapers and to realistic fiction."[3] The narrow socialism practiced by leaders such as Philip Krantz and Daniel De Leon had prevented alliances between socialist and anarchist workers. More importantly for my discussion here, American Yiddish socialism demanded a rigid adherence to an assimilationist position on the question of Jewish identity in the United States. While Jewish socialists in eastern Europe had already begun the formation of political parties, like the Bund and the Paole Zion, that occupied coherent positions midway between socialism and Jewish nationalism, their American counterparts held fast to the view that Jews were fated to become indistinguishable from other working Americans.[4] Whatever provisional organization of Jewish workers might be necessary, the goal of an undivided class culture remained.

American Yiddish journalism, then, was dominated by a single position on Jewish affiliation in the modern world, even as multiple viewpoints were becoming available to the Russian intellectuals who were writing this journalism. Publishing in the Yiddish press in 1897 meant limiting one's consideration of Jewish identity in the United States. As a writer intent on an open inquiry into this subject, Cahan chose to write for audiences who had never explicitly debated the Jewish question and who were uncertain about the racial placement of Jewish immigrants. The world of American fiction offered him, in overlapping fashion, the promise of major authorship and an intellectual hiatus from the obligations and narrow conventions of Yiddish journalism. The point is not that the American literary market allowed him an unlimited imaginative freedom to realize his fictional worlds. Cahan clearly grated against certain preferences of American readers and editors. Rather the American market offered Cahan a greater scope in relation, very specifically, to the question of Jewish collective identity in the United States—the question, that is, of whether Jews would continue to congregate and affiliate with each other in their new home.

According to historian John Higham, anti-Semitism surfaced most powerfully in the American 1890s in three relatively marginal contexts: among patrician intellectuals like Henry Adams and Henry Cabot Lodge—the latter of whom spearheaded the effort in Congress to restrict eastern and southern European immigration; among the urban lower classes; and—most relevantly for the study of Hamlin Garland—among certain segments of the agrarian protest movement. Agrarian radicals often treated the Jew either as the agent of an international finance network supporting the gold standard or as a bourgeois parasite, profiting from the labor of others and making only money rather than useful goods.[5] "Breckstein, on Fifth Avenue," the figure to whom Garland refers in "Up the Coolly," has his origins, it would seem, in the idea of the parasitic Jew, the enemy of the "producing classes." For most reading Americans, however, anti-Semitism was best kept outside the public discourse, limited to the elite clubs, vacation resorts, and private schools where cultural homogeneity had always been a given.[6] In the 1890s, the emergence of a Jewish middle class was making such homogeneity hard to maintain quietly. Yet as Higham describes the mood, the American business classes continued to distinguish exclusive social practices from openly bigoted rhetorical formulations, and the de facto segregation of Jews and gentiles in civil society from anti-Semitic governmental legislation. "[I]n the late nineteenth century a remarkably friendly attitude toward Jews still prevailed widely," Higham explains. "[A]nti-Semitic attitudes were often covert and usually blurred by a lingering respect. Many Americans were both pro- and anti-Jewish at the same time."[7] One might say that for many, the goal was to purge public rhetoric of anti-Semitism and to keep privileged social spaces free of all Jews. In relation to the literary regionalism of the period, the unresolved question raised by this ambivalence was whether immigrant Jews had the same status as other "minor" white subjects or whether Jewishness, like blackness, constituted a racial and cultural exception.

Thus, in acting as the privileged interpreter of the Jewish population, Cahan did not simply forfeit his intellectual liberty. More accurately, he accepted some constraints in order to rid himself of others. If he wanted to publish in the American press, he no doubt needed to grapple with the demands of a local-color readership. But because Americans were themselves unsure about the racial and national status of the new immigrants, Cahan too could remain undecided about the outcome of the Jewish exodus to America. He could avoid foreclosing on the question of Jewish identity, allowing himself instead to won-

der and probe how his people would turn out in an environment that was relatively free of violent persecution. Were the Jews best understood as a distinct
people and therefore a separate national group within the working class? Were
Jews themselves—not the working class in general—responsible for their own
political emancipation? Was it ever prudent or necessary to form Jewish alliances across class lines, or to treat Judaism as something more than a set of
religious practices?[8] When these questions were raised in the context of European anti-Semitism, the answers pointed more clearly toward the political
and cultural autonomy of the Jewish working class. What had fascinated Cahan and other Jewish socialists about America was the possibility that here, for
the first time, a genuine internationalism might be achieved. America, which
had left its doors open to persecuted Jewry for most of the nineteenth century,
posed the Jewish question all over again and held out the promise of eradicat-
ing it once and for all. By using the American rather than the Yiddish press as
his medium of publicity, Cahan could test his early faith in America as the great
emancipator of world Jewry. He could more freely ponder the viability of the
universalist ideal and the persistence of Jewishness in his new context.[9]

Reforming the Reformers: Historical Movement and Consciousness

From the start, Cahan's experiment in English betrayed discomfort toward his
new audience and a willingness to critique its prevailing modes of reception.
His 1898 novella *The Imported Bridegroom* begins with a description of a young
Americanized woman named Flora reading a Dickens novel and languishing
in the security of her parlor: "She sat in her rocker, in front of the parlor stove,
absorbed in *Little Dorrit*. Her well-groomed girlish form was enveloped in a
kindly warmth whose tender embrace tinged her interest in the narrative with
a triumphant consciousness of the snowstorm outside. . . . Flora let the book
rest on her lap and fixed her gaze on the twinkling scarlet of the stove-glass.
The thickening twilight, the warmth of the apartment, and the atmosphere of
the novel blended together, and for some moments Flora felt far away from
herself."[10]

Flora's depiction in the above passage, as a dreamer enveloped in her own
cocoon of comfort, suggests bad reading habits. In his critical writings, Cahan
defines realism as against "the story of adventure and plot," which he considers "the aesthetic diet of children."[11] While romance provides only escape and
frivolous pleasure, realism—through its "lifelikeness" and simplicity of expression—highlights virtues and vices, progressive and backward tendencies,

so that an audience improves its understanding of the world and its capacity for meaningful action. Looking to Russian literature as his model, he views realist literature as "a criticism of life," a mode of writing designed both to reflect life and to redirect it.[12] "[A] work of art must also be a work of education," he writes. "'Art for art's sake' is out of the question in [Russia], where the poem must take the place of the editorial, and where the story-teller, who does not make his fiction a criticism of life, is looked upon as something like a public officer who betrays his trust."[13] In order to achieve such education, however, the serious storyteller required an equally serious reader, with the capacity to pay close attention to the "criticism" in the text. Flora fails in this respect, for she cares much less about the lessons in the novel she reads than about the scene of her own reading and the sense of imaginative flight she experiences. In Cahan's mind, her reading practices contradict the novel she is reading. Amy Dorrit, the heroine of *Little Dorrit*, distinguishes herself by refusing to emulate the wealthy classes even though she has the financial means to do so. Flora Stroon, in contrast, employs Dickens's novel as a prop to raise her status and to distinguish herself from her peers. Cahan presents Flora to us in a theatrical setting of her own design—a "back parlor, which she had appropriated for a sort of boudoir" (*IB*, 93). Within this setting, reading becomes a stimulus for escaping the most pressing contemporary realities, for ignoring the relevant "criticisms" of *Little Dorrit* as they pertain to an immigrant's life in New York.

Flora is, in a sense, doubly guilty in this novella. Cahan stigmatizes her first as a social aspirant, whose version of bourgeois domesticity lacks the authenticity of an American original. Her failure to achieve the refinement she covets emerges the first time we hear her speak: "'Just comin' from the synagogue, papa?' she greeted him affectionately in English. 'This settles your fast, don't it?'" (*IB*, 95). The shoddiness of Flora's English grammar compromises her pursuit of an American home and confirms her marginal status in relation to the "sophisticated" 1890s reader.

But Cahan is not nearly so friendly to this reader as he may first appear. Lincoln Steffens, Cahan's editor at the *Commercial Advertiser* between 1897 and 1902, describes how Cahan brought "the question of realism in the arts" from the East Side into the newspaper's office and how he "made incessant propaganda among us for the Marxian program and for Russian realism."[14] Steffens's comments suggest that Hutchins Hapgood, who also wrote for the *Commercial Advertiser,* quoted directly from Cahan when he included the following remarks in *The Spirit of the Ghetto*, attributing them to "an impassioned critic" partial to Russian realism.[15] "Now and then, indeed, I see indications of real art in your writers—great images, great characters, great truth—but all merely

in suggestion. . . . You prefer an exciting plot to a great delineation of character. . . . I love you all. You are clever, good fellows, but you are children, talented, to be sure, but wayward and vagrant children in the fields of art."[16] If the
literary public sphere in America was the domain of juvenile producers and
consumers, in the opening of *The Imported Bridegroom*, the infantilizing agent
is the female American reader, curled up in her sheltered parlor.[17] Flora, in
other words, stands accused not simply of imitating, but of imitating a model
of escapist domesticity that is already flawed. Cahan may allow his own readers to mock Flora's inauthentic construction of an intimate private space.
Covertly, however, he warns them of the threat to great literature posed not by
Jewish women but by a feminized reading public, intent on entertainment and
imaginative flight. Cahan's mistrust of women is difficult to miss in his initial
portrayal of Flora. Harder to notice is his mistrust of the American reading
public, whose deficiencies unfortunately become gendered in this narrative.
Without proper supervision—without male writers like Cahan to teach rather
than pander to them—readers like Flora threaten to deprive the best European
and American novels of their capacity for real illumination.

From Cahan's perspective, this resistance to illumination on the part of
American readers presented a special predicament for Jewish writers intent on
writing about fellow Jews. If American readers were allowed their fantasies
about the urban slum and the "minor" status of those who inhabited it, literature about Jews could become a trifling, nostalgic affair. His function as the
American literary representative of Jewish immigrants required that he reeducate that public through "criticisms of life." Such criticisms might then contribute to the processes of historical change taking place within the Jewish
quarter.

Cahan's intention to reeducate American editors and readers as interpreters of the Jewish people emerges with sharp clarity in "Rabbi Eliezer's
Christmas," published by *Scribner's Magazine* in 1899. This story begins with a
satire of two uptown women who work in a settlement house but whose interest in the slum clearly exceeds reform and uplift. Cahan reminds his readers that the "enthusiasm" of Miss Bemis "was not exclusively philanthropic.
She had recently become infatuated with a literary family and had been hunt-
ing after types ever since."[18] Rabbi Eliezer, a former scribe who now owns a
newspaper stand and a circulating library, is a perfect example of such a picturesque type, for his eyes—in the words of Miss Bemis—"seem as if they were
looking out of a tomb half a mile away." In Miss Bemis's view, Rabbi Eliezer is
merely a souvenir of a time that has long since passed. Cahan, who clearly
wishes to expose the dehumanization that informs the perceptions of reform-

minded slummers, describes Miss Bemis as "tingling with compassion and with something very like the sensation of an entomologist come upon a rare insect."[19]

The two women stop and talk to the scribe-turned-bookseller. After learning that his stock of printed matter is too slim to allow him to make a decent living, they give him twenty dollars "to bring his stock up to the standard."[20] The rest of the story addresses Rabbi Eliezer's anxiety over his acceptance of the money on Christmas Day, which he believes may compromise his Judaism. For Cahan, however, there is clearly more at stake than Rabbi Eliezer's *religious* integrity. This rabbi deals in the production and distribution of print, while his two patrons treat him as if he were a figure in a literary text, fodder for the "literary family" and its pursuit of "types." By accepting the twenty dollars from the two women, Rabbi Eliezer enters the American literary marketplace, where characters such as himself so often get turned into curios and where writers like himself must often assert themselves in order to secure a fair share of autonomy. The twenty-dollar gift may allow Rabbi Eliezer to achieve success in a mass market print economy. But it means very little if he remains beholden to readers like Miss Bemis, who prefer that he continue to play the part of an anachronistic scribe.

It is in some sense surprising that a story with the potential to challenge literary slummers should find its way into a magazine like *Scribner's*, which often catered to them.[21] What makes the story palatable in this instance, however, are the six illustrations, none of which correspond to the written text immediately surrounding them. The text begins with the caricature of the two slummers, but the first picture points the reader to the middle of the story. The caption, which reads, "Why should you be afraid to tell us how much?" refers to a brief moment when the two women have already departed the scene and a group of "market-people" crowd around to inquire about the sum of the gift (see fig. 1). The picture implies that the story's theme revolves around Jewish avarice, and this impression is fortified by illustrations 3 through 5. The final illustration, as well as the second one, treats the Rabbi as a benevolent relic from another world (see fig. 2). The last caption reads, "He went on whispering and nodding his beautiful old head."[22] Clearly, the story with the pictures and captions gives a different impression than the one without them. In the unillustrated version, Rabbi Eliezer stands torn between an Old World lifestyle that he has partially outgrown and a modern economy of literary slumming that threatens to strip him of autonomy. In the best of all future worlds, he will reject both these possibilities and become a modern subject with at least a measure of control over his own representation. According to the pictures, how-

Fig. 1. "Rabbi Eliezer's Christmas," title page illustration by W. J. Glackens, *Scribner's Magazine* 26 (December 1899): 661.

ever, Rabbi Eliezer's potential transformation entails no modernization and no adverse pressure from the literary market, only the outbreak of his own greediness. In the best of worlds, he will suppress his greed and simply nod "his beautiful old head," accepting the charitable gift without allowing it to whet his appetite for more money and status.

"Rabbi Eliezer's Christmas" is a stark example of a story that critiques some of the assumptions of American readers only to qualify the initial challenge, in this case through the illustrations. Such tension arises in Cahan's work as he negotiates between desires to reach an American readership and to reeducate them on the historical development of American Jewry. Cahan understood his writing as a record of Jewish American modernization. He wished to show new audiences that Jewish people were adapting to a context full of possibility, where traditions needed to be discarded or drastically reworked. Anachronism had little place in his depictions of contemporary American Jews. In an article on the chief rabbi of New York, for instance, Cahan explains that "Rabbi Joseph remained the man of the third century he had been brought up to be, while his

Fig. 2. "Rabbi Eliezer's Christmas," illustration by W. J. Glackens, *Scribner's Magazine* 26 (December 1899): 667.

fellow country people . . . were in hourly contact with the culture of the nineteenth century. A gap was yawning between the chief rabbi and his people, one which symbolized a most interesting chapter in the history of Israel."[23] In the American chapter of their history, Jews were nineteenth-century subjects, having "grown up" out of the historical period dominated by the ideas of the Talmud. Whether Jewishness would be shed entirely or whether it would reemerge adapted to the New World, in a form that was perhaps vaguely reminiscent of the old religious one but marked by the rupture of migration—this was the issue to ponder. What Cahan believed, without doubt, was that the way of life associated with eastern European Jewry was not viable in the United States.

If much of the literature categorized as local color abetted the process of national consolidation by representing, as Amy Kaplan aptly states, "rural 'others' as both a nostalgic point of origin and a measure of cosmopolitan development," Cahan's fiction is anomalous.[24] What distinguishes his work is not simply the substitution of the urban for the rural other but the clear distinction he makes between the Lower East Side and the point of origin to which

Kaplan refers in the above quotation. Cahan's fictive families and communities reveal a willingness on his part to make some concessions but not others in his effort to instruct American readers on the course of Jewish American history. While his characters appear marginal and incompletely Americanized, they do not belong to a premodern folk world cut off from modernity. Cahan's ghetto is characterized more by the absence of the folk world than by its determining presence. Flora Stroon's father, Asriel, longs for his native Pravly, but he cannot recover the town as he once knew it even when he returns there. "He looks at Pravly," Cahan writes, "and his soul is pining for Pravly—for the one of thirty-five years ago, of which this is only a reflection" (*IB*, 103). Cahan's abrupt insertion of the present tense emphasizes the futility of trying to overcome the temporal gap, for Asriel is situated quite clearly in a New World history. This history inevitably inflects and outstrips his memory, so that—as with Yekl, David Levinsky, Rabbi Eliezer, and others in Cahan's fiction—his current recollections appear estranged from the objective world being imagined.[25] At times, one has the sense that Asriel's return to Pravly and his purchase of a Talmudic scholar who resides there is an American rite of passage; his attempt to appropriate his Jewish origins is motivated not by abiding ties to these origins, but by a desire to prove his spiritual legitimacy and economic potency to his peers. Thus, in attempting to trace himself back to his cultural roots, he returns relentlessly, boomerang-style, to the present.

The temporal interruption that his characters undergo is crucial to understanding both Cahan's intellectual project and his authorial ideal. In order to imagine himself as a writer of significance, teaching readers about matters of global import, Cahan needed to portray Jewish immigrants as "major" historical people, with the capacity to affect the contemporary context in which they lived. Hutchins Hapgood, whose exposé often transmits the ideas and sentiments of his guide and fellow journalist, makes the connection between major literary status and major historical status fairly clear when he compares Cahan to other ghetto writers and decides that "Cahan's work is more developed and more mature as art than that of the other men, who remain essentially sketch writers." Cahan "emphasiz[es] the changed character and habits of the Russian Jew in New York, describing the conditions of immigration, and depicting the clash between the old and the new ghetto and the way the former insensibly changes into the latter. In this respect, Cahan presents a great contrast to the simple Libin, who merely tells in a heartfelt passionate way the life of the poor sweatshop Jew in the city, without consciously taking into account the relative nature of the phenomena."[26] This evaluation was certainly shared by Cahan himself, and it reveals both a willingness to localize the work of other

Jewish writers and an anxious refusal to submit his own to the same limits. To treat his characters as undeveloped folk, rooted in a circumscribed place and a timeless origin, was to risk devaluing his own work. Cahan very deliberately confronts readers who might understand his fiction simply as an adaptation of local color conventions to an immigrant population. What the stories suggest is the writer's distaste for minoritizing both his literary subjects and himself as a writer.

The Imported Bridegroom: Cosmopolitanism and the Trace of Identity

Cahan's sense of himself as an author rested on his insistence that Jews were subject to modern historical processes and capable of contributing to them. This insistence qualified him as an aesthetic educator in English, using narrative "lifelikeness" to alter the perceptions of his American literary public. But Cahan did not simply argue in his work for the modernization of American Jewry. What is crucial to my treatment of his work is that he problematized the very process that he represented. If his fiction gives us a collection of Jews aspiring more or less authentically to be Americans (as, for instance, in the case of Flora), it presents, even more prominently, Jews whose authenticity as Jews is unresolved and perplexing. For Cahan, modernity is the agent that makes Jewish affiliation less certain. As his characters become part of the American labor force, trade in the American market, and read in public libraries, the religious laws and rituals that governed their previous communities lose at least some of their authority. With the breakdown of the traditional authority, questions arise about the kind of communities these modern American Jews will form and join. As with Asriel Stroon, modernity threatens to turn Jewishness into mere nostalgia, forcing those who claim it to prove that it is socially significant, something more than a meaningless vestige. Insisting on the temporal interruption experienced by his immigrant characters, Cahan raises the question of their Jewish cultural continuity and sets the stage for his narrative exploration of modern identity and community.

Given the publishing options available to him, this exploration could take place for Cahan only in English. In 1890 the Hebrew Federation of Labor, a fragile alliance of Jewish workers, issued a statement of aims and purposes that encapsulates the tenor of Yiddish socialist rhetoric in the United States during much of the 1890s: "There is no Jewish question in America," the statement insisted. "The only Jewish question we recognize is the question, how to prevent the development of such 'Jewish questions.' Only because we alone,

Yiddish-speaking citizens, can have an influence among the Jewish immi-grants; only because we speak their language and are familiar with their lives—only because of this, are we organizing this special Jewish body. The Yiddish language is our tool; one of our goals is to erase all divisions between Jew and non-Jew in the world of workers."[27] The federation's statement underscores a cherished belief among almost all the Yiddish-speaking socialists who had em-igrated from Russia. These intellectuals, many of whom had been participants in the Russian revolutionary movement, believed, in Abraham Cahan's words, that there was "a political meaning [to] their journey to America." They were not simply abandoning the Revolution, not "running away like an ordinary im-migrant."[28] On the contrary, America offered an end to the Jewish question and an opportunity for a universalist working-class movement. In order for this vi-sion to be realized—in order for the Jewish masses to be weaned from cultural isolation and constituted as fully developed class subjects—socialist theory needed to remain pure in its content. As Irving Howe wrote, "before the charge of 'nationalism,' courageous men quailed, as their grandfathers might have quailed before charges of heresy."[29]

In his willingness to reconsider the outcome of the Jewish exodus to Amer-ica, Cahan took the risk of allowing the genie of Jewish separatism out of the bottle. He did so, however, in a relatively protected context, out of reach of the majority of the immigrant community. His reluctance to express his unre-solved thoughts in Yiddish—to betray any such uncertainty in front of a Jew-ish audience while "socialism in its narrow sense" still prevailed—reflects the dominance of a particular approach toward language and political leadership among Jewish socialist intellectuals. Heavily influenced by Russian revolu-tionary populism, these leaders struggled to subordinate the immediate means of political action to its universalist ends, the specifically Jewish medium to the socialist message.[30] Ideally, Yiddish needed to be apprehended as a neutral vehicle, doing little more than transporting the message of secular learning, assimilation, and class struggle. As Cahan wrote in the July 1896 edition of *Di Tsukunft*, a highbrow monthly, "healthy propaganda in Yiddish will bring the workers to socialism and [English,] the language of the country."[31] Of course in actuality, the Yiddish writing of Russian expatriates often signified the pres-ence of a Jewish identity, uniting people of different geographical origins, re-ligious practices, dress codes, and linguistic variations. The means of class struggle could easily become its ends, and vice versa. Readers partial to the idea of a coherent Jewish community could easily absorb the socialist content of the Yiddish press into Jewish culture, treating the principle of internationalism not as a defining aspiration but (in contradictory fashion) as a contributing part of the common ethnic tradition. In their anxious attempt to prevent such inversions, the writers and editors of the Yiddish press sought to dispel from their discourse any doubt over the ultimate fate of American Jewry. The good socialist writer had to compensate for the unintended effects of the medium by purifying his message. To do anything less *in Yiddish* would have been to offer the Jewish masses a flawed education.

By the middle of the 1890s, however, Cahan had clear reasons to question the assimilationist conclusions of his peers. The continued persecution of eastern European Jews reminded immigrants of the context they had fled and the kinship between their own lives and the lives of those who remained. Moreover, the international socialist movement had repeatedly abandoned the victims of pogroms and official discrimination, leaving American Jews with a sense of common cause and responsibility. In 1891, as the representative of both the United Hebrew Trades and the Jewish section of the Socialist Labor Party, Cahan had been exposed to the movement's attitude toward anti-Semitism at the second congress of the Socialist International in Brussels. He had gone to Europe with the intention of placing "the Jewish question" on the agenda and convincing the delegates to demonstrate their support for Jewish labor worldwide. In order to preempt any accusation of nationalism, he had described his two organizations in the most orthodox socialist terms: "We are very pleased that our workers stand together with all other workers and do not separate themselves. . . . The quicker we merge with our American brothers, the quicker we can make disappear the national grouping."[32] After refusing to withdraw the issue of the Jewish question from the agenda, Cahan made his plea: "All the Russian newspapers attack the Jews and claim that the socialist workers detest them. . . . It is asked that you deny this, to say that you are the enemies of all exploiters, whether Christians or Jews—and that you have as much sympathy for Jewish workers as for Christian workers."[33] Rather than appearing too partial to Jewish interests, the delegates (many of them Jewish themselves) passed a weak, equivocal resolution condemning both philo- and anti-Semitism.

If the international socialist movement was an unreliable political ally, so too was the U.S. Congress. Although the majority of reading Americans in the 1890s preferred tacit social exclusion of Jews to an outright restrictionist government policy, patrician congressional leaders, led by William Cabot Lodge, were seeking to reduce the number of immigrants from southern and eastern Europe, having already curtailed Chinese immigration in the 1880s and early 1890s. After considering several restrictionist proposals in the first part of the decade, Congress passed a bill in 1896–97 making literacy the criterion of entry. Grover Cleveland vetoed the bill, but support for the measure and others like it prompted Cahan to write an article for the *Atlantic Monthly* defending "The Russian Jew in America." "The question of limiting immigration engages the attention of Congress at frequent intervals, and bills aiming at reform in this direction are brought before the Senate and the House."[34] He went on to refute the nativist charges against Russian immigrants and to describe the many qualities that made them praiseworthy newcomers and residents. Clearly, the lawmakers' indifference to persecuted Jews and the threat of a spreading nativism reminded him once again of the obligation connecting him to his European counterparts. As long as European Jews were being victimized in Russia and neglected in the United States, they needed Jewish representatives like Cahan to secure their access to political emancipation.

As Cahan was coming to terms with American Jewry's collective obligation to the victims of European anti-Semitism, he was witnessing, in addition, the emotional dependence that American Jews could display toward newcomers from the Old World. American Jews who embraced their adopted country as a site of political freedom and economic opportunity also feared it for its capacity to deprive them of spiritual authenticity. On the Lower East Side, the antidote to the experience of loss so characteristic of the period was the importation of Old World figures to serve as replacements and souvenirs. As Cahan explained in his article on New York's "chief rabbi," "the refugees imported many of the celebrities of the old Ghettoes of Russia, Poland, Galicia, and Roumania. They did not rest until they had secured the best synagogue singers, the leading wedding band, and every Yiddish actor known to fame."[35] One of the primary questions that puzzled Cahan in his 1898 novella *The Imported Bridegroom* was how, exactly, these coveted tokens of the Old World would emerge from their trial of immigration. Their situation was defined by contradiction— by emergent ethnic affiliations dedicated at times to their own undoing. Expected to avail themselves of all that the New World offered and yet obliged simultaneously to serve as conduits to a point of Jewish origin, the celebrities faced bewildering pressures from their equally bewildered American importers.

The celebrity in question in *The Imported Bridegroom* is a Talmudic scholar, brought to the New World by a businessman in order to marry the businessman's daughter. At the beginning of the novella, Asriel Stroon has become worried over the state of his soul and determined to recapture an authentic Jewish life, which he associates with the Polish town of his birth, Pravly. His daughter Flora, though, dreams of marrying "an educated American gentleman" and moving uptown (*IB*, 94). Asriel journeys to Pravly, wins the Talmudic scholar for his daughter by outbidding a rival, and returns to New York certain that his own Jewish identity has been secured. Flora rejects the scholar Shaya at first, but soon recognizes his intellectual talent and begins to see him as the American doctor whom she had imagined marrying. As Shaya takes to reading secular books and visiting libraries outside the ghetto, the suspense of the story begins to hinge on the question of his destiny. Will he emerge finally as a model of cultural continuity, as Asriel wishes him to do? Or will Flora succeed in molding him into a genteel American doctor?

Cahan poses the question of Jewish identity in America by constructing his benchmark immigrant as a whimsical character, free of any governing idea about his own destiny.[36] In Pravly, where conditions funnel him toward a career as a Talmudic scholar, he indulges in playfulness unbefitting a pious Jew; and in America, after beginning his adaptation, he expresses himself as a Jew whenever he is moved to do so. While unpacking his books, "his attention was arrested by a celebrated passage. Without changing his posture, he proceeded to glance it over, until, completely absorbed, he fell to humming the words, in that peculiar singsong, accompanied by indescribable controversial gesticulations, which seem to be as indispensable in reading Talmud as a pair of eyes" (*IB*, 125–26). The description of Shaya studying the Talmud with and through his body accommodates an audience in search of picturesque ghetto scenes. But it is significant also for the suddenness with which Shaya is "arrested," the immediacy of his religious desire, and the absence of a life ambition to determine his expression—all of which render his picturesqueness less stable than it might otherwise be. Shaya becomes in this description a supremely mimetic and historically revealing character. Through him, Cahan aspires to portray, as György Lukács writes of Walter Scott, "[t]he typically human terms in which great historical trends become tangible."[37] In other words, Shaya's rudderless will allows the most powerful agency in relation to the Jews, whether it be the inherited cultural experience of the European Diaspora or the impact of a more secular American context, to speak transparently through his actions. As Shaya goes, so go the American Jews.

Shaya's value as a Talmudic scholar in New York provides at least some incentive for him to retain his Old World Jewishness. Asriel, his benefactor, wants nothing more than to spend his money supporting the boy in a life of study. When we first meet Asriel, he is "tugging nervously at his white beard" (*IB*, 95), unsure of his identity and of his place in the world to come. In order to secure the balance in his spiritual account, he must exchange what he has gained during his thirty-five years in America, namely his capital, for what he has lost, his Jewishness as an unquestionable possession. "Alas! he had been so taken up with earthly title deeds that he had given but little thought to such deeds as would entitle him to a 'share in the World-to Come'" (98). Because his own practice of Judaism generates only a dubious spiritual currency un-transportable to the next world, he purchases a more capable producer of good deeds from Pravly. In this respect, Asriel thinks not only like an employer own-ing the products of someone else's labor, but like an immigrant anticipating the struggles of adaptation that he will doubtlessly face once again upon dy-ing. Searching for the bounty that will make him native in his final home, he begins the process of adapting to the *next* world by attempting to repossess the Old World in the New.

The contradiction in Asriel's scheme is that it depends both on transport-ing Shaya intact, outside of history, and on importing him very concretely into America. Asriel can buy the young scholar as a producer of good deeds, but he must first profit from him in America, where Shaya has as much right to re-make himself as Asriel does to prepare himself for the next world. Asriel plays the fool because he fails to consider that just as he himself and his scheme for redemption have been defined by experiences specific to business and trans-plantation in America, so too the spiritual prodigy will change his goals and values in response to his new context. "You are taking a precious stone with you, Reb Asriel. Hold it dear," says the leader of the Pravly congregation (*IB*, 119). Precious perhaps, but, as the narrative unfolds, more clay than stone. De-spite Asriel's desire to preserve the young scholar, he himself must see to it that Shaya conforms well enough to attract Flora: "Asriel lived in the hope that when Shaya had learned some English and the ways of Flora's circle, she would get to like him. . . . He provided him with a teacher, and trusted the rest to time and God." Sensing that the teacher poses a threat, however, Asriel im-mediately reins him in, urging him not to "take [Shaya] too far into those Gen-tile books" (134). Although he fires the teacher soon after hiring him, he is helpless against the young scholar's consuming desire for a modern secular ed-ucation. Shaya goes "too far" in this education and becomes, in the words of a pious peddler at synagogue, "an appikoros," an atheist.

As Asriel's dream of spiritual recovery collapses, so does the hope of es-tablishing his desired home in America. The story of his Americanization be-comes, in fact, an account of recurring homelessness. He leaves the synagogue after learning of Shaya's new beliefs and practices and finds himself, much like a newly arrived immigrant, entirely alienated from his surroundings: "The clamor of the street peddlers, and the whole maze of squalor and noise through which he was now scurrying, he appeared to hear and to view at a great dis-tance, as if it were on the other side of a broad river, he hurrying on his lonely way along the deserted bank opposite" (*IB*, 149). While it might be tempting to read the "bank opposite" as a metaphor for the Old World, we have by this point in the novella already witnessed Asriel's sense of estrangement in Pravly, where "his heart [is] contracted with homesickness for America" (111). As a result of the skewed process of Americanization he undergoes, the coveted home for Asriel is neither the New World nor the Old, but rather the Old *within* the New—a place in Cahan's imaginings that belongs to the category of romance and short duration. Despite its appeal, America is an unreliable and deceitful mediator, because it elicits a spiritual desire to possess the past, only to seduce the very figure who stands in as a synecdoche for the recoverable past. In response to this seduction, Asriel decides at the end of the novella to resettle in Palestine. "America is now treife to me. I can't show my head," he says to the pious housekeeper whom he plans to marry. "[L]et us put up a canopy and set out on our journey. I want to be born again" (158).[38]

In the minds of most Jews in the 1890s, however, the idealistic colonists in Palestine faced inevitable disappointment rather than spiritual rebirth.[39] Palestine was a primitive environment, which could not be made to sustain either the European Jewish tradition or the lifestyles of American urban dwellers, let alone Asriel's need to have one inside the other. If he began the story worried that Jewishness adapted to the New World was not portable to the next, he has discovered sadly that what seems portable to the next world is not viable anywhere in the new one. The combined attractions and deprivations of America have condemned him to the fate of a perpetual stranger, thwarted by all places of settlement in his quest to have new and old together and untouched by one another.

Whereas Asriel's ideas of an American home derive from an image of his native Polish town, Flora pursues an American home that has its antecedents in the domestic spaces of the uptown bourgeoisie. Her dream of a refined home turns on her "vague ideal" of "an educated American gentleman" (*IB*, 94). At the beginning of the novel, she seems to place little weight on the ethnic background of her gentleman. The important thing is that he belong to the professional classes and that he look and talk like an American. Her desire for a life indistinguishable from that of a bourgeois gentile woman even casts doubt initially on the significance of her Jewishness. Early on, we learn that Asriel's religious rigor is "unintelligible" to Flora and that "she looked on [his praying] with the sympathetic reverence of a Christian visiting a Jewish synagogue on the Day of Atonement" (96). If belonging to a culture means knowing it—if, that is, being reveals itself through familiarity and comprehension—Flora's claim to Jewish identity appears at first in question. But Cahan does not wish

to conclude, at least at this point in the novella, that the loss of religious beliefs and practices translates into the loss of cultural belonging. Flora's trajectory once she meets her imported bridegroom offsets the initial impression,
giving to her "vague ideal" a kind of ethnic concreteness. What appeals to her
about Shaya, it seems, is his potential to become not merely an American gentleman, but an American gentleman with Jewish origins. The doubleness of
the affiliation makes all the difference to her, for it invests her imagined home
with both refinement *and* intimacy.

Given the link that Cahan has already established between Flora's aspirations for status and her reading practices, it seems fitting that the scene in
which Shaya becomes part of her bourgeois life romance is a scene of reading,
in which Flora supervises as Shaya performs out loud in his new language: "He
was in a fever of impatience to inhale the whole of the Gentile language—definitions, spelling, pronunciation, and all—with one desperate effort. . . . Presently she leaned forward to see a mispronounced word for herself. Their heads
found themselves close together. . . . She had an impulse to withdraw her face,
but felt benumbed. He went on patting her, until, meeting with no resistance,
his lips touched her cheek in a gingerly kiss. . . . their hearts, each conscious
of the other's beatings, throbbed wildly" (*IB*, 138). On the one hand, the episode is defined by transgression and transformation, for Shaya, unbeknownst
to his importer Asriel, responds simultaneously to the temptation of gentile
books and the physical attraction of his female tutor. But on the other hand, as
Shaya crosses one cultural boundary in this scene, his crossing allows Flora to
honor and uphold another. The romance of reading together hinges for Flora
not only on leading Shaya into her own forbidden world of secular books but
on the promise of sharing that very world with a fellow Jew. More concretely,
her desire is mediated by the textual tradition they both enter and by the linguistic resemblance that they already possess. This pair can read together in
English and carry on their discussions in Yiddish. Despite Flora's inflection,
which "[is] so decidedly American that to Shaya it sound[s] at once like his native tongue and the language of gentiles," her Yiddish "[is] Yiddish enough" for
him (123). From her perspective, Shaya's Yiddish is a perfect oral complement
to his ambition and aptitude in written English. Months after the couple's engagement, "[h]e proceeded to expound, in Yiddish, what he had been reading
on Acoustics, she listening to his enthusiastic popularization with docile, lov-
ing inattention" (143).

Flora's disposition in this quotation comments tellingly on the part the
young scholar has come to play in her romance, but it suggests also that something has changed in their relationship since the first scene of reading and kiss-

ing. Whereas Flora was previously the English-language tutor, here Shaya has become the teacher of Western science, very much in the way of a Yiddish newspaper intent on uplifting the uneducated through "popularization."[40] Shaya has clearly outgrown his initial need for a coach. More importantly, Flora's "inattention" recalls the book resting in her lap in the opening scene of the novel, and it suggests to us a potential problem with this union. These book lovers have a very different relationship to books and language. For Shaya, Yiddish serves to promote not so much communion in the private domain, but understanding of the world. In order to profit from the critical insights provided by English-language texts, Jews translate these texts for one another and discuss them in the tongue they know best. But the goal of translation and discussion is of course a substantive worldly education, and in this respect, Flora proves a limited partner. Just as she pays scant attention to the lessons implied by *Little Dorrit*, she neglects the content of Shaya's spoken Yiddish, embracing it instead as a token of his cultural resemblance to her. According to Flora's assumptions, the semiotic significance of language as a part of the home—its capacity to provide refinement in the case of *Little Dorrit*, warmth and familiarity in the case of Shaya's explanation—trumps the larger criticism it carries. Flora deprives language of its educative function, confining it to the site of its utterance and apprehension rather than using it as a tool to comprehend the world as it is and as it might be.

As a reader, then, Flora not only buys into the childishness of the American literary public sphere; she also threatens to reduce Jewish intellectual discourse to the same level. Yiddish on her lips and in her ears becomes a language of disengagement and invisibility—not simply spoken *in* the Jewish home, but completely suffused and hidden by the domestic realm. It helps to define her ideal home *as distinct from* the complex, heterogeneous reality of the American scene, and it thrives on the insularity that American domestic life offers. What emerges through the romance narrative that Flora attempts to author is the potential reciprocity between Jewish culture and the secluded space of the bourgeois American family. The former makes the domestic more homey, while the latter provides a private and protected space for sustaining elements of Jewishness.

In *The Imported Bridegroom* this marriage of ethnic and private space appears to conflict with the desires of the intellectually inclined, publicly minded Jewish male. Shaya wishes to use his Yiddish in order to widen the scope of his own and his interlocutor's knowledge and, in doing so, to set the stage for full Jewish participation in the modern world. Equally important, Shaya chafes against the home's exclusion of a multinational American reality. Just after the couple's secular wedding at a city court, Flora's romance collapses when she finds Shaya in the attic apartment of his tutor, studying a book on Auguste Comte with a cosmopolitan reading group:

> A tin can was hissing on the flat top of a little parlor stove, and some of the company were sipping Russian tea from tumblers, each with a slice of lemon floating in it. The group was made up of a middle-aged man with a handsome and intensely intellectual Scotch face, who was a laborer by day and a philosopher by night; a Swedish tailor with the face of a Catholic priest; a Zurich PhD in blue eyeglasses; a young Hindoo who eked out a wretched existence by selling first-rate articles to second-rate weeklies, and several Russian Jews, all of them insatiable debaters and most of them with university or gymnasium diplomas. The group met every Thursday to read and discuss Harriet Martineau's *August Comte,* under the guidance of the Scotchman, who was a leading spirit in positivist circles. (*IB,* 160)

The scene is clearly modeled on events from Cahan's own life as a bachelor and newly arrived immigrant. He reports in his autobiography that "a frequent visitor to [his] attic quarters was Edward King . . . a short stout Scotchman, with jolly round face, baldheaded and good-natured. . . . He would often come to my attic with two positivist friends. On such occasions I would invite some of my Russian friends and in my attic room we would read and talk and drink tea brewed on my stove. King's friends were an educated French shoemaker and a dark-skinned Hindu university graduate."[41] In his life and in his novella, Cahan idealizes "the world" brought into the home and made concrete as a local community. As he describes it in his fiction, this community thrives on the intimacy of its scale—the tea giving rise to the talk, for instance—and its commerce with outside audiences and populations. In both his life and his novella, however, what Cahan ends up excluding from this hybrid public-private community is women.

From a feminist perspective, the exclusion of women obviously compromises the conception of the local community offered at the end of *The Imported Bridegroom.* Cahan flirts with a fascinating alternative to the nineteenth-century assumption of completely separate private and public spheres—and with the overlap between this assumption and an emergent model of ethnicity in the United States. But in suggesting this alternative, he envisions his leading female character isolated and inconsequential, a gossamer on the fringe of all social spaces. Rather than asserting herself within Shaya's community, rather than undergoing a transformation of her own, Flora clings to her dream of a purely Jewish, purely private space—a dream that she has no chance of fulfilling, given the direction in which Jewish American history (as embodied by Shaya) moves in this narrative. Cahan leaves Flora at the end of the novel with a future devoid of significant social relations: "A nightmare of desolation and jealousy choked her—jealousy of the Scotchman's book, of the Little-Russian shirt, of the empty tea-glasses with the slices of lemon on their bottoms, of the whole excited crowd, and of Shaya's entire future, from which she seemed excluded" (*IB*, 162). Flora becomes, much like her father, displaced by the process that she herself has abetted, as Shaya finds both the options that his new family pursues—the resurrected Old World community and the Jewish domestic one—divorced from the reality that surrounds him.

This reality would seem, then, to demand that Shaya give up his sense of Jewishness entirely. His fate at the end of the novella, alongside Flora's and Asriel's marginality, seems at first to be a comment on the inevitable disappearance of Jewish distinctiveness in America. The novella, in other words, appears to give expression to the orthodox socialist understanding of the American exodus: Jews (in spite of their women and nostalgic old men) will make their home in America by becoming indistinguishable from other Americans. Yet Shaya's behavior in the final scene complicates such a reading. In a passage that recalls the description of the young scholar engaged in Talmudic study, we learn that "he became engrossed in the reading; and only half-conscious of Flora's presence, he sat leaning forward, his mouth wide open, his face rapt, and his fingers quietly reproducing the mental gymnastics of Comte's system in the air" (*IB*, 160). The text is no longer the Talmud and the language no longer Hebrew, but Shaya's physical engagement in his reading reminds us of his identity as a Jewish man. Modernization in the American ghetto here entails replacing the object of study but retaining the Jewish form—the gestures, the obliviousness to what is outside the text, the mouthed words. As I have suggested, this distinction between a secular, internationalist content and a specifically Jewish mode of conveying it was central to the Yiddish-speaking socialists. These staunch cosmopolitans justified their use of a Jewish language by treating it as a highly functional first step, to be discarded as soon as the masses were ready. In the above description, however, the visible Jewish form seems an indelible part of Shaya's expression, one that persists in spite of interfering with the larger project of communicating with non-Jews. While the bodily language may help Shaya apprehend what he reads, it threatens to detract from the collective interpretation of Comte's text. Fully immersed in intellectual debate, Shaya is depicted "making a vehement gesture of despair at somebody else's absurdities" and then "taking the book from the Scotchman's hand . . . in a feverish search of what struck him as a misinterpreted passage" (161).

Cahan offers us a glimpse of a future in which Jewish forms are sustained regardless of the uneasy tension that exists between them and the internationalist goals of socialism. Moreover, the single-sex nature of the cosmopolitan community at the end of the novella ensures that Jewish manners travel into modernity even as the beliefs and rituals they once carried fall away. Cahan assumes that Jewish men like Shaya will participate in communities that are not only cosmopolitan but inherently resistant to miscegenation. Although Shaya goes "too far" for either Asriel or Flora, in other words, the plot of the novella denies him access to gentile women and therefore prevents him from going all the way. What informs this plot direction is the idea that while Jewishness may not always have a separate place to call home in America, it will continue to reside very separately in the body, frustrating any desire for a conclusive answer on the question of Jewish belonging. Rather than situating his story definitively as an internationalist response to the Jewish question, Cahan equivocates in the end: Shaya loses religion and refuses a Jewish domestic life but appears to avoid squandering his cultural inheritance. His identity remains insulated against a potentially corrupting desire for gentile things and people, a desire that leads him back to the tutor and into the male cosmopolitan community but never to an intermarriage. In the last scene, Cahan suggests that for a time Jews may reproduce with other Jews and receive the secular world, its books and human representatives, as the objects of their passion. But this precarious response to the question of Jewish social relations is no final answer either. Perhaps the most telling comment on Shaya's future comes from Shaya himself: "You don't know me yet. I tell you you don't begin to know me" (*IB*, 159). His remark is addressed to Flora, but he might as well be speaking to the author as well. *The Imported Bridegroom* gives full expression to Cahan's uncertainty over the possible outcomes of Jewish relocation in America.

"The Apostate of Chego-Chegg": Spoiled Romance and Compromised Relations

The Imported Bridegroom is unique in Cahan's fictional oeuvre for the emphasis it places on a multinational community, but it is typical in its treatment of a failed romance, a frustrated marriage plot. The list of fictions that fall in one way or another into this category is long. "A Providential Match" (1895), *Yekl* (1896), "Circumstances" (1897), "The Apostate from Chego-Chegg" (1899), "The Daughter of Reb Avrom Leib" (1900), *The White Terror and the Red* (1905), and *The Rise of David Levinsky* (1917)—all of these deal in the failure to realize love in marriage, whether the failure takes the form of a troubled marriage, a separation, or the inability to establish a romantic union in the first place. In *The Imported Bridegroom*, the collapse of the marriage plot gives rise to a same-sex alternative, which is itself tinged with romance. For Shaya does not enter the community of intellectuals prosaically; rather he is seduced by the English-language tutor, who, by the end of the novella, occupies the position of Flora's rival suitor. In the scene in which Asriel discovers his prodigy's secular life-style, Cahan figures that lifestyle in the language of a clandestine affair. We learn that Asriel "panted with hatred and thrilled with a detective-like passion to catch Shaya in the act of some grave violation of the Mosaic Law. . . . He dis-covered that Shaya's frequent companion was his former teacher of English, whom he often visited in his attic room on Clinton Street. . . . After tracing Shaya to the Clinton Street house Asriel stood waiting around a corner, at a vantage point from which he could see the windows of the two garret rooms one of which was the supposed scene of the young man's ungodly pursuits" (*IB*, 151). Here, the center of secular and sexual temptation moves from Flora to the tutor, as America the seducer, who has "robbed [Asriel] of [his] glory" (154), takes on a male form. In many of the other fictions mentioned above, however, no such promising substitution takes place. Romance fizzles, and characters find no adequate surrogate. They resign themselves to marriages that never did and never will take on the aura of romance.

Critics have suggested that this recurring theme has its roots in Cahan's own fraught marriage. Thus, in reference to the short story "Circumstances," Ronald Sanders writes that "its 'autobiographical' elements become less definite, but it seems quite clear that Cahan's marriage, though it ultimately survived, had known a good deal of crisis by this time."[42] Further on, he ex-plains Shaya's choice to talk Comte on his wedding night as a veiled indicator of the character's and Cahan's own sexual dysfunction, suggesting that the ti-tle plays with the aural similarity between *imported* and *impotent*. What I hope to add to this account is the notion that both the troubled plot of Cahan's mar-ried life and the equally fraught romance plots of his fiction develop out of and, in turn, reinforce his quandary as a Jewish American writer, choosing between models of family that inevitably conflict with one or another desire for com-munity.

No literary form is more closely linked to the processes of modern com-munal formation than the romance. As Doris Sommer has revealed in *Foun-dational Fictions*, for instance, it is no coincidence that the writers of Latin American romance novels were political leaders much like Cahan. As found-ing figures in nations that had recently established independence, these writ-ers saw literature as a helpful tool for winning over the populations that they and their fellow creoles now governed. Rather than ruling through coercion as their European predecessors had done, these new leaders legitimated their nation-building projects by grounding them in the rhetoric of marital love.

"Without a proper genealogy to root them in the Land," Sommer explains, "the creoles had at least to establish conjugal and then paternity rights. . . . They had to win America's heart and body so that the fathers could found her and reproduce themselves as cultivated men. To be legitimate, their love had to be mutual; even if the fathers set the tone, the mothers had to reciprocate." Love rhetoric celebrated consensual alliances across class, ethnic, and regional boundaries, "invest[ing] private passions with public purpose" and patriotism with all the heat and fervor of romance.[43] It established the creole father as the mutually agreed upon head of the household, and, by an allegorical leap, it encouraged others to view him (and the institutions to which he was connected) as a democratically sanctioned representative, taking care of the nation's history. In the novels that Sommer discusses, plots ending in blissful marital union become natural at the very moment when national unions between heretofore unrelated or antagonistic populations become sacred.

Cahan's situation was of course vastly different from that of his Latin American counterparts. While they wrote about characters with whom readers might themselves form romantic alliances, Cahan's characters were, for much of the American literary public, undesirable partners and somewhat marginal participants in the nation's history. Cahan, in other words, was in no position to consolidate his adopted nation by authorizing romantic desire between Jews and middle-class Americans, even if that had been his wish. What he could do fairly freely, however, was to place his characters in potentially romantic relation to each other and to non-Jewish *immigrant* characters—and to use the resulting plots to comment on the natural course of Jewish belonging in American history.

Like the Latin American novelists, Cahan was writing *about* populations that were new to both the concept of an abstract affiliation (whether ethnic, national, working-class, or universal) and the discourse of romantic love. Their allegiances had been to people from their hometown, their fellow *landsmen*, not to people from other parts of Europe who, when they were encountered, spoke an unfamiliar form of Yiddish and practiced Judaism in an unfamiliar way. For those invested in maintaining and reproducing orthodox communities over time, the rhetoric of love posed a clear danger, because it encouraged young people to choose their own life partners and to treat the authority of their original community as an obstacle for romance to overcome. Love called for the revision of local attachments in coordination with the compelling reality of abstract, imagined commitments. As Cahan's autobiography describes, "the word 'love' was not used [in Russia] with reference to Jews. If a Jewish bridegroom loves his bride, one said, 'He wants her,' or 'She pleases him,' or 'He faints for her.' But love—love was for gentiles, primarily wealthy gentry."[44] No surprise, then, that Cahan often figured the initiation into modernity as an ecstatic conversion from traditional Jewish life to romantic experience, whether that experience involved a woman (as in *The Rise of David Levinsky*) or an idea:[45] "In *Family Joy*, Tolstoy portrays the piety that possesses the heroine after she falls in love and is loved. . . . This is what happened to me in the first weeks of my conversion to socialism. I walked in a daze as one newly in love."[46] It was abundantly clear to Cahan that as a modernizing people, Jews could achieve the transcendence of love in their worldly relations. The problem was figuring out how—given the historical trajectory of the Jewish people and their communal associations—love and marriage should be realized, in what direction they flowed most naturally.

Cahan had attempted to address the issue at the end of *The Imported Bridegroom* by constructing his main character as an endogamous atheist, whose renunciation of tradition and passionate attraction to secularism belies a lingering Jewish identity. In his subsequent story, "The Apostate from Chego-Chegg," Cahan tests the persistence of identity more extensively, asking in effect what happens to Jewishness in the case of an intermarriage. The appikoros (atheist) can lay claim to Jewish identity by participating in its biological reproduction, but what of the apostate, the *meshumedeste*, who takes on a gentile spouse and converts to the spouse's religion? Does the union in which she is involved come naturally to her? Does it lead to the desire for inclusion in the spouse's gentile community? Is there any basis at all for calling the *meshumedeste* and her offspring Jewish? In this story, the *meshumedeste* represents the ultimate contradiction between essence and practice. Her actions jeopardize not only her own being as a Jew but Jewish being more generally. Yet according to the logic of cultural inheritance, she remains a member of the group by birth—thinking, feeling, and desiring accordingly. Cahan poses the central question in the very first line of the story. Michalina, a Jewish immigrant from Poland who has married a Christian peasant from her hometown, declares to herself, "So this is America, and I am a Jewess no longer!"[47] The entire story reads as an exploration of the accuracy of this hypothesis and, by extension, as a further inquiry into the possibility that Jews of the future, free of European tribalism, will no longer desire relations with other Jews.

Cahan's choice of a Polish immigrant as the husband of his apostate helps to dramatize this possibility, tying the story to a history of nationalist labor conflict in Europe. The story responds, in part, to an ongoing struggle during the late 1890s between the Jewish Labor Bund and the Polish Socialist Party. The Bund had been instrumental in the formation of the Russian Social Democratic Workers' Party, from which it later broke away. After the Bund's founding in 1897, leaders of the Polish Socialist Party had accused the new party not only of fomenting Jewish nationalism but of abandoning Polish and Lithuanian workers in their struggle for independence from Russia. Bund leaders countered by insisting that the Polish Socialist Party had never done anything for the Jewish proletariat except slander and threaten it.[48] The conflict, which continued to the end of the century, was given extensive coverage in the Yiddish American press. "The Apostate from Chego-Chegg" implicitly considers whether the friction between the two political groups reflects an inherent incompatibility between Jewish and Polish workers or whether this tribal opposition is contextual and destined to be overcome in America. Like his peers in Europe, Cahan seems motivated by the fear that communal ties to an eastern European peasantry will degrade the status of the Jewish worker. But he seems equally concerned that unnecessary exclusion of Poles from working-class alliances stems from a parochialism inconsistent with the goals of socialism and the best ideals of America.

He begins by dividing Michalina's desire schematically down the middle. "She was yearning for her Gentile husband and their common birthplace, and she was yearning for her father's house and her Jewish past." Whereas the Jewish past and the European birthplace were one and the same in *The Imported Bridegroom*, here the Jewish past signifies something older, rooted in a group experience accumulated over time rather than an individual life history. Despite the initial indication of conflicted desires, this group experience becomes the major determining agent over the course of the first few pages. It affords Michalina a perspective on her own condition that her husband does not and cannot have. "She was a *meshumedeste*," Cahan tells us: "something beyond the vituperative resources of Gentile speech. The bonfires of the Inquisition had burned into her people a point of view to which Wincas was a stranger. Years of religious persecution and enforced clannishness had taught them to look upon the Jew who deserts his faith for that of his oppressors with a horror and a loathing which the Gentile brain could not conceive" ("AC," 94). The capacity for full comprehension of her status within the Jewish community reminds Michalina that she is not only an outsider by virtue of her action, but more importantly an insider by virtue of her knowledge. The Inquisition, as a synecdoche for diasporic experience, has left its scar in the form of a peculiar outlook, passed along through the generations. When, sitting by a road, she finally does see a Jew named Rabbi Nehemiah passing by, she follows him, "as if he were tied to her heart" (97), to a nearby Jewish settlement called Burkdale, where she is subsequently discovered and stigmatized as the *meshumedeste* of Chego-Chegg. Rather than binding her to her husband, this episode has the effect of intensifying Michalina's attachment to the Jewish community and her alienation from non-Jewish Poles.

If the group experience she has inherited provides a privileged perspective on her own condition, a viewpoint unavailable to Wincas and Chego-Chegg, it appears also to create an economic strain between the groups, leading them toward distinct occupations in America, separate communities, and contrasting positions on Cahan's imaginary historical map. The Long Island villages featured in this story belong to entirely different socioeconomic systems. Chego-Chegg, we are told, "was surrounded by farms which yielded the Polish peasants their livelihood. Their pay was about a dollar a day, but the potatoes were the principal part of their food, and this they got from their American employers free. Nearly every peasant owned a fiddle or a banjo. A local politician had humorously dubbed the settlement Chego-Chegg (this was his phonetic summary of the Polish language), and the name clung" ("AC," 96). This agricultural, quasi-feudal arrangement contrasts with the Jewish suburb of Burkdale, which "owed its existence to the 'Land Improvement Company,' to the president of which, Madison Burke, it owed its name. Some tailoring contractors had moved their 'sweatshops' here, after a prolonged strike in New York, and there were, besides, some fifty or sixty peddlers who spent the week scouring the island for custom and who came here for the two Sabbath days— their own and that of their Christian patrons. The improvised little town was lively with the whir of sewing machines and the many-colored display of shop windows" (97).

In this story, Jews have an aptitude for urban living and adaptation to the wider American world that Poles do not possess. While the name of the Jewish suburb points to the modern vision of a presidential founder, the name of the Polish town evokes the population's entrenchment in a clumsy language. Compared to "Chego-Chegg," the name Madison Burke not only alludes to the stories of Americanization unfolding in the town, it also gives to the Jewish residents of the town the racist blessing of white influence. For Madison's counterpart is "[a] young negro . . . twanging a banjo to a crowd of simpering Poles . . . who got the peasants to forsake their accordions, or even fiddles, for banjos. He was the civilizing and Americanizing genius of the place, although he had learned to jabber Polish long before any of his pupils picked up a dozen English words" ("AC," 99). The "young negro" confirms the whiteness of Jew-

ish workers, while suggesting a combined racial and temporal separation between the two populations. The Jewish residents of Burkdale, having achieved
a measure of class consciousness in their New York labor dispute, represent a
stage of development that is both advanced and white. The Polish peasantry,
in contrast, remain mired in a primitive condition, not yet ready to participate
in the struggle of labor against capital.

The distinction between a blackened feudal nation tied to agriculture and
an evolved people accustomed to commerce, migration, and class conflict
leads to obvious difficulties in the context of a marriage. Michalina has been
taught to regard her husband's people as a "a race like unto an ass," and Cahan
does little at the beginning of the story to contradict this view, portraying Wincas as a creature of the farm, who inhales the breeze when it brings "his native
village to his nostrils" ("AC," 99). Plagued by a debilitating homesickness, Wincas aspires to nothing more than the reproduction of his old life. When
Michalina prevails on him "to press coats, which was far more profitable than
working on a farm," he returns predictably to farming because "[t]he soil called
him back" (101). Michalina, on the other hand, spends much of her time at
"[t]he little railroad-station about midway between the two settlements" (99),
where she watches longingly as Jewish passengers embark on and return from
their journeys. As a community of peddlers, small-scale manufacturers, and
shop owners, Burkdale thrives on its open borders and its relations with other
contemporary places. Michalina yearns to be part of the settlement and the
progressive intercourse that continuously regenerates it.

What seems odd about Burkdale is the apparent agreement between its
Jewish ethnicity and the mobility of its residents, as if intercourse with other
communities places a greater premium on preserving group difference while
difference promotes the impulse to keep on traveling. In other words, Jewish
worldliness appears at times to depend on Jewish endogamy, the latter ensuring that Burkdale will be the product of a deterritorialized national history. In
the beginning of "The Apostate of Chego-Chegg," Cahan considers that Jews
are modern insofar as they possess both an inherited identity and a capacity to
interact with the people of other nations. What allows these two traits to coexist in this case is the itinerant history of the Jewish people, the diasporic experience that has been transmitted genealogically to Michalina and the Burkdale residents.

No sooner has this understanding of modernity been proposed, however,
than it is unsettled by a shift in plot. Cahan moves from the position of historical philosopher, recording the advanced stage of his nation's history, to a more
intimate role as the chronicler of daily Jewish American life. As he does so, he

reveals the difficulty and ambivalence inherent in forming unions that are both intra-ethnic and inflected by a cosmopolitan orientation. Rabbi Nehemiah, whom Michalina had followed to Burkdale "as if he were tied to her heart" ("AC," 97), returns to the narrative, transformed from his original incarnation as a Jeremiah warning Burkdale residents against "[s]moking on the Sabbath, staying away from the synagogue, . . . or ogling somebody else's wife" (98). When he bumps into Michalina at the railway station, he has shaved his beard, clipped his hair, donned a derby hat, and become a peddler much like the other residents of Burkdale. More importantly, he has rejected his former religious beliefs and converted to orthodox melting-pot Americanism. "Religion is all humbug," he tells Michalina. "There are no Jews and no Gentiles, missus. This is America. All are noblemen here, and all are brothers—children of one mother—Nature, dear little missus" (100). Such Pauline rhetoric suggests that the modernization of American Jews might come at the cost of a gnawing contradiction between universalist beliefs in humankind's oneness and endogamous practices.[49] If American ideology invites Jews to wander away from their original communities, it does not yet (in 1899, when the story is written) sanction an inevitable return to Jewishness. Nehemiah the Atheist, as he now calls himself, suggests to us that the physical mobility allowed by a democracy is not nearly so innocent toward Jewish culture as Michalina first perceives it. He implies that Jews are modernized not by the inherited memory of their own itinerant history but by the more radical movement and transformation promised by their adopted country. Americanism is more radical than collective memory precisely because in exerting its influence, it brooks no limits of national boundary. Brought to its logical end, Americanism runs counter to any project dedicated to the consolidation of a distinctive people, even one defined as "American."

It is no surprise, then, that Michalina stops her interlocutor in the middle of his lesson on liberal inclusiveness and urges him to be quiet: "'S-s-s-sh!' she interrupted imploringly. 'Why should you speak like that? Don't, oh, don't!'" ("AC," 100). Nehemiah's lesson disrupts her notion of Burkdale as a harmonious enclave, embodying both progress and Jewish continuity, and it compromises Nehemiah himself as a desirable object, capable of restoring her to her own people. Because his universalist principles encourage romance across ethnic lines, they are poor mediation for a union between two Jews. The same sequence of events is repeated in a subsequent conversation, in which Nehemiah attempts to use Petrarch as a vehicle of seduction: "It's only a story I read. It's about a great man who was in love with a beautiful woman all his life. She was married to another man and true to him, yet the stranger loved her.

His soul was bewitched. He sang of her, he dreamed of her. The man's name was Petrarca and the woman's was Laura." After he insists that Michalina is his Laura ("Laura mine!"), she cries out for him to "Stop that!" Cahan glosses this statement by noting that "[a]t that moment he was repulsive" (100). Just as American ideology clashes with the desire for a Jewish union, so too does the rhetoric of love. Exposed simultaneously to new populations and to the triangulated structure of love, Jewish subjects could easily figure the insular culture of their birth as the very thing that romance needed to transgress. As Sommer notes in relation to Latin American romance fiction, "Erotic interest in these novels owes its intensity to the very prohibitions against the lovers' union across racial and regional lines. . . . the enormity of the social abuse, the unethical power of the obstacle, invests the love story with an almost sublime sense of transcendent purpose."[50] In "The Apostate of Chego-Chegg," the "unethical authority" of the insular European Jewish village has been replaced by an endogamous ethnic culture, typified by suburban Burkdale, which appears just as insular and authoritarian. In either case, there is no easy fit between romantic love and marriage *within* one's own group. The possibility of participating in the creation of a more inclusive community, constituted by relations that are more authentically consensual, makes the intra-ethnic union seem prosaic, coercive, and antiquated. It makes sense, then, that Michalina is repulsed by Nehemiah at the very moment that he attempts to plot their relation as a romance. In doing so, he calls attention to his own inadequacy as an object of romantic desire.

The plot that emerges, then, hinges on a triangle involving Wincas, Nehemiah, and Michalina. What is unconventional about this plot is that neither of the relationships appears to have the stuff of a binding union. Wincas lacks inherited group experience and the knowledge that comes with it; Nehemiah measures up poorly to the romantic criteria implicit in his own rhetoric. Nevertheless, for much of the remainder of the story, Cahan plays with the possibility of returning Michalina and her newborn child to Jewish culture through a marriage to Nehemiah. Pleading his own case, Nehemiah reminds Michalina (and informs the audience) that Jewish law does not recognize her marriage to Wincas: "You are a Jewess. Mind, I don't believe in the Talmud; but, according to the Talmud, your marriage does not count. Yes, you are unmarried!" ("AC," 102). This interpretation is confirmed and expanded when Michalina visits a rabbi on the Lower East Side, who pronounces that her baby girl also remains Jewish according to religious law, since "children follow their mother" (103). Unlike a male *meshumed*, Michalina can restore not only herself but also her child to Judaism. Cahan's story depends on the viability of her attempt to undo all of the effects of her own apostasy. Because this attempt is entirely legal according to Jewish law, the women of Burkdale give their full endorsement to the union and pool their resources so that the couple can marry and escape to London.

In the discussion with the rabbi and the ensuing planning of an elopement, Cahan exposes another seed of romantic possibility. The rabbi reminds Michalina of "the laws of the land—of America," which "must be obeyed" ("AC," 103), and the women of Burkdale treat this body of law as the authority that must be overcome in the escape plot. Had Cahan wished to press harder on this structural possibility, he might have provided an explicit commentary on the threat posed by American cultural and legal authority to the survival of Jewish identity. According to this understanding of ethnicity, melting-pot ideology, together with the law that reflects and informs it, stands in the way (unethically, to use Sommer's language) of Jews choosing other Jews as marital partners and fellow citizens of a community. In order to reassert this choice as a romantic and morally valuable one, the Burkdale women must treat the idea of the melting pot as, quite literally, the law of the land. Once they have convinced Michalina that the melting pot inhibits Jewish consent, they can draw on the rhetoric of romance to correct the damage that America has done to their newly formed Jewish community. Thus pitted against American doctrine and custom, Jewish desire for other Jews can begin to seem natural once again.

But if this particular narrative interpretation is along the lines of what the Burkdale women have in mind, it is certainly beyond the rhetorical capacity of Nehemiah, who prefers his futile combination of Petrarch and Crèvecoeur. And it merits no more than a muted suggestion in the larger story that Cahan wishes to tell. For a character like Michalina, the mandate from within the Jewish community to marry a coreligionist has at least the weight and authority that the "law" to assimilate through intermarriage has in the larger national context. Having grown up with an orthodox father, she inevitably views Talmudic law as the primary obstacle to love once romantic love becomes a factor in her relational decisions. The Burkdale women, that is, employ a remedy for intermarriage that is itself a major source of the original infection. In trying to convince Michalina that her romantic desire flows most naturally toward a fellow Jew, these women suffer from a nostalgic delusion similar to the one that affects Asriel Stroon. Whereas Asriel attempts to recapture the Old World community within his New World context of status and upward mobility, the Burkdale women imagine the damage inflicted on Jewish communal relations fully repaired by modern romance—with the couple, the object of repair, transferred back for safety's sake to its former European terrain. In both cases, Jewish Americans repress the impact of the New World context at their own psychological peril.

In the end, Michalina sees Wincas wandering around in search of her and, on the verge of departure for London, resists the Burkdale women in deciding to return to him. In explaining Wincas's anxiety and his hint of suspicion, Cahan writes that "[w]ater and oil won't swap secrets even when in the same bottle": Wincas, in other words, can only intuit the plan of escape from Michalina's behavior, since cultural difference prevents both him and his fellow Poles in Chego-Chegg from obtaining knowledge about the Jewish community. But although Michalina has knowledge that is inaccessible to her Polish husband—although, as the inverse of Shaya, she feels affectively tied to other Jews while being allied in a reproductive partnership with a gentile—she cannot be redeemed through reunion with the Jewish people of Burkdale. After deciding on Wincas and promising to pay back the Burkdale women for the money they expended on boat tickets, "her own Yiddish sounded like a foreign tongue to her" ("AC," 104). It is as if Chego-Chegg and the suburban community that had momentarily accepted her again are equally alien to her. "Nobody will give me anything but misery," she has already cried out, "nobody, nobody, nobody!" (102). Torn between desires for competing models of community, Cahan and his heroine seem to feel that marital choices lead inevitably to unhappiness and longing.

At the root of Michalina's emotional suspension lies Cahan's hesitation over plotting the course of Jewish American history. He begins the story with the hypothesis that "this is America, and [Michalina] is a Jew no longer" ("AC," 94); through the Lower East Side rabbi, he injects the opposite theory, "Once a Jew, forever a Jew" (103); and he concludes the story with a tautology that makes both previous statements true, despite the obvious contradiction: "A *meshumedeste* will be a *meshumedeste*," says the leader of the Burkdale women (104). The unplaceable *meshumedeste*, both Jew and non-Jew, reflects Cahan's uncertainty over what constitutes productive desire and, accordingly, what norms ought to govern the formation of local community for American Jews. Whereas *The Imported Bridegroom* hints in the end at the fragility of the multinational collective, here Cahan casts doubt on the foundation of an all-Jewish community, which, given its predilection for romance, will continue to breed future *meshumedestes* destined to be *meshumedestes*. In "The Apostate of Chego-Chegg," all desire is unproductive, insofar as it stands in the way of a necessary type of local community. America is the land of compromised relations. What marks this story is Cahan's doubt and regret toward both of the historical outcomes he considers.

Relocation to the Yiddish Press

Giving expression to such doubt and regret was a crucial part of Cahan's project in English. Yet this expression came with new pressures, and possibilities for misreading, that Cahan did not have to face as a Yiddish writer. In his review of the *Imported Bridegroom* collection, William Dean Howells underscores these pressures when he wonders whether Cahan will "pass beyond his present environment out into the larger American world, or will master our life as he mastered our language."[51] For Cahan, the present environment of Jewish America was nothing to "pass beyond," since it could itself lay claim to a valuable share of modernity. Cahan could attempt to reeducate his American public, but if a reader like Howells continued to treat the world of his fiction as only a minor literary challenge, what hope could he maintain for the literate masses? A sense of futility doubtlessly played at least some role in his return to the world of Yiddish journalism, and specifically to the *Jewish Daily Forward*, in 1902. American audiences had granted Cahan a literary space for exploring questions of communal affiliation, but they had complicated his quest to chronicle the progressive movement of Jewish American history. He was willing to struggle with these "children in the fields of art" for a period of time, but he did not wish to risk his entire career on such endeavor.

Moreover, several important developments had altered the course of the Yiddish socialist press by 1902 and had given Cahan good reason to consider making use of it once again. Foremost among these was the Dreyfus Affair, which occupied the Lower East Side papers between the summer of 1898 and the spring of 1899. Whereas previously the only legitimate socialist position on the Jewish question had been the orthodox Marxist belief in total assimilation, Dreyfus helped to bring such uniformity to an end. Of the two major Yiddish socialist papers of the time, *Dos Abend Blatt*, the paper controlled by Philip Krantz, followed the French socialist deputies in dismissing the entire affair as an entirely bourgeois conflict. But the *Jewish Daily Forward*, under the leadership of Louis Miller and Abraham Leissin, embraced the position of Jean Jaurès, who had become a staunch defender of Dreyfus by the summer of 1898.[52] Leissin, who had absorbed the ideas of the Bund before coming to the United States in 1897, was particularly influential. As Jonathan Frankel explains, "[he] was apparently the first man to describe in detail the ideology and achievements of the Bund to the New York public," and "[t]he Dreyfus Affair . . . enabled [him] for the first time to present the public at large with his ideas on the Jewish question."[53] While Leissin was skeptical toward any idea of solidarity between the bourgeoisie and the working class, he insisted that Jewish workers had as much reason for and right to nationality (in the present pre-socialist period) as the workers of any other nation. According to Frankel, the *Forward* as a whole moved to this position in the wake of the 1903 Kishinev pogrom. But by 1900, the year in which the Bund established its first branch in New York, the fragile ideological coherence of Yiddish socialism had already begun to break down.[54] To argue in Yiddish for specifically Jewish working-class interests was no longer, necessarily, to offer a flawed education. Writing in 1906, Jacob Milch, a member of the old guard, lamented that "[u]ntil recently the intellectual life of the great East Side of New York was absorbed mainly in social questions of a general nature, or, to be more correct, in Socialism," but that recent events in Europe and the new immigration had brought "a mosaic of theories and movements" to the East Side.[55]

This mosaic was important to Cahan not because he was a committed nationalist but rather because he was a pragmatist, who found something lacking in all the ideologies he confronted and preferred to attach himself to movements depending on the demands of a particular historical moment. In 1903, after the Kishinev pogrom, he advocated strong alliances with wealthier Jews for the purpose of aiding immigration to the United States. But between 1905 and 1907, perhaps in response to the proliferation of nationalist groups, he coaxed the *Forward* back toward a more cosmopolitan, class-based position.[56] This desire to move across an ideological spectrum, to resist any permanent positioning of the political self, informs his fiction in English. It also prevents us from treating his decision to write for American audiences as a kind of spiritual fall—a Faustian bargain with the dominant reading formation in the United States. The Yiddish socialist press of the 1890s threatened to compromise Cahan's literary project as much as the major monthly magazines that published his English-language work. Cahan accepted some of the conventions imposed upon him by the major monthlies, but he did so in order to accommodate his ongoing and unresolved meditation on Jewish identity. Furthermore, rather than simply capitulating to these conventions, he treated the theme of modernity's influence on immigrants as a crucial component of his project to educate American readers.

Paying attention to the shifts in Cahan's account of identity and to his views on the temporal location of Jewish immigrants forces us to confront an authorial subject whose orientation toward two different public cultures is defined by challenge and self-revision. In relation to socialist debates on Jewish identity, Cahan questions the assimilationist position, but he never commits finally to the belief that Jews will reorganize themselves in all-Jewish communities as they lose their religious orthodoxy. A character like Michalina feels the pull of such communities without ever situating herself decisively. Nor does Shaya, with his persistent exhibitions of Jewishness, rest easily and contentedly in his multinational community. Responding to the fact that such figures of uncertainty and ambivalence could only materialize outside the debates in Yiddish, Cahan moved to another public sphere, where he weighed the nature of Jewish communal belonging within a modern national context. In relation to an American audience intent on a literary tour of "the Jewish colony," he worked to present Jewish immigrants as rapidly developing people, contemporary urban figures irreducible to souvenirs. Like Hamlin Garland, he unsettled the contemporary belief that a population's marginality pointed to its parochialism and historical immaturity. Contesting the assumptions of his American readers and moving restlessly between positions on the Jewish question, Cahan distinguished himself not as a partisan but as a skeptical thinker, an ideological migrant exploring multiple conceptions of Jewish citizenship in the modern world. Committed to understanding the Jewish resettlement in turn-of-the-century America, he was, equally, reluctant to plot its end.

4

AN INTERLUDE

Mary Austin's Southwestern Protest and the Politics of the New Regionalism

IN APRIL 1926 THE ARCHAEOLOGIST EDGAR HEWETT, DIRECTOR OF THE New Mexico State Museum and the School of American Research, proposed the idea for a "Culture Center of the Southwest," to be located on land just outside of Santa Fe. His plan was to create an institutional alliance between his School of American Research, which specialized in southwestern archaeology, and the Southwest Federation of Women's Clubs, an organization spanning ten states. Catering mostly to the women who would spend time there, the Culture Center would serve as both a leisurely retreat and a venue for adult education, becoming something like a "summer university" during the busiest season.[1]

For Hewett, the plan appeared to be only one in a series of campaigns undertaken in a spirit of collaboration since the Atchison, Topeka, and Santa Fe Railroad had begun promoting the Southwest as a tourist attraction in 1895. Hewett, along with Frank Springer, had founded the New Mexico State Museum in 1907, presiding over its relocation to a larger site and its emergence as the recognized authority on cultural matters pertaining to the Southwest. Working in conjunction with the Railroad and with the tour organizing Fred Harvey Enterprises, the museum drew talented artists to the region by providing them with studio space, exhibit space, and national and international promotions. It also housed the School of American Research, which directed archaeological excavations and ethnographic studies and displays. Under the umbrella of the museum, the disciplines of southwestern art, ethnology, and archaeology all developed together in a relatively seamless and coordinated fashion.[2] There was, therefore, little reason to anticipate that any of Santa Fe's constituencies would resist the Culture Center plan.

What Hewett failed to consider was the growing prominence of transplanted writers, who, by the very nature of their craft, were far less dependent on the museum for work space and public displays than were painters and sculptors. As Mary Austin, Alice Corbin Henderson, Witter Bynner, and Mabel Dodge Luhan assumed the most powerful positions in the art colonies of the region, the museum's hegemony over the knowledge industry began to crumble, breaking down finally over the Culture Center plan.[3] The "yearners," as the writers came to be called, opposed the project on the grounds that Santa Fe would be overrun by Main Street America, its local difference compromised and its culture transformed into a cheap imitation of the real thing. These writers were proponents of a "new regionalism" that rejected late-nineteenth-century "local color" as the inauthentic offspring of East Coast, metropolitan audiences.[4] Wary of tourism's effects on local communities, they cringed at the thought of having Santa Fe so visibly subjected to the exigencies of the American mass market. With Mary Austin as their leader, they formed the Old Santa Fe Association to coordinate a national campaign against the establishment of the center. Members of the association wrote articles for eastern newspapers, gave speeches to civic clubs, enlisted the support of powerful friends outside the region, and sent hundreds of protest letters to local officers affiliated with the Federation of Women's Clubs. By the end of the year, the federation had capitulated to the artists and had withdrawn from the project.[5]

The Culture Center controversy occurred at a pivotal moment in the history of literary regionalism, as one dominant model for depicting the local community was giving way to another. In the early postbellum stages of nation-building, audiences of regionalism had only limited familiarity with the populations to which they were being introduced. They were, furthermore, often newcomers to tourism in general and its scenes of regional consumption. If a text like *The Country of the Pointed Firs* provided readers with access to communities that seemed untouched by the economy and manners of the metropole, the social and economic differences of such communities needed to be carefully managed. Those who came into contact, whether in literature or in life, with populations at the frontiers of America's expanded networks sought repeated assurances that they were encountering these folks in a comprehensible and unthreatening form. They wanted visible reminders that the populations they visited would accommodate themselves to visitation and, in addition, that they themselves would not lose their "civilization." The Bowden reunion scene in *Country* hinges, in fact, on a careful balancing between Dunnet Landing's ethnic purity and its visible desire to bond with and please the touristic narrator so as to fulfill its own ethics of visitation. Edgar Hewett and the other organizers of the Culture Center plan believed in the appropriateness of this model for the twentieth century. They assumed, in effect, that the needs of the American consumer had remained unchanged since the early postbellum stages of nation-building and that a Culture Center, presided over by experts and situated in a town that catered to tourists, would make the sights of the Southwest that much more appealing to the region's visitors.

The Culture Center controversy is thus a valuable tool for understanding the chronological development of American regionalism. For Austin and the other yearners, the model of regionalist encounter that the Culture Center implicitly supported rested on a skewed application of realist aesthetics. Under the visible influence of the mass market, the Culture Center would encourage travelers to mistake metropolitan ideas of southwestern places, people, and art for the region itself. In this way it would corrupt the raw material of tourism. In response, the job of the "new regionalist" was to limit the altering effects of the market, tend to local difference, and restore faith in the possibility of an authentic encounter with the other.

At stake in Austin's struggle for authority with the southwestern knowledge institutions, however, was not simply the degree of realism achieved by the regional artist or writer, but a vision of community as well. The Culture Center controversy allows us to understand the relationship between the "new regionalism" in art and the national conception of local belonging to which it was joined. For both Garland and Cahan, the postbellum model of regionalism had effectively diminished the power of local populations and, by association, the literary stature of those who represented them. Too often, the regionalist writing that appeared in the major magazines presented its populations as unconcerned with modern markets and incapable of national governance. For Austin and the "new regionalists," the problem with local color was not at all that it denied public influence to fringe communities, but rather that it compromised their cultural difference. The job of the artist was to reproduce the community in its pristine form, prior to its mass market exposure. Only through the process of saving and reproducing the organic community would the nation ever recover from the ills of modernity. Above all, the conflict over the Culture Center concerned the nation's social organization. What forms of family and community should the producers of southwestern culture help to generate and sustain? How, in turn, should the visitor or the literary tourist be interpellated—as a genteel housewife with a decorator's interest in the primitive, or as a social activist with the responsibility to preserve and transmit an ethic of organic community? For Austin and many of the other transplants who made up Santa Fe's art colony, women possessed an inherent talent for building community. Allowed to flourish as authorities in culture, their devotion to the untouched regional community would lead to a wide-ranging national transformation, a process that the Culture Center would necessarily preempt.

Contesting the Culture Center

From the vantage point of any booster of the region attempting to keep up with the trends, Hewett's proposition for a Culture Center in Santa Fe reflected an obsolete understanding of southwestern tourism. The industry had changed since the end of World War I. Previously, the Railroad and its affiliate the Fred Harvey Company had organized visits to the region around centralized sites, where the primitive could be seen and purchased within the reassuring context of a domestic setting. Those who toured the region by train came into contact with Native American products and artisans at places like the Indian House in Albuquerque and the Hopi House near the Grand Canyon, both of which were administered by the Harvey Company and situated in close proximity to the rail station. These sites taught visitors how to make indigenous artifacts conform to the standards of a domestic interior, and how to use the Indian for spiritual revitalization without becoming one. The message, as Leah Dilworth puts it, writing about Mack Sennett's prewar film *The Tourists* (1912), was "that in the encounter with the primitive other, it is best to keep one's distance and not to 'go native,' to stick to one's own side of the tracks, so to speak."[6] At other points of their visit, prewar tourists were invited to access Native American culture via the mediation of Anglo artists. The Railroad's advertising wing subsidized artists by purchasing their work and offering them free transportation "because [it] had found that a favored tourist attraction was viewing painters at work in their studios rendering colorful new Mexican landscapes and Pueblo scenes."[7] Responding to what they believed were the desires of tourists and forming these desires to match the limitations of rail travel, promoters constructed the scene of regional consumption as a settled outpost of civilization, marking it with the felt presence of the Anglo tourist, the painter, and the interior decorator.

With the advent of the automobile as an alternative means of travel, however, the Railroad confronted its deficiency as a tour guide for the more adventurous. Those with an appetite for a less mediated encounter with indigenous communities could now reject the train and explore on their own. The Railroad and the Harvey Company responded, in turn, with an enormously successful innovation called the "Indian Detour," which took cross-country travelers on two- or three-day motor trips to pueblos in the region and then brought them back to the rail station. The Indian Detour, which departed for the first time on May 15, 1926, in the midst of the Culture Center controversy, allowed the Railroad to keep pace for at least a time with the changing nature of tourism in the twentieth century (see fig. 3).[8]

Fig. 3. Back cover of a tourist brochure issued by the Atchison, Topeka, and Santa Fe Railway Company in May 1925, one year before the Indian Detour.

Mary Austin undoubtedly found the Detour an improvement on previous modes of travel: she used it not only as the title of a 1929 article in the *Bookman* but also as a metaphor to describe the experience of southwestern artists, whose work, she believed, had been authorized by direct contact with Native Americans. Unlike the work that the prewar Railroad had subsidized, the art that Austin celebrated concealed the signs of a mediating presence, so that "a wet gleam of arroyo and rearing cliff leap as freshly, as completely disentangled from the foreground as if it had just proceeded out of the in-knowing thought of the All-Father." The goal for the artist was to achieve a "disentanglement from an over-Europeanized subjective foreground" in order to offer the consumer an entrance into the indigenous life of the region rather than a perspective outside of it.[9] The Detour in its purest form meant leaving Anglo life for a period of time and sustaining an immersion in an environment perceived as primitive. It required of regional consumers that they join the artist in journeying to what seemed an uncorrupted source, resolutely unchanged by outside visitation. In Austin's view, only a collaborative detour by artist and consumer could preserve the aboriginal authenticity that remained a trademark of the region.

By the end of the 1920s, then, the dominant mode of representing and receiving the Southwest had clearly shifted. The Railroad had adapted itself to technologies that changed the way people traveled, and in the process, it was participating in the formation of new and more skeptical types of art producers and consumers. In this context, Mary Austin secured her authority as a political and an aesthetic representative by displaying her own intimacy with regional cultures and by publicly opposing a project like the Culture Center, which made the market's displacement of the indigenous all too evident. Her views on restraining the influx of the market in order to preserve the region's aura, indeed its marketability, were often supported by moneyed interests in the Santa Fe community. Thus, in her major article of protest against the Culture Center, she notes the backing of "an important contingent of the 'business men,' doctors, lawyers, merchants, educators, at Santa Fe" in describing "the sharp edge of a sword dividing the ways of community thought." As the *Santa Fe New Mexican* put it, those on Austin's side of the sharp edge were after "the kind of growth and the kind of business that [were] making Santa Fe substantial and prosperous, without impairing the assets."[10]

"Women's Genius" and the Politics of the New Regionalism

But if this was the climate that ensured Austin's success as leader of the Old Santa Fe Association, her investment in the Culture Center controversy far exceeded the motive of developing and sustaining tourism in New Mexico. At issue in her insistence on authentic contact between Anglo-American consumers and aboriginal communities was, most crucially, the nation's destiny. Austin spoke for a cross-section of American regionalists and folklorists who believed that urbanization, technology, and mass networks of communication were corroding American civil society.[11] From the "new regionalist" perspective, local artists needed to transmit culture and geography in indigenous form rather than adapt it in formulaic fashion to a mass audience, determined in its tastes by a metropolitan elite. Such conformity to mass networks led to atomized relations between individuals and, ultimately, to apocalyptic historical events such as World War I. By contrast, the preservation of organic communities such as those of the Southwest was crucial to the drama of national redemption, to the "re-settlement" of America as Lewis Mumford put it in *The Golden Day*. Austin saw herself and her fellow artists as prophets of redemption, warning against the consequences of a mass-mediated society and directing American subjects toward a therapeutic collective end. "Preeminently the novelist's gift is that of access to the collective mind," she writes in an essay titled "The American Form of the Novel." "Whoever lays hold on the collective mind at the node from which issues the green bough of constructive change, finds himself impelled toward what is later discovered to be the prophetic form." Austin's peers were often willing to grant her this status as American prophet, able to heal a disabled civil society by pointing it toward a promising destination. Henry Smith explained that "[t]he important thing about a prophet is that he has the insight into the state of his tribe, and out of that insight speaks thoughts needful to be heard by his fellows. It is in this sense that Mrs. Austin's characteristic works are prophetic writings."[12]

Austin had earned her prominent position in the regionalist movement by writing with sensitivity and great craft about a Western desert environment. *The Land of Little Rain*, published in 1903, was a short masterpiece of nature writing, dedicated in an uncompromising way to the intricacies of a region located just east of the Sierra Nevadas in the Mojave Desert of southern California.[13] With intimate attention to detail, Austin recorded the diverse ecosystem of the region, which included small mammals (rats, chipmunks, squirrels, and badgers), scavengers (buzzards, vultures, and coyotes), painted lizards, owls, bobcats, and wolves, and for flora, obscure shrubs and flowering herbs, great pine trees in the mountains, creosote, and mesquite. Human communities appear in the text in the form of a mining camp called "Jimville," several Paiute "campoodies," and the Mexican town of El Pueblo de Las Uvas.[14] Compared to her work in the 1920s, however, *The Land of Little Rain* seems relatively unconcerned with the articulation of a social vision for the local community. In other words, Austin does not write about these local communities as models to emulate or reject or refine, but as instances of desert life to be observed closely and with a measure of suspended judgment. Human communities surface as contributors to an interdependent ecosystem, which needs to be encountered in its full living diversity. At times, they add to this diversity by allowing cultural influences from outside the region to flourish. On Mexican Independence Day, for instance, the village of El Pueblo de Las Uvas sings "everything, America, the Marseillaise, for the sake of the French shepherds hereabout, the hymn of Cuba, and the Chilian national air to comfort two families of that land."[15] But Austin never lingers long enough on such features to convey a set of standards for local community life. In *The Land of Little Rain*, her attention to the entirety of the desert ecosystem points to a tradition of regionalism focused less on the nature of American civil society and much more on the uncompromised appreciation of a complex, multifaceted place.

By the time of the Culture Center controversy, however, the focus of Austin's regionalism, along with the "new regionalism" more generally, had clearly shifted to the "state of [the] tribe," as Henry Smith put it.[16] From Austin's perspective, a prophet like herself needed to identify a collective destiny for her people. Doing so meant tapping into what in *Everyman's Genius* (1923) she called "the deep self," the container of racial memory. The group inherited and then repressed a set of traits and experiences from the past, and the prophet's job was in part to recover these latent possessions. Racial archaeology, however, was only half the battle. Genius had to be "thought of as continually at work modifying the life process, as between the racial tendency and the environment."[17] For Austin, a brilliant and exceptional national destiny rested on the coupling of racial continuity and geographical adaptation as codeterminants of national identity. These two sources of nationality were intertwined and at the same time often in tension.[18] In *Everyman's Genius* the former—that is, the embrace of racial descent and the resistance to miscegenation—takes precedence, because "a Jew or a Serb or a Slav, however much Americanism his immediate-self may take on, when he begins to draw upon his deep-self will find himself able to reach only the experience of his racial past."[19] Those who can draw upon an Anglo-Saxon deep self, she implies here, are those who can both become American and transmit Americanism to their offspring. Yet if American is something that one becomes through residence, Austin must at times value the forfeiture of an original identity rather than its preservation. Thus, in *The American Rhythm* (1923), she privileges the "emotional kick away from the old habits of work and society,"[20] suggesting that nationalization depends on a moment of rupture and cultural forgetting. As Leah Dilworth, drawing on Walter Benn Michaels's work, has argued, Austin's celebration of Indians must be seen in the context of her cultural nationalism. Indians, despite threats to the homogeneity of their gene pool and to the diversity of their cultures, appeared to have realized themselves as the products of Austin's Americanizing agents. They were at once "the purest race we know anything about" and a group that "has been long habituated to the American environment."[21]

   While Austin could never quite determine which agent was primarily responsible for Americanization and which people as a consequence were eligible for citizenship, she was much more certain about the form the ideal nation would ultimately take. The result of refashioning the nation was neither an acceptance of the rationalized networks that precluded identification and intimacy nor their replacement with a single organic community at the national level. Rather, she envisioned a diversity of such communities distributed neatly across the country, easily distinguishable from one another by the influences of their respective local geographies. According to Austin's map, a high degree of cultural pluralism was the very sign of an autochthonous people. Such pluralism did not descend into racial difference or political animosity, provided that Americans guarded their cultures against unassimilable foreign incursions while allowing the territorial integrity of the United States—as if all parts of the land shared a mystical and undefined essence—to inform their blood and shape their destiny. Indian life, then, provided a vision not only of an aboriginal past but also of a national future composed of Americanized cultures, distinctive from one another and yet linked by the contiguity of their territories and an immanent racial memory.

In Austin's understanding of the Americanization process, the landscape functioned as an active feminine presence in relation to the nation's communities, disciplining otherwise fragmented subjects into cooperative arrangements. Thus, in *The Land of Journey's Ending* (1924), she describes a Pueblo society in which water shortage leads to the collaboration of a proximate population:

> When a crop can flourish handsomely on the run-off of natural watersheds, a family may subsist satisfactorily by itself for everything except its social occasions. But when a river is to be diverted in its course to irrigate the fields, then, by the same tie that they bind the river to the service of the corn, men bind themselves by the tie of the indivisible utility. Rain falls on radical and conservative alike, but the mother ditch makes communists of them all. That is, it makes for cooperative effort with psychological implications, to which the term "communism" is a clumsy, crab-like approach.[22]

The clumsiness of the term derives from its associations with political struggle, which is precisely what the mother ditch—through its elevation of community at the expense of the individual family—eliminates as a threat. Here, in the feminization of a geographic agent that forges a community, one begins to see how Austin's feminism merges not only with her environmental concerns but with her nationalist ones as well.

Austin had spent a large part of her literary-political career protesting the exclusion of women from public life and proposing policy changes, such as the establishment of community kitchens, that would improve their condition. Like many ex-suffragists in the 1920s, she was unimpressed with the results of enfranchisement and at times appalled by the failure of women to sustain the momentum of social change.[23] In an article for the *North American Review* (1923), she lamented that "[w]ith the ballot in their hands, the influence of American women in international relations, in domestic policies, in education, in literature and the arts and religion and science, is still largely indirect." The indirectness of female influence was a problem not only for women, but for the nation as a whole, for it precluded "the amelioration of social conditions through the interpenetration of the social organism by woman thought."[24] Austin often attributed the atomized state of the nation to a system that misconstrued the essential differences between the sexes. "Man is the perpetual adventurer," she insists, "who by a long process of stupidity has been made over into a kind of social hermaphrodite, a male-mother, whose sole duty and occupation it is to trot back and forth between his job and his offspring with the expected morsel."[25] "Women's genius," in contrast, "may take protean forms, but its mode will be almost universally to seek fulfillment in group service rather than in personal adventure."[26] The gender implications in the passage pertaining to the mother ditch become clearer in this light. In the same way that the southwestern environment could mother a group of disparate families into a community, women were the catalysts and caretakers of the social organism, the third determinant, as it were, in the process of Americanization. A nation that restricted women's communal talents to the nuclear family was denying its own realization as a people fully diversified by geography and linked by a common territory.

In her autobiography, *Earth Horizon*, Austin directs much of her protest against the circumscribed domestic space of the bourgeois family, which becomes an apt metaphor for any object that confines the female self, restricting its movement and surrounding it with the most artificial ornamentation. Interestingly, her response to domestic interiors leads to a system of literary categorization:

> What Mary knew after "Ivanhoe," completely and absolutely knew, was that she wanted to write books "with footnotes-and-appendix." She wanted to write books that you could walk around in. [F]rom that time she had a criterion: books were either to be walked about in, or "paper on the wall." The phrase she probably plucked out of the common speech. Wall-paper had but recently made its way from the genteel East. There was none of it in Mary's house, but Grandpa had it on the parlor, and the year that Mary was born, he began to stock it along with the other oddities of furnishings such as were offered in drugstores of the period. It was the way of people, when they wished to pay a modish compliment, to tell you your clothes fit "like the paper on the wall"; pasted flat over an artificially firmed outline. It was about this time that "glove-fitting" corsets came into vogue. What Mary meant by a wall-paper book was one you couldn't walk around in, as you did in "Alice in Wonderland" or "Ivanhoe," with notes.[27]

The advent of wallpaper in the Midwest is here associated simultaneously with the importation of genteel culture from the East and with close-fitting corsets that imprison the body. For Austin, the primary attributes of the pervasive Victorian home are its limited space and its alienating decorations. The phenomenon of wallpaper manages to conflate both of these characteristics. Books that belong in the wallpaper category are those with a diminished size and scope (the domestic fiction and local-color sketches, for instance, that many of Austin's nineteenth-century predecessors had been encouraged to write) and those that feel prescribed by alien convention. In either case, they do a kind of violence to the natural self, which is defined by its distance from conjoined sites of cultural (East Coast) and patriarchal (domestic) authority.[28]

Throughout the autobiography, the developing artist chafes against these sites of authority, whether they are represented by men or by the Victorian women of her mother's generation. Thus, her mother's "interest in 'Art' as a possible livelihood was completely disappointed by Mary's refusal to utilize it for the only purpose of which [her mother] could conceive in connection with Art as an education, for the enlivening and adornment of the home." And later on, with reference to her relocation to New York, she comments on "the unwillingness of men editors to step out of [women writers'] way. There was a growing interest in the experiences of women, as women, and a marked disposition of men to determine what should and should not be written."[29]

These cultural pundits pressed female artistic production into perversions of its natural inclination, but they were even more damaging to the female consumer, who, Austin believed, had been stripped of her capacity for discrimination. As a 1922 article for the *Bookman* makes clear, nowhere was the depletion of the female consumer more apparent than in the women's clubs, where culture was still being disseminated according to the Chautauqua model of adult education. "It is a humiliating admission for so confirmed a feminist as myself to make," she writes, "but a survey of what is actually transacting among the organized and federated groups of women from whom creative social reaction might have been expected, shows them, in respect to literature, art, and education, very much in the state of conscientious attendants at concerts who have to wait until the conductor turns around to know when to applaud the orchestra."[30] Women were not the only ones to suffer under these conditions, however, for "[i]t cannot . . . be assumed that men sitting together as an organized body to hear any available author read from or talk about his work, will produce any sort of result which will be found competent to support a creditable national literature." What women must begin to respond to "is not the book after it is written, nor the personality of the author who writes it, but the process by which a really vital book gets itself produced out of our communal experience."[31] In this article, Austin creates a correspondence between two social trends: on the one hand, women have been turned into passive consumers of art with a diminished tendency to exercise their own judgment, and on the other hand, the national culture has become dominated by figures who fail to promote collective consciousness, or what Austin calls "woman-mindedness in our literature and art."[32] The article depicts a cycle of passive female consumption and deracinated cultural production, the primary location of which lies within the institution of the women's club.

Austin's opposition to these clubs would have applied equally well to the Harvey Indian houses of the Southwest and to the early marketing of the region in general. For the Harvey Company had brought the Indian pueblo into the safe confines of a neatly organized domestic setting, where the primitive appeared to serve the home and where women were appealed to as consumers and home decorators. A Harvey guide to the Pueblo Indian, entitled *First Families of the Southwest* (1920), comments on the company's marketing strategy through the chapter titles it employs: "How the Indian Women Do the Cooking," "Indian Women Who Command the Household," "Where Woman Is the Perpetuator of the Arts," "The Pima Women, Who Make Baskets," to name just a few.[33] Such guides suggested that women could improve and regenerate their homes through inclusion of the primitive. Marketing the region effectively meant circulating images of native female artists, whose crafts, according to the experts, were intended not as expressions of a community's culture but as objects for household use and display. George Wharton James, whose books on Indian basketry provided valuable counsel to Anglo-American consumers, made the significance of the indigenous female artist explicit: "Where the maker of a basket has a definite use for the work of her hands it means something to her more than a mere money-getting proposition. Something of herself, her life, her thought, is put into that which she expects to use in her home life."[34]

As early as *The Land of Little Rain*, Austin was already writing against the notion that Indian women were ideal homemakers. In the chapter titled "The Basket Maker," she profiles an Indian artist named Seyavi who "made baskets for the satisfaction of desire,—for that is a house-bred theory of art that makes anything more of it."[35] By the time of *The American Rhythm*, Austin had shifted her focus away from collectible baskets and pottery entirely, preferring to focus instead on chants and legends, verbal products that did not accommodate themselves to the display case. The outcome she opposed was the production of the Southwest as an institutional extension of the bourgeois domestic realm—a site that, in effect, wall-papered the female visitor and the Native American producer simultaneously. It was exactly this kind of region that Austin viewed as the inevitable outcome of the Culture Center plan, designed as it was in the same spirit as the Harvey Indian houses. A region epitomized by the Culture Center would restrict Anglo women to their twinned roles as passive consumers and household managers, while forcing Native American artists to repackage their work in accordance with alien cultural conventions. The danger was that women, taught to read the Southwest by male authorities, would value it in turn only as a means of adorning the home. For Austin, such pedagogy and practice were a waste of both regional and female potential for realizing an autochthonous American people.

It is no surprise, then, that Austin voiced her protest to the Culture Center in a rhetoric that pits the "culture" of women's clubs against the indigenous Southwest and that identifies the effect of the one on the other as a process of distortion and domestication. In the *New Republic* article opposing the Culture Center, she begins by situating the proposed development within a history of Chautauqua institutions, characterized by "the pleasant air diffused by lectures and superficial predigested study courses and the presence on platforms of distinguished personalities politely stepping down the results of their labor to the comprehension of unlaboring audiences." Her only hope is that "the General Federation of Women's Clubs . . . may not feel itself so necessitous in the matter that it must make a cuckoo's nest of the most distinctive and creatively distinguished town in the Southwest, to incubate its own cultural expression."[36] From Austin's perspective, the nest built by the Culture Center would inflict its damage on three interrelated projects: on the preservation of regional communities, which would become uprooted and "fitted" to the wall-papered domestic realm; on the authorization of the female consumer, who would be kept from discovering her natural self in the role of the public mother; and finally, and most comprehensively, on the reformation of the nation's civic society.

What the nation desperately needed, according to Austin, was Americanizing contact with an indigenous population distinguished for purity of blood and absorption of local geographies. In order for the indigenous communities of the Southwest to have any national value, mediators were needed to reproduce the lifestyles and artistic expressions of a given community in their original, purely local forms. Such a process of intact transmission called for the talents of Anglo-American women. Gifted with the innate ability to forge collectivity, women were, in Austin's view, ideally positioned to convey the cultural essence of a community to an ailing nation of alienated individuals. Healing the nation in this manner required that Anglo women first reject the guidance of male knowledge purveyors who privileged the isolated patriarchal family. Austin pointed readers to the corruption that took place when native populations and female consumers were subordinated to the standards of the patriarchal home and thereby deprived of the chance to absorb and express the spirit of the local community. What she failed to note, however, were the limitations that homogenous local communities could themselves impose on modern individuals, both women and men, Native and Anglo. Willa Cather, in her writing on southwestern communities and her insistence on the place of the nomadic artist within such communities, would make these limitations apparent.

5

ART OBJECTS AND THE OPEN COMMUNITY
IN WILLA CATHER'S SOUTHWEST

AT ABOUT THE TIME OF THE CULTURE CENTER CONTROVERSY, A QUIeter conflict over regional representation was germinating in Mary Austin's own house. In late June 1926, Austin, undergoing surgery in St. Louis, had given Willa Cather access to her Santa Fe house as a refuge in which to write, and Cather, who was in the midst of researching and writing *Death Comes for the Archbishop*, had gone there in the mornings with much pleasure.[1] When Austin read the novel that was published the following year, she was less than pleased about her own generosity. "Miss Cather," she explains in her autobiography *Earth Horizon* (1932), "used my house to write in, but she did not tell me what she was doing. When it was finished, I was very much distressed to find that she had given her allegiance to the French blood of the archbishop; she had sympathized with his desire to build a French cathedral in a Spanish town."[2] And in a 1932 article published in the *English Journal*, she emphatically declares that Cather's sympathetic treatment of a French Jesuit priest "removes [the novel] from the category of regional literature."[3] For Austin, Cather's novel of the nineteenth-century Southwest made a dubious contribution to the building of indigenous regional communities within the United States. Was Cather's novel grounded in an American region or wasn't it? Set in a fictional landscape characterized by dynamic cultural convergence and centered around characters who were French in origin and nomadic by nature, it seemed to belong simultaneously to several territories and several national histories.[4]

Cather's novel, and Austin's reaction to it, suggest the need to account for yet another dimension to the struggle over how best to mediate the encounter between the native Southwest and the audiences who consumed it. If Mary Austin emerged as the primary regional spokesperson in the middle of the 1920s, adjudicating questions of public policy and aesthetic authenticity, her authority depended not simply on wresting power from the knowledge institutions of the Southwest but also on staving off implicit challenges to her mode of representation by figures such as Cather. Austin and the other yearners had treated the building of geographically specific local communities as the appropriate social end of both Anglo and native experience in the Southwest. Cather, in contrast, valued experience of the region, and of regional art, precisely for its refusal to be delimited by any project or end outside of the experiencing subject. Cather's work often celebrates subjects whose inner lives exceed their immediate physical surroundings and the communities in which they presently participate. At times she qualifies the range of the nomadic inner life by assuming the subject's return to a national or ethnic origin. But in *Archbishop*, lives do not always conform to the plot of cultural return. Cather's novel features both characters defined by a persistent passion for relocation and local communities designed to accommodate them.

Whereas Garland and Cahan brought the value of empowering modern local communities into regionalist writing, Cather recognized the limits that modern local communities could themselves place on emancipated thought and action. In *Archbishop*, such thought and action depends for its ongoing existence on the durability of artwork, architectural monuments, and religious shrines. Art objects become the guarantors of an individual subject who both participates in a local community and is capable of attachments with people outside of it. Drawing from Hannah Arendt's thoughts on the ethical importance of the art object, I propose in this chapter that together, Cather and Arendt comment powerfully on the place of the aesthetic category in contemporary visions of local belonging and the need to promote and defend it.

Cultural Utility and the Value of Artwork

Cather shared with Austin a belief that the artist had a crucial role to play in bringing the Southwest to the public's attention. Austin's hope was that artists, and specifically female artists, would ultimately realize themselves in group service, as social workers promoting a national commitment to sedentary organic communities. For the nation to become a people dispersed neatly along local lines, art had to evolve into a practice that served a collective function—a "woman-minded" practice expressive of an underlying American rhythm. In the writings not only of Austin but of other southwestern regionalists as well, art needed to shape American citizens into an autochthonous people, members of tightly unified regional communities. It is not surprising, then, that southwestern artists often imagined their work as an extension of their political activism on behalf of the Indian, for both practices shared the same project of social reorganization. A letter to Austin from Mabel Dodge Luhan, encouraging her to "get busy and write" in order that the nation would continue to invest itself in the politics of Indian rights, makes this merging of practices explicit:

> The country almost has seemed to go *indian*. . . . Is it possible that the lit-tle drop of indian *in* every one awakened and answered the call? Any way— what was *latent* is now awake and conscious and must be kept awake and nourished until vigorous and undeniable. We want *interest* and *apprecia-tion* of the indian life and culture to become part of our *conscious* racial mind. . . . This publicity is invaluable. That it began in politics does not prevent its being channelled into aesthetics. . . . Keep the indian *in* the public eye and soon he will be an integral part of the public welfare.[5]

Luhan establishes here that a common interest in Indian rights derives not from the provisional affiliation of dissimilar subjects but from the shared des-tiny of group members—from the latent drop of Indian on its way to becom-ing fully conscious. The country joins together because it already belongs to-gether, and, through the immediate political goal of Indian rights, it realizes the ordained agreement as the foundation of its beliefs and actions.[6] In the world as Luhan imagines it, political and artistic "publicity" (as she terms her activism) can be collapsed into one another without any loss to the subject. The two are interchangeable insofar as the subject is always already political, prior to any choice or action. Art serves to remind audience members of the collective commitment—to nation and local community simultaneously— that, according to new regionalists, defines and ennobles them.

Whether Austin understood this commitment as genetically or historically ordained, present materially in the blood or as a governing principle that the nation needed to realize fully over time, she too believed that the legitimacy and the value of art resided in its usefulness as a social instrument, designed at once to remind a people of its common destiny and to help a proximate pop-ulation coalesce as a local community. In an addendum to the 1930 edition of *The American Rhythm*, she conveys her faith in a progressive evolution toward aesthetic utility and in the centrality of women artists in achieving it: "It should not, however, appear at all astonishing that the more pronounced util-itarianism of women should have turned the lyric invention to social use; to have demanded of it that it should prove itself in being made to 'work' more directly than through its affectiveness in raising the plane of male activity. That poetry can be made to work successfully, to exhibit, as it were, life preserva-tive inherencies, is a group discovery of the utmost ancientness."[7] Like Luhan, Austin makes art the carrier of a group identity. Art is the vehicle responsible for circulating this identity to the various units of the social organism so that all activities—be they political, economic, or cultural—ultimately express the same collective consciousness. In Austin's contemporary world, the broader circulation of a given community's identity would ideally serve two collectivities. By bringing socially useful art to the public's attention, American artists of the Southwest could both preserve a particular group's identity and disseminate a national ethos of strong locality, promoting total participation across the nation in consolidated communities.

Nothing could have been further from Willa Cather's ideas on art, and indeed from her ideas on the value of southwestern art in particular. In an unpublished essay that could easily serve as a rejoinder to Luhan's letter, she writes that "unless [the artist] is more interested in his own little story and his foolish little people than in the Preservation of the Indian or Sex or Tuberculosis, then he ought to be working in a laboratory or a bureau."[8] What Cather insists on throughout her essays on aesthetics is the autonomy of artistic practice, evidence of which can be found in any human setting. In answering a query about "a new term in criticism: the Art of 'Escape,'" she explains that "this definition is for the moment used in a derogatory sense, implying an evasion of duty," but she asks rhetorically, "What has art ever been but escape?"[9] She makes her case by pointing to the pottery produced by Native American women—the same women whom Austin celebrated for their devotion to group welfare:

> Hundreds of years ago, . . . the Indian women in the old rock-perched pueblos of the Southwest were painting geometrical patterns on the jars in which they carried water up from the streams. Why did they take the trouble? These people lived under the perpetual threat of drought and famine; they often shaped their graceful cooking pots when they had nothing to cook in them. Anyone who looks over a collection of prehistoric Indian pottery dug up from old burial-mounds knows at once that the potters experimented with form and colour to gratify something that had no concern with food and shelter. The major arts (poetry, painting, architecture, sculpture, music) have a pedigree all their own. They did not come into being as a means of increasing the game supply or promoting tribal security. They sprang from an unaccountable predilection of the one unaccountable thing in man.[10]

The artwork of these women, who were experimenters with form and color, must be located not in the genealogy of the group, according to Cather, but in the discrete pedigree of the major arts. While Cather does not deny the influence of race in this essay, she does contest its determination of aesthetics. The geometrical designs that she invokes spring not from a thing in Indians but from a "thing in man," and they share no identity with what Austin called the "life preservative" activities of a group. Because they have neither origin nor

end in tribal culture, they attest to the transcendent humanity of the producers, who are not only the most human, but "of all men the most individual" as
well.[11] Cather goes on to mention several European artists (including Courbet
and Shelley) who dabbled in politics but were "'useful,' if you like that word,
only as all true poets are, because they refresh and recharge the spirit of those
who can read their language." Exempt from "considerations and purposes
which have nothing to do with spontaneous invention,"[12] the artwork, for
Cather, represents the end of one subjective experience (on the production
side) and the beginning (on the reception side) of a separate, but equally "use-
less," one.

According to the conception that emerges here, the artist can only achieve
anything worthwhile by imagining herself as a producer who is unrestricted
by national or racial culture. As Louise Bogan wrote in an article that para-
phrased an interview with Cather, "No one can convince her that sociological
reasons can explain the appearance of great writers in certain places at certain
times. Greatness, to her mind, is up to the individual; the culture into which
he is born can be of little help and less hindrance to the complete, freely functioning artist."[13] Inherited culture could not make the artist, nor could it in-
hibit her. This view of culture's limited sway provides perhaps the best context
for understanding Cather's contradictory attitudes toward Jews. For while she
could produce damning representations of Jews, she could also embrace Jewish artists, such as David Hochstein and Yehudi Menuhin, and use them as
character models in her work.[14] Such a discrepancy suggests that throughout
her career, the one Jew who was more human than Jewish for Cather was the
Jewish artist. Culture, as it was coming to be defined in the first decades of the
twentieth century, was never, to her mind, the content of great art.[15] Art was
an expression of an autonomous agent, who had freed herself from inherited
culture in order to discover the spiritual gift granted to her as a human being.

In Cather's fiction, however, this approach to aesthetics often coexists un-
easily with an approach to culture that confines individuals for at least some
of their lives to a national or racial category. Cather's work leads us to wonder
whether art is for her an exceptional practice, which allows only a temporary
escape from a world otherwise governed by inheritance. Thus, in *Death Comes
for the Archbishop*, Father Latour, after being served an onion soup on Christmas Day, remarks to Father Vaillant, his fellow priest and his chef for the day,
that "in all this vast country between the Mississippi and the Pacific Ocean,
there is probably not another human being who could make a soup like this."
"Not unless he is a Frenchman," Vaillant responds. Yet in the very next chapter, Latour loses this Frenchness when he allows himself to be imaginatively
transported to the Orient by a bell of Moorish descent.[16] Such experiences are

defined in this text not as occasional flights of touristic fancy but as the normative behavior of a nomadic personality. A kind of cycle emerges, then, in which cultural identity is established, only to be stripped of its agency by the freely functioning subject. What, then, is the relationship between the nomadic practices and beliefs associated with art and the more ingrained ones (such as cooking) that derive from an inherited identity? The question at issue here is whether Cather's nomads inevitably return to a culture of origin.[17]

Part of the point I wish to make in the readings that follow is that this return can by no means be taken for granted. Cather's insistence on the autonomy of the aesthetic subject contributes to a broad and consequential ethics: the artist's lack of a defining extrinsic end is embodied for her in the material work, and the work, in turn, signals the human subject's fundamental freedom from any particular destiny. Through art, Cather gives primary position to a subject who is inexhaustible even as this subject commits to a particular collective endeavor. Although some of Cather's essays seem to suggest that the freely functioning artist operates in a social vacuum, *Death Comes for the Archbishop* opens up the possibility of an alternative to this view. It offers us artistic characters whose thoughts and actions have no predictable destiny but at the same time clearly respond to the southwestern communities in which the characters take part. The novel, therefore, provides a way of conceiving art as both informed by the generative conditions of collective life and freed from the obligation to serve a particular group interest. Juxtaposed with an aesthetic that treats all endeavor—artistic as well as political—as an instrument in the service of a communal project, Cather's notion of aesthetic experience takes on urgency. It attends to a subject whose imaginative pursuits extend well beyond the defining limits of a group, whose very existence therefore underwrites two related ideas: that collective agreements are not natural but contingent on dialogue and that engagement with an outside world has value for those who enter into these communal agreements. As a means of protecting this mode of subjectivity, art for Cather has a necessary place in any community.

Thinking, Making, and Belonging in Cather's Regional World

Hannah Arendt's understanding of art and its significance, as described in *The Human Condition*, helps to clarify at least some of what is at stake for Cather. Like Cather, Arendt conceives artwork as the product of a thought process liberated from utilitarian concerns. "The immediate source of the art work is the human capacity for thought," she writes, and she quickly distinguishes between thought, which "has neither an end nor aim outside itself," and cognition, which "always pursues a definite aim."[18] The purely thinking man feels compromised by the end of production and therefore leaves no material trace of his activity. By contrast, art, a hybrid practice, derives not simply from the desire to think, but in addition from the desire to make things, to supplement a world of objects.

While artists belong to the tribe of *homo faber*, or man the producer, Arendt distinguishes them from producers who make objects for use, such as chairs and tables. Whereas chair-makers design their objects to serve a specific function, artists refuse to consecrate either their own thought processes or the material objects that embody them to a designated end. In this way, they help to keep in check the moral standard of utility, which in its dominating form reduces all beings and things to means, rendering them disposable and subjecting them to destruction. For Arendt, the threat is "not instrumentality, the use of means to achieve an end, as such, but rather the generalization of the fabrication experience in which usefulness and utility are established as the ultimate standards for life and the world of men." The artwork begins to take shape in her theory as a curb on two different types of *homo faber:* capitalist producers who treat all things, including their own creations, as disposable raw material for future production, and overly romantic revolutionaries, who posit no permanent institutions as the end of their violent actions. In both cases, "while only fabrication . . . is capable of building a world, this same world becomes as worthless as the employed material, a mere means for further ends, if the standards which governed its coming into being are permitted to rule it after its establishment."[19] Arendt incorporates autonomous artistic practice into an ethics concerned not only with the status of the subject, whose emancipation in thought depends on the limitation of instrumental thinking, but with the object world as well, where the work of art, by its very nature, promotes the durability of the world and the ontological value of certain things in and of themselves.

Arendt's focus is on the things that are produced by the freely functioning artist, but Cather's primary concern in *Archbishop* is the emancipated subject, whose inner experience constitutes the origin of the lasting artwork. Like Mary Austin, Cather is preoccupied with the authenticity of artistic endeavor, its capacity to generate and to draw on that which is irreducible in the artist's life. But in Cather, what is authentic or irreducible in the artist is not the presence of a shared geographical or genealogical source, but of inner experience that transcends both of them. Whereas in Austin authentic art testifies to the evacuation of self and the transmission of an identity rooted primarily in blood or land, Cather traces art to a state of intense imagination and affect, one that liberates the experiencing subject from any particular extrinsic origin or end.

It makes sense, then, that her two major characters are missionary priests who repeatedly displace themselves, departing from locations that previously limited the scope of their inner horizons. Through migration and travel—first from France to Ohio, then from Ohio to New Mexico, and finally within the Southwest and Mexico—the priests become psychically mobile subjects, in their imaginations intent on moving even when they are settling physically in a place. Thus, Jean Marie Latour, Cather's archbishop, wakes up one morning in Santa Fe to the ringing of a bell, which transports him to Rome and then further east, to "Jerusalem, perhaps, though he had never been there." He compares this event to a previous experience in New Orleans, when "an old woman with a basket of yellow flowers" had "dropped [him], cassock and all, into a garden in the south of France where he had been sent one winter in his childhood. . . . And now this silvery bell note had carried him farther and faster than sound could travel" (*DCA*, 43). Perceptions, desires, and momentary associations that do not pertain to the immediate temporal and spatial coordinates of the region are the very stuff of authentic expression. For such phenomena testify to the extraordinary nature of *inner* life in the Southwest, which for Cather comprises the proper content of regional art. While the southwestern landscape repeatedly stimulates imaginative flight, this flight cannot be reduced to the region, or to any other place for that matter. What makes it potentially aesthetic is that it belongs irreducibly to the mobile, multicentered subject.[20]

Compared to the missionaries' previous homes in Ohio and France, the Southwest is particularly well suited to such a subject. The objects that are most typically southwestern are those with the richest and most ambiguous derivations. While the bell is inscribed in Spanish, Father Vaillant informs his counterpart Latour that "it was pledged to St. Joseph in the wars with the Moors" (*DCA*, 44). This leads Latour to reflect that the Spanish learned their silversmithing from the Moors and that the bell was, "[i]f not actually of Moorish make, copied from their design." Moreover, in accounting for his own psychic associations, Latour points out that the bell is one of many southwestern silver objects with an indefinite origin, for the "Spaniards handed on their skill to the Mexicans, and the Mexicans have taught the Navajos to work silver" (45). Constituted by convergent histories, places, and populations, regional objects help to liberate a cosmopolitan subjectivity from the limits of a single cultural location.

But it is not only these highly textured human artifacts that encourage psychic mobility in the Southwest. Riding back to Santa Fe toward the end of the novel, Latour surveys the landscape and notices that "there was so much sky, more than at sea, more than anywhere else in the world. . . . Elsewhere the sky is the roof of the world; but here the earth was the floor of the sky. The landscape one longed for when one was far away, the thing all about one, the world one actually lived in, was the sky, the sky!" (*DCA*, 232). In the vast, flat spaces of the Southwest, the traveler sees a limitless sky not only when looking up, but also when looking out. If the region is made up in part of objects that belong to many places, then it consists as well of landscapes that have not been "placed" or defined at all. Such sky-filled landscapes, rather than overwhelming and defining the subject, encourage the kind of endless flight that Latour experienced in conjunction with the bell.[21] The natural attributes of the region redeem both residents and visitors not by imposing an autochthonous identity upon them, but by "softly pick[ing] the lock, slid[ing] the bolts, and releas[ing] the prisoned spirit of man into the wind, into the blue and gold, into the morning, into the morning!" (276).

As that quotation suggests, Cather's focus on the region's capacity for spiritual regeneration dovetails with her interest in religious faith. For if the region often serves as an immediate catalyst extricating the subject from any particular worldly destination, faith prepares the subject for such experience by directing his or her thought away from material preoccupations. The religious believer tends to the quality of inner life, valuing its phenomena above all other things in this world. What draws Cather to the lives of these missionary priests in the Southwest is what she later calls the "triumphs of faith" (*DCA*, 278) that take place there. Deprived of worldly comforts such as water, geographic familiarity, and institutional acclaim, the missionaries insist, in spite of their material longings, on the end value of their inner lives. In doing so, they prepare themselves to realize faith in the most emphatic and uncompromised ways.

The Southwest thus offers a setting in which the priests can triumph over their own longings for past comfort and habit. In addition, it offers the priests a communal life free of the restrictive conventions to which they otherwise would have been subject. Beyond the scrutiny of family members and provincial French society, Latour can cultivate and, in turn, give voice to his love for Vaillant without risking social disgrace—without, that is, worrying that he is violating arbitrary moral standards related to an object's gender.[22] As we will see more clearly further on, the archbishop must learn to redirect his love when it becomes exclusively focused on his fellow priest. Early in the novel, however, expatriation on the fringes of the western world, where old communal norms can give way to new ones that reflect the fluidity of love, allows Latour to confess his feelings freely: "Where there is great love there are always miracles," he says to Vaillant. "One might almost say that an apparition is human vision corrected by divine love. I do not see you as you really are, Joseph; I see you through my affection for you" (*DCA*, 50). In order to make space in his life for such intimacy and expression, Latour must deprive himself of relations with his biological family. As with faith, the pursuit of a miraculous, unbounded life of love requires a painful abnegation of desirable ends. He reflects at one point, "as any bachelor nearing fifty might have," that "[i]f he were a parish priest at home, there would be nephews coming to him for help in their Latin or a bit of pocket-money; nieces to run into his garden and . . . keep an eye on his housekeeping" (255). But underneath such a lament lies the conviction that life as parish priest would have been horribly restrictive and monotonous as well. Childlessness is the price that Latour must pay for uninhibited interpersonal experience and the cherished relational ties that result from it.

Those who take the intensity of their subjective lives seriously must not only forfeit certain readily accessible desired objects, then, but also break with the utilitarian values and expectations that too often dominate communal life. There is in this novel a spiritual reward for social superfluousness—a reward that is received within the temporal limits of human life. Achieving the reward, however, requires both courage and skill, stealth and secretiveness, because the subject who values inner life must both risk stigmatization and take care to avoid it. Toward the end of his life, Latour reflects on his own departure from France with Vaillant: "Both the young priests knew that their families would strongly oppose their purpose, so they resolved to reveal it to no one; to make no adieux, but to steal away disguised in civilian's clothes. . . . How clearly the old Archbishop could recall the scene; those two young men in the fields in the grey morning, disguised as if they were criminals, escaping by stealth from their homes" (*DCA*, 284–85). Cather envisions the seminal event of the missionaries' life here as criminal and illicit, something that involves concealing the passionate nature of their commitment so as to ensure its future flourishing. In a similar vein, we are told that Sada, the Mexican slave woman who helps to relieve Latour of his spiritual barrenness, "was carefully watched at home" by the Protestant family that owned her and that she "had slipped out through the stable door and come running up an alley-way to the House of God to pray" (213). Moreover, she wears her rosary beads "tied with a cord around her waist, under her clothes, as the only place she could hide them safely" (216). Sada receives her reward immediately, as she falls to the ground inside the chapel before a statue of Mary, shedding what Latour knows are "tears of ecstasy" (214). In the process, she suggests to us one of the central meanings that attach to the Virgin Mary over the course of the novel. In-

sofar as Marian devotion constitutes religious deviancy in a Protestant country (and particularly at the time in which the novel takes place),[23] such devotion is marked by the same experiences of captivity, secrecy, and transgression that Cather considers crucial to any life that covets and pursues inner
intensity.

Sada's capacity to share an episode of such intensity with Latour—not only
benefiting from his presence but also contributing to his conception of Mary,
as if a conduit connected the two worshipers to each other—points again to
Cather's understanding of art and its relation to cultural difference. For Cather,
subjective experiences that underlie artistic production and passionate religious devotion are not only available to all human subjects, but they are themselves in excess of a particular cultural location. We have already seen that in
this novel, Navajo silver craftsmen work their material in a manner that is not
entirely specific to Navajo tradition. Similarly, as Mexican and European religious practitioners share inspirational agents, they too produce objects that belong to a single history of the church in the Southwest rather than to a given
racial population. Well before the incident with Sada, we encounter the legend of the Virgin of Guadalupe. Juan Diego, a poor sixteenth-century Mexican,
is visited by Mary and then doubted by his Spanish bishop after he relates the
story of this miracle. Mary returns to Juan Diego, however, leaving him this
time with an indelible image of her on the inside of his mantle, so that the
Spanish bishop and his Vicar "instantly [fall] upon their knees" when they see
the man again. This bishop is not the only European who is drawn to the narrative and to the object associated with it. After hearing the story from a priest
who has journeyed to see the portrait of Mary now enshrined at the site of the
miracle, "Father Vaillant was deeply stirred . . . and after the old man had gone
. . . declared to [Latour] that he meant himself to make a pilgrimage to this
shrine at the earliest opportunity" (DCA, 49).

But if Juan Diego's miracle and its aftereffects suggest that all subjects can
potentially escape from their cultures of origin in Cather's Southwest, they are
in another sense a reminder of the limitations that cripple native southwestern populations in this text. Cather's Mexicans and Indians achieve inspired
moments like French and Spanish missionaries, but they rely for the time being on Europeans to ensure consistent memorialization of those moments.
The shrine to Juan Diego's miracle, we are told, is "the one absolutely authen-
ticated appearance of the Blessed Virgin in the New World" (DCA, 46). As a
material sign of a miracle produced by (or through) Mexican hands, then, it is
best considered an exception. The colonialism of Cather's vision is tied to this
question of the religious subject's durability in the region. Without the help of

the institutional European church and its facility in material production, native subjects leave little or no evidence of their extraordinary experiences and thus imperil the survival of the faith.[24]

Much like Arendt, Cather establishes a reciprocal relationship between durable sacred objects on the one hand (cathedrals, painted mantles, silver medals with the figure of the Virgin, for example) and the inner life, here the living faith, on the other. The art object plays a crucial role in the protection of religious life in the Southwest, for the region is not only a source of inspiration, sharing agency with a subject whose inner experience necessarily exceeds local attributes. It is also an assemblage of overwhelming landscapes, religious disorder, and brutal violence, all of which pose an enormous threat to the subject's ongoing imaginative vitality. The missionaries must contend with the region's terrifying potential to erase any trace of the subject entirely. This perception of the Southwest emerges most clearly during Latour's visit to the Acoma Pueblo, during which the bishop despairs that the "shell-like backs behind him might be saved by baptism and divine grace, as undeveloped infants are, but hardly through any experience of their own. . . . When he blessed them and sent them away, it was with a sense of inadequacy and spiritual defeat" (DCA, 100). Here, Acoma Indians are presented as undeveloped infants, victims of the powerful destructive forces that Latour has encountered on the way to the Pueblo. The bishop falls into despondence during and after this visit in part because he foresees the vanishing (spiritual and physical) of the Indian as inevitable and laments his own failure to do anything about it, but also because the Southwest as he now perceives it renders all experiences of transport meaningless as it denies them future life. In doing so, it dooms Latour himself to the kind of cloistered withdrawal practiced by the Spanish priest Fray Balthazar, who was ultimately hurled off the edge of Acoma for indulging his fantasies of the European good life to the detriment of the pueblo's inhabitants. The options appear grim at this point in the novel: one is either completely *of* the region (as the Acomas are) or mired in a circumscribed European setting. If man the maker cannot share space with an agent as powerful as the southwestern landscape, then man the thinker stands no chance either.

This sense of doom and cultural isolation disappears by the end of the novel. As Latour rediscovers the possibility of a fruitful spiritual life in the region, he revises his opinion of Native Americans. "I do not believe, as I once did, that the Indian will perish" (DCA, 297), he says. Yet one is left with the feeling that his rediscovery and his revision are contingent on a tasteful composition of the region according to French principles of form. As another bishop insists at the beginning of the novel, "the Germans classify, but the

French arrange! The French missionaries have a sense of proportion and rational adjustment" (9). It is precisely this sense of proportion and adjustment that the region seems to require at the outset. For Cather begins by describing a beautifully ordered European landscape, where three cardinals and a missionary bishop discuss the need for a new vicarate in New Mexico, which has recently been annexed by the United States. Immediately after this scene, she introduces Latour in the middle of the desert, wandering in what he perceives as a "geometrical nightmare" (18). To be sure, this description points in part to the bishop's unfamiliarity with southwestern geography and to his own need of adaptation. But given what transpires over the course of the novel, it suggests as well that this "country was still waiting to be made into a landscape" (95) and that the French missionaries are responsible for supervising its settlement and composition.

Moreover, prior to such settlement, the threat posed by the region surfaces from within the bodies of regional subjects, so that Latour and Vaillant must protect their parishioners not only from geographic agents, but from biological ones as well. Much of the fifth book of the novel recounts the bishop's effort to assert institutional authority over a Mexican priest, Father Martinez, who flaunts his violation of the celibacy code by pointing out his children. As suggested by the slovenly state of his house—the "young man lying on the floor, fast asleep" (*DCA*, 143), and the "woman's hair that had been indolently tossed into a corner" (149)—Martinez implicates the members of his diocese in his own bodily disorder. For Latour, the deficiency of such a man resides in his refusal to acknowledge the rule of law—his insistence instead on the primacy of his own appetites and the arbitrariness of his own autocratic power.[25]

Cather conveys quite clearly in this section that Martinez and his followers are currently vulnerable to such lawlessness and that its consequence is not a failure of faith in the present—as the Mexican priest himself declares, "Our people are the most devout left in the world" (*DCA*, 147)—but a failure to ensure its future survival. Martinez is a producer exclusively of children, rather than of sacred objects that will outlast them (such as the cathedral that Latour builds at the end of the novel). In effect, he channels his productivity only into the making of subjects, who are themselves destined for worthlessness without objects that attest to their value. After hearing Martinez give mass, Latour reflects that "[r]ightly guided . . . this Mexican might have been a great man. He had an altogether compelling personality, a disturbing, mysterious, magnetic power" (150). Martinez represents not a failure of intellect, then, but quite literally a failure *to make something* of his intellect. What guidance, in the form of a European priest, would provide is more control over both biological reproduction and the raw intensity of the subject, so that the one does not dominate life and the other not only inspires but assumes a lasting external form. The need for such guidance entitles the French to administer the southwestern territory. For the mobile subject cannot emerge reliably until the Frenchmen have ensured the region's arrangement, attaining control over agencies that compete with the subject and inculcating an ethic of durability.

Clearly the most appealing way to Americanize the Southwest according to Cather's particular style of colonialism is to place the region in French hands. Anglo American administrators, unlike Martinez, produce inanimate objects in this novel, and yet they ignore the need to make *sacred* things and to designate them as such. They fail to ensure that some objects, manmade as well as natural, are kept from being used up. At the end of his life, Latour reflects that "the year 1880 had begun a period of incongruous American building. Now, half the plaza square was still adobe, and half was flimsy wooden buildings with double porches, scroll-work and jack-straw posts and bannisters painted white." The flimsiness and incongruousness of such architecture conveys the message that neither the buildings themselves, nor the subjects who built them, nor the "half-circle of carnelian-coloured hills" (*DCA*, 271) that surround them have any persistent value; all of these entities are only raw material for the meaningless cycles of destruction and production that the instrumentalist producer visits on the region.

To please Mary Austin, Cather might have suggested that the antidote to this American building was more adobe-style houses, in keeping with local tradition and the previous identity of the town. Instead, Cather applauds her archbishop for constructing a cathedral that, while adapted to the natural land, is Midi Romanesque in style. Seen from afar, "the Cathedral lay against the pine-splashed slopes as against a curtain." But when one "drove slowly nearer, the backbone of the hills sank gradually, and the towers rose clear into the blue air, while the body of the church still lay against the mountain" (*DCA*, 272). Cather negotiates carefully here between the church's organic incorporation into the land ("the backbone of the hills") and its status as an artificial addition ("the towers . . ."). Unlike the flimsy wooden buildings, the solid and agreeable cathedral testifies to the value that she places on the durable human artwork, in balance with the natural world (see figs. 4 and 5).

As we can see, then, the cathedral is a crucial figure in this novel in part for its function as a lasting manmade object. It attests both to the need for things that mark the spiritual subject's presence over time and to the role of the French in providing such well-made things. The work itself would seem, in this sense, to emanate from Latour's French identity. When we begin to con-

Fig. 4. St. Francis Cathedral, Santa Fe, New Mexico, from a distance. St. Francis was the model for the cathedral in *Archbishop*. Photograph taken between 1905 and 1915 by H. S. Poley. Denver Public Library, Western *History* / Genealogy Collection, P-1350.

sider the monument as the product of its builder's accumulated experience, however, its status as a specifically French object becomes less certain. The cathedral gives material form to the history of the church in the Southwest, to the many experiences of faith that Latour has been absorbing and collecting over the course of the novel. Insofar as those experiences resist cultural location, one would expect the church to do so as well. In emphasizing both its Midi Romanesque style and its adaptation to the southwestern landscape, Cather complicates the identity of the monument. Is it best considered a French artwork within the Southwest or, instead, an object much like the bell, lacking a fixed cultural identity?

Cather foregrounds the cathedral's expressive ambiguity: from one angle, the most crucial feature of the church is its southwestern setting, while another angle reveals its Midi Romanesque towers. But if we can read the cathedral as being less French for the importance of its setting, we can also read it as being more French. In justification for his choice of style, Latour tells Vail-

Fig. 5. St. Francis Cathedral, Santa Fe, New Mexico, February 1943. Photograph by John Collier. Library of Congress, Prints and Photographs Division, FSA/OWI Collection, LC-USW33-019175-C.

lant that "[o]ur own Midi Romanesque is the right style for this country" (*DCA*, 243). Why exactly it might be the right style is never fully articulated, but the glimpse we get of the final product suggests that its rightness can be traced to its inherent adaptability. Since Midi Romanesque can be accommodated to any scene, it has the potential to look good anywhere it appears. In the same way that French architecture seems to agree naturally with any local geography, so too in the later stages of the novel the French tongue becomes literally something of a lingua franca, ideally suited to translating and preserving regional facts and legends. In relation to such verbal artifacts, Latour wishes that "he had had the leisure to write them down, that he could have arrested their flight by throwing about them the light and elastic mesh of the French tongue" (277). Here the French missionaries import a form that is exceptional not only for its durability but also for its elasticity—a quality that informs the cathedral as well. If Frenchness does not conflict either with the regional landscape that frames it or with the unbounded inner experiences that it potentially represents, then as a builder of a monument to the southwestern church, Father Latour can retain both his inherited identity and his cosmopolitanism. He can embrace the carnelian hills and the faith of parishioners like Juan Diego while remaining a loyal Frenchman. In effect, he can have his exile and his return simultaneously.[26] Throughout this text, there is a tension between the mode of subjectivity that feeds artistic practice or religious faith and the one that is determined by a cultural identity. In many of the final pages of *Archbishop*, Cather attempts to reconcile the two by focusing on what she considers an intrinsically capacious inherited identity, one that is fully realized through the experience of cultural mobility.

Such a solution, however, is in no way a final answer in a novel that meditates so incessantly on the "freely-functioning artist" and the experiences that underwrite her or his practice. To accept the premise that the less French one becomes, the more faithful one is to French identity, is to view the subject's mobility within predetermined limits, to render it a mere function of a cultural placement that is always naggingly around, never permitting a position outside of it. Because Cather's ideas on aesthetics require her to secure this outside position for at least some of her characters, she often resolves the tension between the two modes of subjectivity by erasing the influence of cultural identity entirely and by treating the genealogical family as a provisional rather than a necessary type of community. Her characters form powerful affective bonds across lines of descent, both in response to the miraculous subjective experiences that I have discussed and in order to enable them. In forming such bonds, they call into question the relevance and the value of an inherited identity. The sense of communities shuffled with one another, in fact, defines the opening scene of the novel, in which the missionary who pleads the case of Father Latour is "Irish by birth, French by ancestry—a man of wide wanderings and notable achievement in the New World," while the host cardinal has a Spanish face "much modified through his English mother" (*DCA*, 5). Furthermore, of the people whom Latour considers major players in his life, three of the five who are mentioned (Kit Carson and the two Olivareses) take part in interracial marriages.[27]

For his part, Father Joseph is the character most clearly associated with the recurring episodes of family rupture, which achieve an almost archetypal significance in this text.[28] Cather explains that "it was the discipline of his life to break ties; to say farewell and move on into the unknown" (*DCA*, 248). The scene in which the two priests depart from their families with the intention of leaving their homeland surfaces three times in the final third of the book, once through Vaillant's memory and twice later through Latour's. Vaillant reflects that his was "a close-knit family" and that the departure was "the hardest act of his life; to leave his country, to part from his dear sister and his father. . . . That parting was not a parting, but an escape—a running away, a betrayal of family trust for the sake of a higher trust" (204). In this instance Vaillant tears himself away only because Latour is present to remind him of "a higher trust," but later in their lives as missionaries, their roles become reversed. The same capacity for attachment that makes leaving so painful for Vaillant allows him to forge new bonds, to insert himself fully into the communities he encounters: "Wherever he went, he soon made friends that took the place of country and family. But Jean, who was at ease in any society and always the flower of courtesy, could not form new ties" (253).

Latour's social deficiency is noticeable only in the New World, where he strives to recreate a French family with Vaillant even if at times it means compromising the cultivation of his own love and that of others. The original scene of rupture replays itself not only in memory, then, but in a new form as Vaillant struggles to define the New World French family as a provisional one, which can give way when need be to a sustained emotional investment in other communities. The problem with Latour's desire for his friend is not that it is homoerotic, in other words, but that it threatens to render both himself and Vaillant fully stationary—to deny the world a figure with an appetite for the unfamiliar and himself a more versatile subjectivity. In effect, Latour frees his love from the aim of biological reproduction and from the mandate to desire only the opposite sex, but not from the model of an enclosed family—not from the notion that love should be limited according to one's race or nation.

As Susan Rosowski has argued, the kind of love that Cather ultimately celebrates in this novel—the kind, I would add, that conflicts both with Latour's attempt to deepen the roots of the New World French family and with Cather's own uneven assumption of an inherited cultural identity—is the theological virtue of agape. Unlike eros, agape exceeds attraction to any particular object or to any one community, thus constituting a desire without restriction, extensive to all humanity.[29] This is precisely the type of love that Vaillant embraces when he insists for the first time on leaving Santa Fe. "I have almost become a Mexican!" he exclaims. "I am *their man!*" (*DCA*, 208). In saying so, he implies first that he has reimagined his own national identity—an implication that is reaffirmed when he returns from Colorado to raise money among the Mexicans and experiences himself as "[o]nce again among his own people" (259); and second that he is not Latour's man, that he is theirs for now and not his. Latour, in turn, expresses his reluctant acceptance of his friend's claim by approaching the tamarisk tree in the garden where they sit and breaking off "a spray of the lilac-coloured flowers to punctuate and seal, as it were, his renunciation" (209). The tamarisk has already been aligned with the Mexican population, so that Latour's gesture comments not only on his own separation from Vaillant but on the latter's affiliation with this people as well. Latour effectively removes the one obstacle preventing his friend from becoming like "the tree of the people, . . . like one of the family in every Mexican household" (202). When a Mexican woman appears in the garden moments later, Vaillant sends what can be construed as another gentle message to his superior. "Magdalena, Magdalena, my child, come here and talk to us for a little. Two men grow lonely when they see nobody but each other" (210). It is a message, and a model of open community, that Latour himself takes to heart several months later, when he promises Sada that "I will remember you in my silent supplications before the altar as I do my own sisters and nieces" (217).

For Cather, the source of the movement—driving Vaillant to insist on his own departure, inspiring Latour to rethink his family, and allowing Sada to escape from her restrictive one—is the Virgin Mary. We have already seen that Marian devotion evokes the secrecy and transgression of a valued inner life. Part of what it affords the worshiper as reward is an extended period of rebirth, a period in which an old skin is shed and a new one has not yet taken its place. The Virgin's capacity to regenerate her followers leads Father Vaillant to sanctify the month of May as the one most appropriate to her worship. Recovering from his illness during "the month of Mary," he relishes the chance "to worship with the ardour of a young religious, for whom religion is pure personal devotion, unalloyed by expediency and the benumbing cares of a missionary's work" (DCA, 203). But the month of Mary is more than a contained period of emancipated contemplation, for in Vaillant's life spiritual rebirth always leads to action that alters the destiny of his life. It was in May, we are told, that he left his "close-knit family," and in May once again that he spoils Latour's attempt to reconstruct the French family on American soil. Cather's ambivalence over the culture concept as a tool for organizing communal life emerges most clearly in her fascination with what she calls the "beautiful concept of Mary" (218), which reflects and provokes affective bonding between those who do not share a language, a lifestyle, a community of origin, or even a religion. What defines their sense of connectedness is simply the common need and the common capacity to fraternize with other human creatures. One scholar of Mariology has written that there exists for those who revere her a "bond of motherhood that attached her to her son and to the whole human race through him."[30] Yet for Cather, Mary's relation to the human aggregate seems to precede any mediation by Christ or by the faith constructed around him. Reflecting on the Mexicans of his parish and their devotion to Mary, Latour notes that they "were not the first to pour out their love in this simple fashion. . . . Long before Her years on earth, in the long twilight between the

Fall and the Redemption, the pagan sculptors were always trying to achieve the image of a goddess who should yet be a woman" (257). What is immaculate, finally, about Mary is that she exists throughout time and across cultures to remind people of their potential to forge relations with each other.

The Artwork and the Cosmopolitan Local Subject

In *Death Comes for the Archbishop,* Mary is the muse that inspires not simply intensified subjective experiences, not simply an ethic of universal belonging, but a reciprocal relation between the two. In trying to conceive her, the pagan sculptors, if they are anything like Latour and Vaillant, will realize at some point that she visits most reliably where the channels between communities remain open and that her visits, in turn, promote passage through such channels. Cather's muse seems to merge seamlessly with the natural attributes of the region, as if the Southwest is itself an extension of her. When Latour reflects on the southwestern air, which "released the prisoned spirit of man into the wind, into the blue and gold" (DCA, 276), he dissolves the religious muse into the environmental one, since the former, we have already been told, appeared to Juan Diego "clad in blue and gold" (47) and was reproduced on his mantle "in robes of blue and rose and gold" (49).[31] Like Austin with her mother-ditch, then, Cather drops her female muse into the region, associating her metonymically with qualities like wind and air and sunlight.

Yet the fact that Cather's muse fits no finite, earthly form tells us much about the differences between the two writers and the kinds of possibility that each one saw in the region. Austin's mother-ditch, like the land in general, taught subjects to privilege the indigenous community over both the individual subject and the domestic family. Whatever hardship a population suffered at the hands of a brutal environment was probably worth it in the long run, insofar as its members settled more deeply into their cooperative arrangement around the ditch, realizing a group destiny in their collective response to a common local habitat. That single destiny was not the only one that counted for Austin. As populations immersed themselves in local American landscapes, they imbibed a national identity that inhered throughout the contiguous territory. Differentiation by locality signaled not disunion, but an autochthonous nation. Tied together by a common land, the nation acquired consistency in direct proportion to its geo-cultural variation. According to Austin's vision, appropriate regional representation helped to achieve two perfectly compatible communal ends—one local and one national. By containing women and corrupting model indigenous folk, the Culture Center jeopardized both of these ends.

For Cather, the end of regional representation was neither the local nor the national community, but the cosmopolitan local subject. A place characterized by wide-open landscapes and the convergence of previously disparate populations deserved to be celebrated as a home for psychic nomads, for people who chafed against what Cather called "the hard molds of American provincialism."[32] It is fitting, then, that her female muse and the heart of her region resided in the sky, where both visitor and resident had an ongoing reminder of their boundlessness. In Cather's Southwest, a person came to realize that he was in excess of the project(s) to which he was committed, the culture into which he was born, and the world that was immediately available to his senses. This excess, or irreducibility, is in Cather's text the source of the subject's sacredness and the point of departure for the lasting artwork. As an enduring tribute to an experience characterized by such irreducibility, the artwork not only reflects the sacred subject but also secures a permanent place in the world for her. That is to say, the durable artwork reminds all who encounter it that the world honors and cherishes contemplative freedom enough to memorialize an instance of it, to treat that instance as meaningful rather than evanescent.

In *Archbishop,* the production of art and the future of the sacred subject in the Southwest is contingent on the arrival of the French priests. Clearly, Cather's vision both justifies European administration of the Southwest and ignores what Austin called "the tragic implications" of the French Jesuit influence in the middle of the nineteenth century.[33] Yet I would also argue that once we bracket out European settlement as a condition for the sustained practice of art, Cather offers us an illuminating treatment of the ethical role that aesthetics can play within a local community.

I concede that the idea of an inherited culture as the ordained end of a subject's life does not simply disappear in Cather's text. At certain moments, as for example in the observation of the cathedral, the original culture appears to constitute not only a point of departure for the regional artist but also an inevitable point of return, one that frames and thus ultimately informs all of the subject's experiences. Yet the culture concept is fundamentally incompatible with Cather's emphasis on irreducible subjectivity, and I have tried to show as well that the inconsistency often leads her to question "culture" as a principle of belonging—to propose instead a more fluid type of social organization and a "public mother" who disregards original identity in favor of a love that is always extending itself. Cather's text testifies to the abiding ethical importance of the unencumbered subject, whose presence as a concept contradicts the belief that people belong to groups and take on collective ends prior to choosing these ends. The point is not that such a subject is compromised by participation in a community or by commitment to a group objective, but that he remains in excess of the group, capable of changing his affiliation, even as he participates and commits himself.

To remind ourselves of this excess in the current context of literary criticism would mean to value those places in a text where the subject's historical situation becomes uncertain, where the project or the "logic" that appeared to govern the unfolding of the text is suddenly destabilized by another aim, an unpredictable thought. It would also mean challenging the claim that art objects function exactly as other useful social objects do and that the category of the aesthetic is therefore fully collapsible into the primary ends of historical action and analysis—namely those that relate to racial, class, gender, and national formation. According to such a conception, there is really no ethical need for the art object to exist at all, insofar as it performs work that could be more effectually accomplished in other social documents.[34] Put to the test, most cultural critics would probably agree that the arts have an important place in any imaginable historical context. Cather and Arendt help us to say why this might be so.

For both of these writers, the art object is worthy because it conveys the meaningfulness of contemplation and, in doing so, encourages those who encounter the artwork to value the thinking subject as well. I would take issue with Cather's assumption that a mobile subjectivity becomes compromised when it aligns itself or is aligned with a movement for social justice or political change, or when it dwells too much on the material conditions that surround it. For these ends do not place *exceptional* limits on the subject. Insofar as they expose the contingency of previous assumptions, in fact, they often help to liberate thought, opening it up to new horizons. In a similar vein, a critic who finds evidence of an ideology or a group consciousness in an artwork does not spoil its artfulness, provided that the object is also recognized as a valuable end itself, never finally reducible to a collective purpose at play in it. Cather's skepticism toward the ethics of utility does, however, remind us that it makes ethical sense to avoid treating art simply as an instrument of one or several political projects. The objects we designate as aesthetic become part of an archive of fluid, unroutinized thought, one that will change over time but that should always remain open and accessible to artists who reject intellectual complacency. Such an archive imparts the idea that citizens have no specific historical destiny, only communities to which they provisionally belong.

6

JUSTICE AND THE GLOBAL FOLK COMMUNITY IN ZORA NEALE HURSTON

IN HER FIRST PUBLISHED STORY, "JOHN REDDING GOES TO SEA" (1921), Zora Neale Hurston introduces a character whose type reappears at crucial moments in her work. John Redding, "an imaginative child and fond of day-dreams," aspires to leave the southern village where he was born and see "the wide world." While his dreams do not distinguish him from the previous generation, his expressiveness does, and John becomes—if for only a brief period before his death—a speaker for the inner life of those who came before him. As his father states, "Ah have them same feelings exactly, but Ah can't find no words lak you do. It seems lak you an' me see wid de same eyes, hear wid de same ears an' even feel de same inside. Only thing you kin talk it an' Ah can't. But anyhow you speaks for me, so whut's the difference?"[1]

Hurston concerns herself here with the capacity of a speaker to do verbal justice to a neglected and misrepresented people. The passage calls to mind the often cited moment of her mother's death in Hurston's autobiography, when Hurston's mother, rendered incapable of speech by her illness, looks to her daughter "for a voice."[2] To speak for people like her mother is also, in Hurston's work, to speak against interpretations that have denied them the fair treatment in print to which they are entitled. "The Gilded Six-Bits" (1933), for instance, a story about a Florida working-class couple, addresses a woman's infidelity and the emotional conflicts that take place within both partners as she struggles with her guilt and he with the need to forgive and love again. A white store clerk, who encounters the man after he has rescued his love from resentment, offers an interpretation typical of plantation fiction: "Wisht I could be like these darkies. Laughin' all the time. Nothin' worries 'em."[3] Here the blatantly false testimony of the clerk authorizes Hurston's story as compensation for the verbal injuries inflicted by past writers and interpreters.

In all of these instances, Hurston evinces an awareness that culture workers have a role to play in repairing representational damage. She herself had to compensate for the negative definitions that had in the past denied dignity to people like her own mother and John Redding's father.[4] Yet despite her awareness of this obligation, Hurston's attitude toward the issue of cultural repair is often characterized by attention to her own limitations. A primary question for her throughout her career is how to conceive of the justice she renders and how to position herself in relation to the southern populations she ostensibly serves. Who is she to judge how the people whom she studies should be recognized in public? Is Eatonville, the community where she was born and the one to which she returns repeatedly in her work, merely an object for redemption, waiting passively to be delivered into its rightful place by a city-dweller who no longer lives there? Hurston's inquiry into the role of the artist figure in relation to the local community revolves around this issue of aesthetic justice. Addressing the issue adequately, as we will see, leads her to place demands not simply on the artist, but on the community as well.

Few authors have pondered the theme of justice more explicitly and incessantly than Hurston. "Spunk" (1926), "The Bone of Contention" (unpublished), *Jonah's Gourd Vine* (1934), *Their Eyes Were Watching God* (1937), and *The Conscience of the Court* (1950) all hinge on court cases, and they invite us to consider not merely a legal decision but also the court's method of deciding. Through these trials, Hurston proposes methods of judgment that apply to her own authorial treatment of characters. Yet her approach to justice is anything but consistent over the course of her career. In the early stages, she often seems to approach her work believing that literature can create, in fiction and perhaps through fiction, a justly proportional world. The short story "Sweat" offers a telling example of her early attraction to this idea.[5] Delia, the main character of the story, suffers the harassment and repeated infidelity of her husband, Sykes, who does not work and resents Delia for doing the laundry of white people for pay. Aware of his wife's fear of snakes, he brings home a rattlesnake to torment her. But the snake ends up biting and killing Sykes instead, and Delia watches as her husband slowly dies. The story ends with a punishment that makes the world legible and returns it to a condition of rectitude. It is the kind of ending that stands in stark contrast to the death of Tea Cake in *Their Eyes Were Watching God*, a death that seems a cosmic injustice (to both Janie and Tea Cake) and leaves the world out of proportion, marked as morally and epistemologically incomprehensible.

The lingering sense of an unbalanced and unknowable world in *Their Eyes*—Tea Cake's sudden disease and death and Janie's undeserved state of deprivation—points to a fundamental shift in Hurston's writing. Over the course of the 1930s, she began to rethink what it means to do justice to African Americans, as she pondered exactly what doing justice might mean within the context of the "folk" lives that she observed. No longer simply a static cultural object to be translated or a lost treasure to be recovered, Eatonville, in the hands of those characters whom she admires most, becomes a focal point of judgment itself. As she writes in reference to a porch debate in *Their Eyes*, Eatonville makes a claim for itself as "the center of the world."[6] It provides a "spyglass" from which to look out at objects and inward toward the self: the porch talkers teach us not what to know, but—more valuably and reliably—how to go about knowing.[7] While this spy-glass emerges in its purest form on the porch, it derives from a religious sensibility that exceeds the porch, and it manifests itself in a variety of contexts both within and outside of Eatonville. Like Garland, then, Hurston recognizes that the members of her communities need to be imagined not simply as the passive objects on whose behalf she speaks but as deliberating agents, assessing methods of aesthetic production and reception. She urges us to view Eatonville as a necessary way station, a checkpoint in the imagination, for those who participate in the public conversation on aesthetic justice. Giving voice in this context means not only attempting to reproduce a manner of speaking or a particular message, but recognizing local subjects as shapers of a conversation, with a particular orientation toward knowledge and with the capacity to discipline writers and readers who would judge them in a misguided way.

　　As Hurston explores the religious approach to justice that forms the normative foundation of so much shared experience in fictional Eatonville, her previous conceptual framework for defining the local community becomes unsettled. Like many Harlem Renaissance intellectuals, Hurston had depicted the folk community as the origin of a self-reparative racial tradition, a tradition that could restore a proper proportional relation in the cultural sphere between African Americans and the members of other races. Folk community and middle-class intellectuals stood in reciprocal relation to one another, each one receiving compensation from the other for the damage of misrecognition and nonrecognition, each one providing such compensation as well. As both an injured party and a source of repair for middle-class African Americans, therefore, the folk community was central to the pursuit of racial wholeness.

　　From the perspective of so many Eatonville characters, however, any claim to know the route to psychological wholeness was an act of usurpation, a human trespassing of God's domain. It was a violation of the individual subject's mystery and of the unending, unpredictable collective quest for new experience and knowledge. What made Eatonville distinctive was precisely the fact that it was always unfinished, always subject to the creative reinterpretations of individual members. Hurston's characters thrive on the recognition that human justice is a partial and imperfect endeavor, that no matter the ordering principle, the self, the community, and the world remain more or less in need of more adjustment. To borrow from Wai Chee Dimock's comments on the difference that literature can make in relation to law and philosophy, an Eatonville resident "brings to [the] act of judicial weighing the shadow of an unweighable residue." Such a character points us to "the abiding presence—the desolation as well as consolation—of what remains unredressed, unrecovered, noncorresponding."[8] According to this conception of justice, achieving adequate redress for the damages of misrecognition depends on treating the process of remediation as provisional and open-ended. Rather than the means of restoring psychological wholeness, such an approach to judgment provides necessary compensations with their own inevitable shortfalls.

Hurston foregrounds this process of provisional redress in her first two novels, *Jonah's Gourd Vine* and *Their Eyes Were Watching God*. What emerges as a corollary to it is the image of an *unfolkish* local community, open to a full spectrum of outside influences and resistant to being delimited along racial lines. As in Cather's portrait of collective life in the Southwest, the community must risk its own collapse in encouraging characters to wander, both imaginatively and physically. It must accommodate both the leave-taking of wanderers and the newness that they import upon return. It must make room for the very methods that underlie Hurston's own practice as a literary writer, committed to troubling her ethical judgments. Those who sin most egregiously against community are those who, no matter their just intentions, act as if the wandering of community members can be bounded and delineated once and for all. In acting this way, they encroach with their certain knowledge on the divine territory of the self, which must remain at least partially unclaimed. In addition, they deny the world the benefit of local judgment, and locality the benefit of experience in the world.

The Route to Racial Wholeness

Hurston began publishing regularly at a time when African American writers and critics often worked under the assumption that the arts had a crucial role to play in the pursuit of a just world.[9] In his essay "The Negro in American Literature" from the anthology *The New Negro* (1925), William Braithwaite captures the pervasive faith in the remedial power of the arts: "In the generations that [the Negro] has been so voluminously written or talked about he has been accorded as little artistic justice as social justice. . . . Sustained, serious or deep study of Negro life and character has thus been entirely below the horizons of our national art. Only gradually through the dull purgatory of the Age of Discussion, has Negro life eventually issued forth to an Age of Expression."[10] For Braithwaite, the reflection and partial judgment characteristic of "Discussion" had given way in the twentieth century to the conviction and full translation of "Expression." A great correction in the scheme of African American representation had occurred. Measuring the current portrayals of the race against past distortion and abuse, Braithwaite sustains a powerful hope in the ability of artists and intellectuals to mete out justice through writing.

While Braithwaite rejects the notion of a separate black literature, inflected by the writer's racial origin, he quite readily accepts the notion of a black race, with distinctive experiences and modes of expression. As soon as African Americans become serious writers, in his view, they begin speaking a universal language and cease being racial. For Braithwaite, the folk past retains its importance as a "precious mass of raw material," to be brought into the national literary arena in a form provided by the modern artist.[11] But writers achieve artistic justice by ensuring that all Americans learn to recognize who "the Negro" really is, and such recognition depends most of all on the form of representation employed by the writer. Moving from the "Age of Discussion" to the "Age of Expression" is a matter of acquiring "artistry" more than simply recovering a folk origin, since the origin has already been recovered in previous literature about African Americans. "With [Paul] Dunbar," he writes, "we have our first authentic lyric utterance, an utterance more authentic, I should say, for its faithful rendition of Negro life and character than for any rare or subtle artistry of expression." Jean Toomer represents the pinnacle of American literature, for he "can write about the Negro without the surrender or compromise of the artist's vision."[12] Like Dunbar, Toomer reveals a thinking, feeling people to the American public, but he also distinguishes these people by portraying them within an aesthetic framework not their own.

In establishing a hierarchical relation between Toomer and his "raw material," Braithwaite envisioned himself not simply as a promoter of elevated writing by African Americans but also as an advocate for the folk. In a likeminded depiction of the relationship between "high" and "low" culture, Alain Locke points out that today's poets, "through acquiring ease and simplicity in serious expression, have carried the folk-gift to the altitudes of art." Elsewhere, in a piece on Sterling Brown, Locke describes the work of the modernist as the work of a translator: "One must study the intimate thought of the people who can only state it in an ejaculation, or a metaphor, or at best a proverb, and translate that into an articulate attitude, or a folk philosophy or a daring fable." Left alone, the "folk-gift" seemed mired in time and place, undeserving of the world's attention. As Braithwaite writes, it "gave, unwittingly, greater currency to the popular notion of the Negro as an inferior, superstitious, half-ignorant and servile class of folk."[13] But carried to the "altitudes of art," it became a creative achievement worthy of the highest and most lasting forms of expression and public notice. If persecution in the Jim Crow South could easily result in aesthetic impairment—in the inability of the folk to produce racial expressions of lasting quality—the altitudes of art protected and enshrined the "ejaculation," "metaphor," and "proverb." These altitudes were, in effect, doing double work for Braithwaite, simultaneously demonstrating the capacity of cultivated black writers to participate in a Euro-American aesthetic tradition and sending the message that folk expression deserved enduring representation. The hope was that the urban elite, fluent in the languages of contemporary art, would, as Locke writes, ensure "the revaluation by white and black alike of the Negro in terms of his artistic endowments and cultural contributions."[14] Turning "folk temperament" into an immortal "race soul,"[15] the currency of high modernism would offset the public image of the race as lacking both acculturated intellectual custodians and a repository of folk artifacts worth saving.

In his emphasis on the capacity of African Americans to acquire the attributes of "civilization," Braithwaite echoed the ideas of Hurston's academic mentor, Franz Boas. By the time of her first trip south in February 1927, Hurston had been a student and great admirer of Boas for a year and a half. As her biographer, Robert Hemenway, describes the relationship, "Boas became the most important figure in her academic life, not only because of his great personal magnetism, but also because he recognized her genius immediately and urged her to begin training as a professional anthropologist, concentrating on folklore. His science provided a taxonomy for her childhood memories, and she called Boas 'the greatest anthropologist alive' and 'king of kings.'"[16]

If he provided her with a taxonomy, she—as a talented and committed black scientist—provided him with evidence of his taxonomy's validity. For over the course of the first three decades of the twentieth century, Boas had spoken out repeatedly against white supremacists like Lothrop Stoddard, Madison Grant, and Henry Osborn, whose theories were feeding the national obsession with racial purity. In both academic journals and widely circulated newspapers, Boas was remarkably consistent in his views, arguing that racial generalizations were always flawed because members of a race could not be said to share the same genetic material or to exhibit a reliable consistency in physical characteristics. Races lacked biological unity. "As a matter of fact," he wrote in the New York Times in response to statements by Osborn, "the very concept of a race means that it is a group of a great many individuals varying among themselves in appearance as well as in mental characteristics." Furthermore, no study had ever established a credible connection between the physical features typically associated with a race and the way in which particular organs like the brain functioned. Therefore, he wrote, "[i]t does not matter from which point of view we consider culture[;] its forms are not dependent on race."[17] He concluded that races consisted of multiple hereditary lines, none of which, by virtue of physical features alone, could be designated as inferior or as inherently different in function. Boas's use of empirical evidence of the body and its functions was in this sense analogous to Braithwaite's use of modernist technique. In both cases, the purpose was to offset the prevailing assumption that people of African descent, and the cultural objects that they produced, could not evolve beyond a certain primitive level.

Although all the races had equal potential, according to Boasian theory, all cultures were in no way equally advanced. As Susan Hegeman and Walter Benn Michaels have both recently pointed out, Boas was not a cultural relativist, if by relativism we mean the lack of any absolute standards for measuring the value of cultural beliefs and practices.[18] The goal of anthropology, in fact, was to get outside one's own cultural bias in order not simply to reveal the values of another culture but to view cultures comparatively and to decide, on the basis of a "freedom of judgment," which values and which achievements were more or less developed. Not surprisingly, the values and achievements that Boas's free judgment often described as developed were thoroughly European: technological innovations, developments in scientific knowledge, and the "extension of political units" from small communities to nation-states (and from nation-states to an international governing system) all signified social advancement.[19]

By the time Hurston entered his classes, Boas had not only formulated this scheme of cultural evolution; he had applied it to places like Africa and to populations like African Americans. He concluded that in Africa a relatively high level of civilization had been attained, roughly equivalent in many ways to medieval Europe; that such attainment pointed to the capacities of African Americans; that slavery and subsequent oppression had deprived many southern African Americans of the civilization their ancestors had achieved; and that in migrating northward, the talented members of the race would acquire a much greater degree of civilization than they had ever had in Africa, gradually becoming indistinguishable from whites. The solution to the race problem lay ultimately in a process of biological and cultural miscegenation, which would lead not to the transformation of both races, but to the whitening of African

Americans.[20] Hurston must have seemed, for Boas, an embodiment of this geo-historical scheme: here was a talented woman who had freed herself from Jim Crow conditions and medieval Africa in order to acquire the knowledge that white America, north of the Mason-Dixon, could impart.

Whether or not the academics who were publishing on black folklore and culture in the 1920s drew directly from Boas, his method of offsetting white supremacist rhetoric permeated the field. This method was still important enough in 1925 to gain representation in several places in the *New Negro* collection. In "The Negro's Americanism," Boas's student Melville Herskovits asked "to what extent, if any . . . the Negro genius [had] developed a culture peculiar to it in America," and his response, after observing Harlem carefully, was that it was "a community just like any other American community."[21] For Herskovits, the story of northern blacks was the story of any immigrant group. While "the Negro came to America endowed, as all people are endowed, with a culture," and while that culture had taken on new forms in the South, "[a]ll racial and social elements in our population who live here long enough become acculturated, Americanized in the truest sense of the word, eventually."[22] Harlem was living proof of the race's great capacities, as measured by its potential for full adaptation.

At the same time that Herskovits was addressing the most developed and thus least distinguishable of places, other white folklorists were focusing their attention on the South, where the race was perceived to be at its furthest from Euro-American acculturation. Black difference in the South was not necessarily linked to Africanness, however. In fact, a number of folklorists traced cultural attributes such as superstitious beliefs and patterns of speech to a white folk cultural origin. Newbell Niles Puckett began his *Folk Beliefs of the Southern Negro* by reminding readers that "the Negro has very often become the custodian of many things which contributed to the glory of the Old South," and in his keeping "the master-touch of Chippendale, Sheraton, and others, and the French influence from New Orleans and elsewhere are clearly discernible."[23] Puckett was a poor advocate for the view he expressed, for he was not rigorous enough to avoid treating the black version of folk life as a cheap and degraded substitute. But it is crucial to recognize that Puckett was positioning himself as a progressive, challenging the assumption that superstition was a racial attribute and that blacks, therefore, could not be fully assimilated. Superstition was a hand-me-down, to be discarded by the evolving recipient (white first, black next) over time. "The whites of the South gave up their superstitions all the more quickly," he wrote, "because the Negro took them over. . . . Today Negro race pride is forcing many more or less illiterate Negroes to give up, or at least to subdue and refuse to pass on, the old beliefs for fear of ridicule from the more developed members of their race." Eight years later, the link between superstition and race was still strong enough for Anthony Buttitta, a white journalist, to argue that "certain superstitions . . . are of decided European extraction" and to declare ultimately that "this lore is a thing of the past. The Negro is not as all-believing as he has been shown to be."[24] For both Puckett and Buttitta, the important point to remember was that race neither precluded civilization nor endowed it. Doing justice to the African American folk meant revealing the contingency of their difference, locating them within a history of cultural development originally scripted and produced by white people.

For Hurston and many other African American intellectuals of the 1920s, this antiracism tended to deny the race any meaningful originality, since the point was to prove that African Americans could follow in the footsteps of white cultural innovators. Those, like Hurston, with the access and the will to reproduce the manners, inflections, and knowledge characteristic of high Euro-American civilization were applauded for their capacity to do so. Yet they were applauded as imitators, embodiments of a process in which white people blazed the civilizing trail and black people followed. According to the Boasian scheme, the African American middle class could be perceived only as either insufficiently evolved (products of black southern backwardness) or inauthentically modern (followers of white American trendsetters).

From the perspective of many who wrote in the New Negro anthology, therefore, the Boasian scheme needed to be modified if it was to become sufficiently reparative. What Braithwaite had tended to was the crucial role that the urban elite would play in delivering aesthetic justice to the race. What he had neglected was the damage done to the elite by racial theories predicated on imitation—on the assumption that high culture was derived from white producers and that black people were in the process of adopting it. Thus, when Arthur Schomburg contended that "[t]he American Negro must remake his past in order to make his future," he was referring not to the uncultivated folk (as in Braithwaite's first reference to "the Negro") but to the overly cultivated black reader of the New Negro anthology. Schomburg wrote that "a group tradition must supply *compensation* for persecution, and pride of race the antidote for prejudice. History must *restore* what slavery *took away*, for it is the social *damage* of slavery that the present generation must *repair* and offset." If slaves had been stripped of their ethnic birthright, the first generation of freedmen accepted the loss, believing that upward mobility depended on embracing the norms of the dominant society. For Schomburg, therefore, it was up to the younger generation of artists and intellectuals to give back at least some of the American porridge and reclaim the past. Without public recognition of a racial past, African Americans became vulnerable to the age-old charge that they, unlike white immigrants, were merely good imitators, interlopers in a tradition not their own. Given the status of partial or incomplete American that inevitably accompanied assimilation for African Americans, ownership of a past was not "a luxury" for Schomburg but "a prime social necessity," upon which the dignity and autonomy of the middle class hinged.[25] Regardless of the period or place to which the past referred—whether Africa before slavery or the American South—it belonged to the destiny of the race insofar as it could make race members whole again.

Taken together, the essays by Braithwaite and Schomburg assume the presence of two different types of injuries affecting, on the one hand, the agrarian folk and, on the other, the assimilated urban dweller. With an eye to addressing these injuries in tandem, Alain Locke began to situate African American culture within the framework of a pluralist conception of America. According to the tenets of cultural pluralism articulated by Horace Kallen, differentiation by race or ethnicity was itself a natural part of the American assimilative process.[26] New Negroes who exhibited proficiency in some of the dominant expressive norms still belonged and still contributed to a distinctive tradition forged by black people. The pluralist framework held out the hope that the race might be conceived as both modern and autonomous, developed along parallel lines to other races and nationalities and on the cutting edge of its own self-determined history. If African American culture could take its place alongside "those nascent movements of folk-expression and self-determination which are playing a creative part in the world to-day," neither the folk subject nor the middle-class intellectual would remain merely an injured party. Each would also provide repair to "a damaged group psychology."[27] As contributors to and beneficiaries of aesthetic justice, *folk* and *modernist* would stand in reciprocal relation to one another, situated one on each end of a self-reparative racial tradition, each one both receiving compensation and providing it. By linking the one to the other in a common organic tradition, intellectuals could ensure that cultural reparation would be perfectly commensurate with the injury: the middle class had been denied precisely the autonomy and creative agency that emergence from a self-determining folk could provide, and the folk had been deprived of self-expression in an "articulate" incarnation. Art would secure recognition of the race in its most natural, most complete condition. It would restore psychological wholeness by joining the two halves of the tradition into an integrated cultural unit.[28]

The pursuit of racial wholeness was, in fact, an organizing principle in Hurston's major folklore collection, *Mules and Men* (1935). As an anthropologist and a concert organizer, Hurston had previously positioned her work as a corrective to unfaithful representations of the folk, produced, in her mind, to approximate the tastes of white audiences. In reference to the "neo-spirituals" that were being performed throughout the country, she lamented that "[t]here never has been a presentation of genuine Negro spirituals to any audience anywhere. What is being sung by the concert artists and glee clubs are the works of Negro composers or adaptors *based* on the spirituals. . . . All good work and beautiful, but *not* the spirituals." To counteract the effect of such presentations, she put on a well-publicized concert in New York called *The Great Day,* a revue of blues, spirituals, games, and sermons, all taken from the folklore that she had collected.[29] Yet Hurston's attempt to remain neutral and invisible in bringing folk material into the public domain posed a problem for an intellectual intent on representational justice. The people who created the songs and sermons that she was publicizing needed her expressive mediation, just as she depended on theirs. From Hurston's perspective, these people were more embattled by the degradation of white writers like Roark Bradford and Octavus Roy Cohen than they were by the imitative neospirituals.[30] Writers like Bradford and Cohen reaffirmed the popular conception of African American folk expression as comic material, unworthy of artistic preservation. In response to this predicament, Hurston took a slightly different approach to folklore presentation in *Mules and Men.* Rather than offering her material with little or no authorial intervention, she created a plot around a character named Zora, who returned south to the "crib of negroism," where she was still "just Zora to the neighbors."[31] By framing folklore in the context of its recollection by an educated African American subject, Hurston could situate her account as the representation of a tradition in full, its constituent parts fully compensating for the attributes denied to them.

Despite her suggestion that the "crib of negroism" and the character of Zora stood in perfectly reciprocal relation to one another, however, *Mules and Men* does contain the seeds of an ambivalence, one that becomes more prominent in Hurston's fictional work. Here, too, she begins to examine philosophies of justice that recognize the flaws in human judgment and the blind spots in legal verdicts. Hoodoo, the subject of the second part of the collection, picks up, it seems, where legal justice leaves off. A woman whose husband is shot by a man with "good white folks back of him" visits a hoodoo doctor, who promises that "[w]hen we get through with him, white folks or no white folks, he'll find a tough jury sitting on his case."[32] Another doctor specializes in "law cases" and performs his magic for a man "who was in the Parish prison accused of assault with attempt to murder."[33] Hoodoo clearly functions in this text as an indictment of a deficient American legal system. But beyond that, it implies for Hurston that human creatures are not the grand rectifiers they claim to be, that the achievement of full justice depends on the intervention of "spirits for power more than equal to man." Hoodoo loses its centrality in the first two novels, as Hurston turns to Judeo-Christian notions of supernatural justice. What remains consistent, however, is an ethic of skepticism toward human judgments and remedies.[34] As Hurston studied this skepticism, it began to shape her fiction in a variety of ways. Most significantly, it undercut the prevalent hope among Harlem Renaissance intellectuals that an organic cultural tradition, linking middle-class representatives to a self-determining folk origin, would deliver full repair, psychological wholeness, to a racial group.

The growing importance of this religious skepticism in Hurston's work helps to explain a profound shift in her career: At the end of the 1930s and throughout the 1940s, Hurston renounced her earlier embrace of racial categories.[35] "The solace of easy generalization was taken from me," she writes in reference to this changed approach to race, in a section of her autobiography originally removed by her editor but restored in the recent editions of the work. "This has called for a huge cutting of dead wood on my part."[36] At this point in her career, cutting dead wood meant formulating a critique of identity politics—a critique that scholars have often traced either to academic traditions like pragmatism and Boasian anthropology, or to worldwide historical events like the Great Depression or World War II.[37] The assumption here is that Hurston used her folkloric sources to construct racial difference and that her later challenge to the doctrine of essential difference grew out of interracial and internationalist affiliations. Yet this assumption neglects the possibility that southern African Americans, and their approach to collective life, may also have abetted Hurston's challenge to systems of racial classification. If multiple influences affected the process of "cutting . . . dead wood" and jettisoning "easy generalization," Hurston's perpetual dialogue with communities of the black South was a crucial part of the process. Zora the celebrant of the folk and Zora the skeptic toward race consciousness thus begin to look like one and the same writer. The common link joining the two is the conception of provisional justice exemplified by the Eatonville porch talkers. This conception governs the construction of Hurston's fictive local communities, ensuring that the quest for selfhood remains unfinished and that collective agreements are subject to the knowledge and experience acquired in the individual's journey.

Jonah's Gourd Vine: Migration and the Persistence of Injury

While Hurston points repeatedly in *Mules and Men* to the thinness of legal verdicts, she is clearly interested in something more encompassing than a commentary on Jim Crow law. This wider interest in justice pertains to the rest of her work as well. Throughout her fiction, the verdicts of white-administered courts often seem incomplete rather than grossly unjust, as, for instance, in the case of "Spunk," where a man guilty of seducing a married woman is exonerated for killing the cuckold in self-defense. Moreover, African Americans are in no way only victims and opponents of the white legal court. They construct their own trials to resolve intramural conflicts ("The Bone of Contention"), and, more frequently, as Hurston writes in *Jonah's Gourd Vine,* "the judge and jury [move] to the street corners, the church, the houses."[38] Excluded from the white courthouse, African Americans pass judgments within their own communities.

Yet they pass judgments not in accordance with a single standard, but in a variety of conflicting ways. The mayor of Eatonville, Joe Clarke, issues his verdicts unilaterally, decisively, and with little deliberation. As one character explains in *Their Eyes,* "Some folks needs thrones, and ruling-chairs and crowns tuh make they influence felt. He don't. He's got uh throne in de seat of his pants" (*TE,* 46). Other members of the community become vessels of village gossip, allowing a uniform popular mentality to dictate judgment: "They made burning statements with questions, and killing tools out of laughs. It was mass cruelty. A mood come alive. Words walking without masters; walking altogether like harmony in a song" (2). In contrast, infants judge intuitively, availing themselves of a knowledge that comes much less easily to their parents: "Dat's mah eye color alright but her eyes look at yuh lak she know sumpin. Anybody'd think she's grown. Wonder whut she thinkin' 'bout?" (*JGV,* 115). Finally, Hurston offers us a group of porch talkers who return throughout her fiction to engage not only in outrageous storytelling sessions but also in ethical conversations about the behavior of individuals around them. The participants in these conversations (most frequently Sam Watson, Lige Moss, and Walter Thomas) take divergent points of view and often modify them over the course of the discussion. They are never really without a position, yet neither do they insist on finalizing their verdicts. For these men, it would seem, judgment can take any form it wishes, as long as it avoids any tone or tenor that might terminate the conversation.

As Hurston gives dramatic form to these contrasting methods of human judgment, she simultaneously posits the existence of a higher law. In both *Jonah's Gourd Vine* and *Their Eyes*, the acquisition of knowledge, power, and capital takes place in a world that is immanently informed by God's judgment. God intervenes unpredictably, often to remind human subjects that they do not ultimately control their fates and must, as a consequence, submit to a higher will than their own.

Jonah's Gourd Vine revolves around John Pearson's ongoing refusal to curtail his own desire and entitlement. Born into an environment of extreme poverty and hatred, John achieves great things: he educates himself, marries a woman from a higher class, and moves to the all-black town of Eatonville, where he becomes both mayor and a renowned preacher. From a world of the tightest limitation, he travels to a place of much greater freedom, where "Uh man kin be sumpin' . . . 'thout folks tramplin' all over yuh" (*JGV*, 107). Yet in making the most of his opportunities, he fails to place limits of any kind on himself, ignoring the "tramplin'" that he does as a philandering husband, a neglectful father, and an irresponsible leader of his community.

What John lacks, quite clearly, is the sense of judgment—the wisdom of knowing that because he too will be held accountable at some future moment, he must exercise some restraint in an effort to avoid contributing to the injuries of the world. Life provides the signs of a future justice, awareness of which instills a recurring fear in him. After a storm in which he is knocked unconscious in a river "red as judgment" (*JGV*, 86), he dreams of God "upon his throne," with "burning worlds dropp[ing] from his teeth" (87). But John's great urge is to suppress this fear and to avoid or silence those who might aggravate it. In one of the novel's central scenes, he slaps his first wife, Lucy, after she reminds him that "talk ain't changin' whut you doin'. You can't clean yo'self wid yo' tongue lak uh cat" (128–29).

As a counterpoint to John's rejection of any self-imposed limitation, Lucy calmly and defiantly accepts her mortality, thus tormenting her husband by directing him toward the very judgment he wishes to forget. Rather than take corrective action against her husband, she leaves him with an impression of a life always responsive to the presence of divine will. Just before Lucy's death, in a telling exchange with her daughter Isis, she opts not to kill a spider that has crawled to the ceiling. "De one dat put 'im dere will move 'im in his own time," she says (*JGV*, 129). John does not witness this particular incident, but he knows from her "large bright eyes" that though she feels contempt for him, she chooses not to indulge it. In so choosing, she avoids action that might either compromise her own acceptance of mortal limits or diminish John's fear of a future reckoning. Like the storm, Lucy's eyes work not as punishment for a particular sin here, but as the reflection of a greater will with the capacity to do justice when it pleases. The eyes do not correct an instance of abuse or infidelity, nor do they restore the world to moral order; rather they remind John of a future restoration and of his failure to proceed with the necessary caution. Without such caution, Hurston suggests, human relations become subject to whims of mind and appetites of the body, wholly tenuous and lacking in trust. Exempting himself from judgment, John exacerbates the pain and injury to which his intimates are already subject.

John's refusal to posit any ethical limits for himself stems, at least in part, from his total and unqualified embrace of mobility. In the world into which he is born, a life that means anything at all demands constant movement. All internal boundaries have, therefore, the same distasteful associations as the kind imposed by sharecropping and white supremacy. Hurston structures the entire novel around the flights that John takes, at times in response to external threat and at other times out of habit and a sense of entitlement. Faced with his stepfather's resentment on account of his light skin color and mixed racial origin, he experiences a defining moment at the beginning of the novel: "It came to John like a revelation. Distance was escape" (*JGV*, 47). The same lesson is reinforced several years later, after he beats up his brother-in-law and takes a pig from the property of a neighboring white man. Alf Pearson—John's employer and, Hurston hints, his biological father—advises him that "distance is the only cure for certain diseases" (99), as Jim Crow violence awaits him if he stays in Alabama.

It is no surprise, then, that from the beginning of the novel, John becomes fascinated with trains and their manifold potential for transport. He insists, after first seeing a train, that "it say some words too. Ahm comin' heah plenty mo' times and den Ah tell yuh whut it say" (*JGV*, 16). Education requires literacy not only in words and numbers but in modern methods of transportation, for the capacity to make meaning of such methods will open up John's life text to a range of possible stories. He calls the train "the greatest accumulation of power that he had ever seen," and what impresses him most is that "just anybody could come along and be allowed to get on such a glorified thing" (104). To those who take advantage of it, the train confers its power in spite of caste and class. If he breeds contempt, then, he deserves admiration as well, for through a sense of rightful entitlement, he claims the tools and the space in which to realize his own freedom.

John's determination to make narrative meaning of the train—to interpret it as a vehicle for acquiring dignity and property, security and a less restricted arena for the exercise of talent—positions him as a kind of forerunner to other African American male travelers. In a substantial section toward the end of the novel, Hurston clarifies his seminal status: "A fresh rumor spread over the nation. It said war. It talked of blood and glory—of travel, of North, of Oceans and transports, of white men and black. And black men's feet learned roads. Some said good bye cheerfully . . . others fearfully, with terrors of unknown dangers in their mouths . . . others in their eagerness for distance said nothing. The daybreak found them gone. The wind said North. Trains said North. The tides and tongues said North, and men moved like the great herds before the glaciers" (*JGV*, 147–48). Again, the talking train suggests an experience of anxious, abundant prolepsis—multiple texts of opportunity where there had been no text or only one text before. It functions here also as a commentary on the vital communication that took place between black urban dwellers in the North and their rural counterparts in the South. As *Jonah's Gourd Vine* clearly shows, the rural communities of the South, and individuals like John Pearson, were powerfully reshaped by the letters, rumors, advertisements, and industrial agents that flowed southward from the northern metropolis.[39]

Although Hurston might well have depicted the Great Migration as a purely redemptive event, her account is much more nuanced and shaded: "Whereas in Egypt the coming of the locust made desolation, in the farming South the departure of the Negro laid waste the agricultural industry—crops rotted, houses careened crazily in their utter desertion, and grass grew up in streets. On to the North! The land of promise" (*JGV*, 151). In her deployment of the Exodus narrative, she portrays the Great Migration not simply as an emancipatory event but as a divinely inflicted plague as well, inflicting injury on an entire region, white and black. Those who travel north visit punishment on the white South for its sins, but they fail to usher in a new period of liberation, not for themselves, and certainly not for the family and community members they leave behind. For it is crucial to the novel that those who remain in place, awaiting word and deed from the great interpreters of trains, frequently suffer as a result of the travelers' interpretations. In the context of Jim Crow, the inflated entitlement of black men to compensate themselves for their restricted origins threatens to become unmeasured. As one character complains, "you know we done lost two hund'ed [church] members in three months? . . . Some de folks gone 'thout lettin' de families know, and dey say iss de same way, only wurser, all over de South" (149–50). In seeking indiscriminately to obtain the rewards that life owes to them, such folks deprive family and friends of *their* just rewards. Moreover, as Lucy Pearson knows all too well, these travelers may not achieve the liberating correction they seek if the remedy, in its lack of restraint, is tainted with an awareness of moral guilt.

Needless to say, Hurston's meditation on what she allusively describes at one point as "bad travelin'" (86) certainly implicates John Pearson, who, in migrating while suppressing the sense borne of divine justice, inflicts injury on others and guilt on himself. When he crosses the creek separating his origins from the middle-class village of Notasulga for the first time, he all but forgets his mother, and when he moves to Eatonville, where a "man kin be sumpin'," he fails to contact Lucy for almost a year. By the author's standards, we might infer, John seems to warrant the retribution he receives at the end of his life when he is struck by a train while driving. Death by train is a perfectly adequate punishment for a man who has pursued his own mobility and progress at the expense of his loved ones. Hurston appears to restore moral order to the world, and justice to the folk, by administering a punishment perfectly commensurate with the crime. As in her short story "Sweat," where a snake destroys the man who had been using the animal to terrorize his wife, Hurston turns the instrument of pain into the instrument of punishment, and the perpetrator into the victim.

Yet what makes the end of the novel so compelling, so narratively fraught and so different from "Sweat," is that Hurston makes it exceedingly difficult to imagine John as pure perpetrator or to pass any kind of conclusive moral judgment on him at all. Judging John is a difficult endeavor, not simply because he seems at times justified in seeking his own compensations. More importantly, in his embrace of travel, he acts on behalf of others in his community. The "tides and tongues" moving him are like "glaciers" (*JGV*, 148), as Hurston writes about the Great Migration, because they encompass the desire of others for collective vindication. John, in other words, is an agent of psychic repair not only for himself but for his community as well. His obvious talent for speaking and his upwardly mobile success undermine white assumptions about the value of black culture.[40] John's relationship to his third wife is telling in this respect. Sally Lovelace not only urges him on in his career as preacher; she also buys him a Cadillac and encourages him to visit his old town again. Once there, despite his initial efforts at resistance, he gives in to the advances of a younger woman. Sally invests in John's success, and in his mobility, because it reflects on her as well. Whatever she gains in pride from her investment, however, she seems to lose in solidarity, as John once again indulges his desire for new acquisitions and self-transformation. His dilemma is that he has been asked to perform for his community in two conflicting ways—as its representative spokesman and achiever, commended for distancing himself from his restricted origins, and as a loyal kinsman, criticized for incessant wandering. While he often juggles the two roles poorly, he does so, it seems, without the hope of a fully successful, fully balanced negotiation.[41]

John's death at the end of the novel, therefore, reads as testimony to Hurston's own moral uncertainty about a right course of action for her hero. From one perspective, the train accident reads as an entirely heroic attempt at self-martyrdom. "We preachers is in uh tight fix," he says to one parishioner, in reference to the migration northward. "Us don't know whether tuh g'wan Nawth wid de biggest part of our churches or stay home wid de rest" (*JGV*, 150). John's conflict, and his ultimate decision to stay in the region, suggest that he is the only wanderer from Eatonville prepared to suffer for the general sin of "bad traveling." The sermon he preaches before stepping down from Zion Hope Church encourages us to read his life in this manner.[42]

> I heard de whistle of de damnation train
> Dat pulled out from Garden of Eden loaded wid cargo goin' to hell
> Ran at break-neck speed all de way thru de law
> All de way thru de reign of kings and judges—
> Plowed her way thru de Jurdan
> And on her way to Calvary, when she blew for de switch
> Jesus stood out on her track like a rough-backed mountain
> And she threw her cow-catcher in His side and His blood ditched de train
> He died for our sins. . . .
> That's where I got off de damnation train
> And dat's where you must get off, ha!
>
> (180–81)

There are two actions worthy of note here: First, John has gotten off the damnation train and thus, in the terms set up by the novel, limited himself more rigorously as a traveler. More importantly, he has gotten off after Jesus has knocked the entire cargo of damnation off the track of sin. The image of Jesus as the derailer of a train clearly presages the scene of John's death, and it figures that scene as the culminating act in a narrative of conversion and martyrdom. John reforms himself in order to do for others what Jesus did for him. According to the sermon he preaches, he ultimately strikes the train of damnation, the train of bad travelers, not merely to do penance, but to save the souls of future travelers and, presumably, repair the wounds of their loved ones. In more concrete terms, he sacrifices himself (indeed Hurston makes the death look somewhat intentional) in order to turn his life into a particularly effective metaphor: man struggling to eliminate all of the diffuse pain connected to mobility. The culminating event becomes, in this reading, an effort to erase sin and heal injury before they even take place.

But from another perspective, Hurston never permits us to see John as a successful martyr, for he sins at the same moment that he redeems. Even at his best, when he struggles to correct weaknesses and rid himself of abandon and entitlement, he inflicts his damage on the people closest to him. Before the train accident that ends his life, he discourages Sally from buying him the Cadillac, then protests when she urges him to show it off in Sanford, and finally flagellates himself for the infidelity that he commits: "The car droned, 'ho-o-ome' and tortured the man. False pretender! Outside show to the world!" Here he projects onto the droning car an interpretation virtually opposite from the one he has previously given to the train. At the moment of the accident, moreover, he is "looking inward," thus worrying about the state of his soul and demonstrating that sense of an imminent accountability that he lacks at the beginning of the novel. Despite such signs of struggle and inner limits, however, the infliction of injury persists. John not only commits adultery just before the train accident; he also flees the scene of his crime without saying goodbye to his best friend Hambo, who, upon John's departure, "cried over the stove" and "couldn't eat" (*JGV*, 200). Such actions shroud the train accident in moral ambiguity.

The disparate interpretations to which the accident lends itself—both punishment for John's latest transgressions and redemptive act of self-sacrifice—point us to the conflict that he embodies as a leader of his community, responsible for its uplift and repair. As a sinner trying to do what is best for his community, he forces us to consider his innocence. As a martyr who causes as much suffering as he negates, he is tainted with guilt. Both an innocent transgressor and a blemished martyr, John faces an impossible choice: either miring the history of his community in self-sameness or betraying that community in serving as its public representative. Whatever negotiated solution he enacts will be inadequate. We are a far cry here from the smoothly functioning reciprocity between the agrarian folk and the upwardly mobile members of the race envisioned in *The New Negro* anthology. In the moral world that Hurston creates, there is no instance of "good traveling" to function as an all-out indictment of the mobile protagonist. Ultimately, the novel forces us to acknowledge that the residual injustice John leaves in his wake should be pinned not so much to the man, but in a more fixed and irreparable way, to his job. Hurston suggests that the cycle of injury, in which all of Eatonville's travelers participate, cannot be fully corrected—not by a character seeking recognition for himself and his community, nor by his author passing judgment with her pen. And despite that reality, the traveling must go on.

The World of Provisional Judgment

If John Pearson fails ethically at the beginning of the novel, therefore, his failure lies not so much in his commission of any one sin or set of sins as in the absence of that sense that comes from remembering judgment. What makes this attribute only an undefined sense and not certain knowledge is the inaccessible criteria of judgment, the inscrutability of God's "plan": "As for me," Hurston explains in her autobiography, "I do not pretend to read God's mind. If He has a plan of the Universe worked out to the smallest detail, it would be folly for me to presume to get down on my knees and attempt to revise it."[43] Memento mori is thus a complicated injunction for Hurston. Characters like John must hold themselves to some standard of justice without knowing whether it is the right one—without acting, that is, as if it certainly were the right standard. They must restrict themselves even while coming to terms with the provisionality of their basis for restriction. John's failure to assign any limits to his desire, then, has its sinful counterpart in the certainty with which some members of his congregation determine his guilt and seek his punishment. "He was on trial everywhere," we are told, and "didn't have a chance to speak in his own behalf" (*JGV*, 184). Unlike Lucy, who defends herself through stoic silence but leaves any final judgment of "the spider" in the hands of its maker, this section of the community responds to John's arrogance with its own. As John himself reminds them, "Y'all is de one dat is so much-knowin' dat you kin set in judgment" (122).

The descriptor "much-knowing" clearly means something very different from knowing much, and that difference informs Hurston's critique not only of John's congregation, but also of the white justice system and those who administer it. Without any hesitancy at all, these arbiters hoist themselves into positions of making and enforcing law, as if they were conduits for the word of God. While Hurston implies that an inevitable gap separates human justice systems and their verdicts from the higher ones to which access is at best limited, she does not oppose the possibility of legitimate legal judgment. In the two trial scenes in *Jonah's Gourd Vine*, what leads to the system's inadequacy is not its issuing of verdicts, but its failure to take that gap into consideration.

Rather than doubting their initial conclusions and recognizing the need for a prolonged process of deliberation, the courts render their verdicts without any reflexive questioning at all. This lack of skepticism allows the injurious and violently generalizing verdicts of Jim Crow justice to stand. Faced with such determination, what is the point of testifying? As John explains his silence at the second trial,

> Ah didn't want de white folks tuh hear 'bout nothin' lak dat. . . . Dey thinks wese all ignorant as it is, and dey thinks wese all alike, and dat dey knows us inside and out, but you know better. Dey wouldn't make no great 'miration if you had tol 'em Hattie [his second wife] had all dem mens. Dey spectin' dat. Dey wouldn't zarn 'tween uh woman lak Hattie and one lak Lucy. . . . Dey thinks all colored folks is de same dat way. De only difference dey makes is 'tween uh nigger dat works hard and don't sass 'em, and one dat don't. De hard worker is uh good nigger. De loafer is bad. Otherwise wese all de same. (*JGV*, 168–69)

Such comments also serve to instruct Hurston's white readers on the need to check their own rash judgments. They too must recognize that their conclusions about John's character and about how he can best serve his congregants may need a more extensive revision.[44]

In *Their Eyes*, too, judgments embraced as final and beyond reconsideration seem flimsy. Hurston reveals the religious logic behind her suspicion of human certainty in her contrast at the beginning of the novel between the dead bodies that Janie has just finished burying, "their eyes flung wide open in judgment" (*TE*, 1), and some of the Eatonville community members, who, upon her return, "sat in judgment" and gave voice to "Mouth-Almighty" (2, 5). The profound but illegible expressions on the faces of the "sudden dead" (1) comment on the thin, fabricated knowledge of those who scorn Janie for her overalls, her pride, and her marriage to a younger man. Such pretenders share the assumptions of the court that decides on Janie's innocence at the end of the novel: "The court set and Janie saw the judge who had put on a great robe to listen about her and Tea Cake. . . . Twelve strange men who didn't know a thing about people like Tea Cake and her were going to sit on the thing" (176). Although these men rightly exonerate Janie for the death of her husband, Hurston calls into question the absolute authority they claim and the legitimacy of their method. "There is no middle course," the judge instructs the jury, as he outlines the two options: Janie is either "a poor broken creature" or "a wanton killer" (179). By contrast, adequate knowledge can only be achieved after a lengthy process of suspension and deliberation, in which the knower struggles to accommodate the empirical uniqueness that makes judgment so perilous. As Janie explains to her ideal listener Pheoby just before she embarks on her story, "'tain't no use in me telling you somethin' unless Ah give you de understandin' to go 'long wid it. Unless you see de fur, a mink skin ain't no different from a coon hide" (7).[45]

For Hurston, then, a story's value as mink skin depends on the nuanced telling of speakers like Janie and the suspended judgment of audiences like Pheoby. Such communicative habits share an approach toward knowledge production with the dialogue that takes place on the porch. While Sam Watson, Lige Moss, and Walter Thomas take great pleasure in inserting themselves and their opinions into a conversation, they seem much less interested in making a final statement, or even in persuading their interlocutors, than they do in promoting more talk, more conversational detour, more undoing of previous determinations. Whereas Pheoby waits to see the "fur" of Janie's story, the porch talkers give voice to preliminary judgments but situate them in a discursive process defined by ongoing negation. Whatever provisional end these talkers reach individually must be preceded by an extended discussion, in which a variety of judgments are expressed and challenged. Insofar as such discussions revolve around questions of moral innocence and guilt, the porch offers Hurston a public alternative to the court—a place where manifold conflicting viewpoints and endless qualification take precedence over arrival at a final verdict.[46] Hurston places this system of justice on display after Joe Starks forces a man out of town for stealing his ribbon cane. Sim Jones begins: "It's uh sin and uh shame runnin' dat po' man way from here lak dat. Colored folks oughtn't tuh be so hard on one 'nother" (TE, 45–46). Taking the side of property, Sam Watson counters, "Let colored folks work for what dey get lak everybody else. Nobody ain't stopped Pitts from plantin' de cane he wanted tuh" (46). Joe's action quickly becomes an occasion for assessing his entire manner of governing, as the community realizes itself as a potential check against sovereign power. Yet no one seems bothered when the conversation turns to a different topic without any resolution on the first one. Ambivalence wins out, dictating that Joe's governance remain an open question, subject to ongoing debate.

But there is more than good governance, more even than morality, at stake in the porch talkers' interpretation of justice. For Janie and the talkers themselves, much of the attraction of the porch lies in the drama that unfolds there. By challenging the claims of others and making their own challengeable claims, by postponing resolution through dialogue that recognizes its incompleteness, the talkers create a context for performing any number of conflicting positions. They wink at each other, inhabiting their parts and artfully producing, then extending the conflict. The close relation that Hurston sees between the methods of pursuing legitimate knowledge and those of producing engaging drama emerges perhaps most clearly in a discussion on the relative importance of nature and "caution," instinct and learned behavior. "Lige would come up with a very grave air. . . . Then when he was asked what was the matter in order to start him off, he'd say 'Dis question done 'bout drove me crazy. And Sam, he know so much into things.'" (*TE*, 59). In response, "Sam begins an elaborate show of avoiding the struggle. That draws everybody on the porch into it" (60). As if to call more attention to the performances involved in staging the debate, Hurston describes an exchange concerning the question to be discussed. Clearly the content, which could be any topic that resists resolution, matters less than the method, for Hurston. To put it another way, it is the method that provides the appropriate response to what is ultimately an unanswerable question.[47] As an anthropologist, Hurston had almost surely read and heard an abundance of high academic discourse on the topic of instinct and environment. What Sam and Lige offer to this discussion is not an answer to the question, but a foundation for approaching it, a foundation that can be applied to any number of collective inquiries. The debate provides an occasion both for "play-acting" and for commenting on the limits of any theory. In playing their respective roles and pleasurably prolonging the intellectual conflict, they rehearse the process of doubt, negation, and revision crucial to good judgment.[48]

In the world of the porch talkers, all participants take part in maintaining the openness of the discourse, as they mock their own attempts and those of others to finalize abstraction. In explication of the type of talk that she has described in detail, Hurston writes that "[i]t never ended because there was no end to reach. It was a contest in hyperbole and carried on for no other reason" (*TE*, 59). The statement aptly captures the purposelessness of the porch discourse; yet in its failure to get at the seriousness of the approach in question, the term "purposelessness" is in some ways misleading. In this novel and in Hurston's work as a whole, debates such as the one described above have an ethical importance belied by the insouciance of the porch talkers. These debates are, after all, pitted against both the community's condemnation of figures like John and Janie and institutions like the Jim Crow justice system. The paradox that Hurston brings to the fore in her narrative descriptions of the porch is that the discourse can perform its social purpose only if it commits itself to a radical purposelessness, a playfulness for its own sake.[49] There are, in other words, good reasons to carry on these playful "eternal arguments"

(*TE*, 59), even if those reasons never fix or contain the conversation. By creating and protecting space for open-ended dialogue, by negating the authority of all abstract ends, the porch talkers reinforce a form of thinking and acting that serves a variety of significant uses.

Most immediately, Hurston's embrace of playful talk as an alternative to certainty and fixedness stems from a concern with the self and its need for creative expression. Sam and Lige invent and reinvent their polemical characters as they "argue" over the relative importance of instinct and environment. They avoid the terminating claim in part because such a claim inevitably does violence to the object world. But equally important, such a claim threatens to kill that state of suspension upon which their drama depends and, in doing so, to end the self-maneuvering, the reexpression and qualification, involved in responding to the other's challenges. In making their hyperbolic statements and telling their "lies," the porch talkers recognize the inadequacy of binding judgment to both the world as God's creation and to themselves as free-thinkers, revising old thoughts and bringing new ones into public dialogue. Hurston suggests that the porch talkers value both the open self and the inexhaustible world as ends to be encouraged and that they understand the commitment to these two ends as mutually reinforcing. Taking pleasure in the self as a process of reinvention protects the world from reification; conversely, attention to the world's mysteries and resistances keeps the self in a state of flux.

The story of Matt Bonner's mule provides the clearest illustration of this relation. The mule is, on the one hand, the most abused and depleted being in the entire town. As Sam Watson jokes, "dat mule so skinny till de women is usin' his rib bones fuh uh rub-board, and hangin' things out on his hock-bones tuh dry" (*TE*, 49). Yet what makes the mule so exemplary in the context of the porch talk is its relentless defiance, its refusal to be bridled. Whenever we encounter Matt Bonner, he is either expecting the mule to run off or trying to catch it after it already has. "Been huntin' fuh mah mule. Anybody seen 'im?" he asks, in a statement that captures the creature's most salient characteristic (52). Because storytelling on the porch depends on the elusiveness of a referent, the same "evil disposition" that makes the mule such an unreliable farm instrument positions it as a particularly fruitful narrative object. Matt Bonner's failure to catch the mule and hold it to the farm becomes for Sam, Lige, and Walter a sign of an object defying human apprehension, and therefore an object exceptionally fecund in its potential to generate new meaning and narrative personae. "They had [the mule] up for conversation every day the Lord sent," Hurston describes. "[I]t seemed as if Sam and Lige and Walter could hear and see more about that mule than the whole county put together. . . . There would be more stories about how poor the brute was; his age; his evil disposition and his latest caper. Everybody indulged in mule talk. He was next to the Mayor in prominence, and made better talking" (48, 50). In refusing to be used up by Matt Bonner, the mule draws attention to its value as an abundant source of self-renewal and creative expression—a source that, once identified as such, continues to have its felicitous effect on the town even after the animal dies: "The yaller mule was gone from the town except for the porch talk, and for the children visiting his bleaching bones now and then in the spirit of adventure" (58).

Given the reciprocity between open selves and runaway objects, it seems fitting that the town ultimately grants the mule the status of free citizenship, even celebrating that status with "[n]ew lies . . . about his free-mule doings" (*TE*, 55). In allowing the animal to liberate them from stalled thought and fixed judgment, the porch talkers and their listeners recognize their object as a being in excess of its instrumental (economic) value—in excess too, for that matter, of its historical compensatory value. For if the mule figures prominently in African American history as the failed payback for slavery, tied to the promise of forty acres and to the years of bondage preceding that promise, the mule talkers help to free the mule, in effect, from its symbolic burden as retribution. As a free citizen, the mule need no longer strain to reverse the economic position of the people. The town has released it from any obligation to produce the ease and prosperity that Matt Bonner's ancestors were denied.

The association between the mule's liberation and its release from the debt of slavery comments in interesting ways on Janie's own life history. For as Hurston makes clear from the outset, Janie struggles under the burden that her grandmother, an ex-slave, imposes on her: "Ah was born back due in slavery," her grandmother explains in her signature speech,

> so it wasn't for me to fulfill my dreams of whut a woman oughta be and to do. Dat's one of de hold-backs of slavery. . . . It sho wasn't mah will for things to happen lak they did. Ah even hated de way you was born. But, all de same Ah said thank God, Ah got another chance. Ah wanted to preach a great sermon about colored women sittin' on high, but they wasn't no pulpit for me. . . . So whilst Ah was tendin' you of nights Ah said Ah'd save de text for you. (*TE*, 15–16)

With the family history of rape informing her vision (both Janie and her mother are products of rape), Nanny believes that she can preach her "text" onto her granddaughter's life and thereby protect Janie from becoming "de mule uh de world" (14), reduced to fulfilling the desires of the powerful.[50]

What she fails to realize is that her text places its own restrictions on a new generation of black women, who perceive domestic protection or "high ground" (16) as itself a kind of psychic tyranny—a denial of pleasure, novelty, and playfulness. Nanny's compensation for slavery is Janie's injury, for it leads to new forms of misrecognition that are virtually as demeaning as the old forms. In contrast to the women whom John Pearson has left behind in his travels, Janie has been hitched to the tedious rig of economic progress, consigned to an impoverished identity by the closed texts and calcified dreams of her grandmother.

In the first half of the novel, Janie must not only struggle against the judgments of her grandmother and her first two husbands, all of whom attempt to keep her both literally and figuratively from the porch talking community. In addition, she must contend with her second husband's impact on the outer world, which compromises her quest for knowledge and experience as well. Joe Starks is a settler in the full sense of the word. He arrives in Eatonville with a vision of the town—replete with Sears Roebuck streetlamps, street drains, and a commercial town center—and he proceeds to transform the town in the "godly" way that he sees fit. For Hurston and Janie, the problem with his presumptuousness is not so much the initial transformation of the town as its reification. Joe attempts to negate factors like nature (streetlamps and drains to combat night and water) and democracy (centralized power instead of consensual decision making) that might alter the course that he has prescribed. As one villager aptly explains, "he's a man dat changes everything, but nothin' don't change him" (TE, 46). Joe's refusal to consider that his town map might be incomplete—that indeed the right plan, informed by an awareness of such incompleteness, would allow the land and the polity being transformed to change, in turn, the abstract plan—renders the world unfriendly to the blossoming of self that Janie craves. Joe Starks inflicts his injury on Janie both directly and indirectly: by restricting her as a speaking, thinking subject and by containing the world upon which her free speech and thought depend.

To read the first part of Janie's life as a series of injuries culminating in the settlement of Eatonville is of course to suggest that the second part of her life, with Tea Cake Woods, offers at least the possibility of compensation. In Jonah's Gourd Vine, the primary injuries that need addressing are those suffered by the southern folk population, who have been squeezed by the conditions of their lives and often abandoned by upwardly mobile travelers like John Pearson. In Their Eyes, Hurston focuses primarily (although not exclusively) on the wounds suffered by middle-class African American women, who have been deprived of a fruitful interaction with the world, and of any recognition as creative beings, by the aspiration for property and security. As Janie explains, "Ah got up on de high stool lak [Nanny] told me, but Pheoby, Ah done nearly languished tuh death up dere. Ah felt like de world wuz cryin' extry and Ah ain't read de common news yet" (TE, 109). If the world's cry of "extry" points to an endless supply of newsworthy material—supplements exceeding texts and always eliciting more reading—Janie has been confined to an exclusive and entirely unstimulating text. It is no surprise that her attempt at compensating herself involves "common" people and the texts that they make available to her. As others have noted, the novel appears to hinge on the question of cultural recovery. Janie journeys south to the Everglades in order to recover, via the mediation of Tea Cake and his community of friends, an authentic folk experience of the world. Having been denied contact with the origin of the racial tradition, she attempts to reclaim that origin for the purpose, ultimately, of translating it to Pheoby. Thus, it would seem, contact with the folk supplies the creative self that Janie has been forced to give up, while she in turn makes the folk articulate in her narrative. The reciprocity between folk and New Negro seems, at first glance, exemplary.[51]

Yet this reading of the novel overlooks an important feature of Janie's story. Hurston troubles the process of recovery by refusing to delimit the experience that was denied to Janie and by questioning whether that experience has ever belonged or will ever belong to her. Janie's journey fails to prove what faith in racial identity as a vehicle of justice has so often promised—that the self was once and will again be complete, fully repaired. In the first place, Hurston reminds us several times of the newness and strangeness of the Everglades: "To Janie's strange eyes, everything in the Everglades was big and new" (TE, 123). She "learned what it felt like to be jealous" (130) and later "began to look around and see people and things she hadn't noticed during the season." When Janie heard the "compelling rhythms of the Bahaman drummers, she'd walk over and watch the dances" and "got to like it a lot" (133). She encounters the music as an inquisitive outsider, who must acclimate herself for want of any prior knowledge. Such passages mark the second half of the novel as a story more of discovery than of recovery. The experience that Janie acquires as she seeks compensation for past damages can be traced only to the Everglades and its culture, not to any prior version of the self.

But it is more than just the newness of the Everglades that complicates the adequacy of Janie's compensatory journey. If Janie does not repossess something that once belonged to her, neither can she claim possession of what she sees, hears, and lives for the first time. Unlimited and unpredictable, the natural world of the Everglades defies the type of settlement that Joe Starks imposes on Eatonville and the restriction that Matt Bonner visits on the mule. Hurston's description of Lake Okechobee in the throes of a hurricane evokes both of these instances in depicting a natural force that refuses completely its apprehension: "The monstropolous beast had left his bed. The two hundred miles an hour wind had loosed his chains. He seized hold of his dikes and ran forward until he met the quarters; uprooted them like grass and rushed on after his supposed-to-be conquerors, rolling the dikes, rolling the houses, rolling the people in the houses along with other timbers. The sea was walking the earth with a heavy heel" (*TE*, 153). The potential for unruliness is of course part of the point of the place for Tea Cake and Janie. Much like the porch talkers, they seek out a piece of the world in which the objects of human knowledge repeatedly make manifest their otherness, ensuring the self's release from resolved judgment. In the religious terms of the novel, these characters submit themselves to God's judgment—to the inaccessible agencies that make a once-familiar world unknowable and resistant. In reference to this experience of uncanniness, Hurston informs us that "the wind and water had given life to lots of things that folks think of as dead and given death to so much that had been living things" (151–52). In return for placing themselves amid such forces, these characters realize the freedom and wisdom that derive from a suspended self, unable to close on its own judgments.

If Janie is indeed to have her compensatory freedom, then, her journey must be oriented by recognition of the self's incompleteness. Individual freedom goes hand in hand with acceptance of the world's mystery, and neither one is compatible with a self in pursuit of wholeness. Just as consciousness from the outpost of the Eatonville porch sees itself as immeasurable—"never end[ing] because there was no end to reach" (*TE*, 59)—so too must the subject who seeks to adopt such consciousness. That is to say, if Janie wishes to think and act in accordance with the African American communities that she admires, she must give up the aspiration for an experience delimited as "folk," as racial origin, for such an aspiration is entirely inconsistent with the modes of perception evinced both by the porch talkers and by Tea Cake's circle of friends in the Everglades. What drives the highly allegorical narrative in the Everglades is an awareness, even more pressing than that in *Jonah's Gourd Vine*, that folk communities cannot be neatly contained within a discrete cultural tradition. Insofar as the exemplary members of these communities embrace boundlessness as an aspiration, there is no such thing as folk identity and therefore no origin for a race tradition at all.[52]

Janie must inhabit the subjectivity she covets without placing firm abstract limits on it. Similarly, she must avoid restricting others through abstraction, and particularly those others who embrace the same style of knowledge acquisition that she does. Her relationship with Tea Cake becomes, in this sense, emblematic of her orientation toward the desired object in general. After first meeting him, she spends a good deal of time trying to figure him out, deciding whether he is sincere in his love and whether, because of his age and his class, she can trust him entirely. "In the cool of the afternoon the fiend from hell specially sent to lovers arrived at Janie's ear. Doubt. All the fears that circumstance could provide and the heart feel, attacked her on every side. . . . If only Tea Cake would make her certain!" (*TE*, 103). Tea Cake ultimately confirms his love to Janie, but he never makes her certain about his next move and the degree to which he poses a danger to both of them. Immediately after she meets him in Jacksonville, he leaves with her money and throws a barbecue for his friends. Although he subsequently explains his actions to her, he sets off a few days later to gamble back the money and suffers a knife wound. Like the other objects of interest in this novel, Tea Cake does not allow himself to be caught or apprehended. He submits to agencies of chance (such as gambling), spontaneous emotion, and hurricanes that redirect his life and render him difficult to find, even unfamiliar. In her quest for the folk object, therefore, Janie's freedom is necessarily accompanied by the experience of loss.

By the end of the Everglades narrative, that experience has been established as a defining part of the journey south. Having subjected themselves to the wind and water of the hurricane, Janie and Tea Cake must fight with a mad dog for the flotation services of a cow. Tea Cake sacrifices himself to the dog's bite in order to ensure Janie's survival and, in doing so, becomes virtually possessed by the dog's madness: unable to apprehend "this strange thing in Tea Cake's body" (*TE*, 173), Janie confronts the fact that their mutual submission to God's judgment leads not only to free thought and free discourse but to the transformation of her love object into something incomprehensible. The extent of Tea Cake's mysterious illness, in relation to the knowledge and freedom gained in this instance, brings the sense of a worldly imbalance: "Did He *mean* to do this thing to Tea Cake and her? It wasn't anything she could fight. . . . Her arms went up in a desperate supplication for a minute. It wasn't exactly pleading, it was asking questions. The sky stayed hard looking and quiet so she went inside the house. God would do less than He had in His heart" (169). Whatever cosmic restoration awaits Janie in the afterlife, here she must face the reality of unrecoverable loss intrinsic to her acquired conception of self and world.

This reality remains with her when she returns to Eatonville and recounts her story to Pheoby. Janie understands the story that she transmits to Pheoby as partial, offering not a complete body of knowledge on which to base her identity, but bits of understanding suitable to provisional reflections on the self. Much of her past experience with Tea Cake, in other words, is beyond her possession. Just as Tea Cake himself outstrips all of Janie's attempts at apprehension, so too the memory of their time together and its implications for Janie's future: "The kiss of [Tea Cake's] memory made pictures of love and light against the wall. . . . [Janie] pulled in her horizon like a great fish-net. . . . So much of life in its meshes!" (*TE*, 183–84). Janie's "fish-net" provides access to significant past experiences, but the porousness of its "meshes" and the abundance of its object will not allow her to repossess that experience entirely. Moreover, that same permeability ensures that unforeseen new material will penetrate the fishnet, altering Janie's relationship to its current contents. The final sentences of the novel focus attention not only on what Hurston's heroine knows about the journey she has been on, but on all that eludes her about that journey and where it will ultimately take her.[53] Through her narration to Pheoby, Janie comes to terms with the areas of her life that remain unfamiliar and unclaimed. As Janie's messenger and advocate, Pheoby, in turn, must bring Janie's story, in all its open-endedness, to the community. If she has learned anything from the manner of Janie's telling and the ethics embedded in the story, she will remind the community that the story's meaning for the future of Eatonville residents, and the kind of recognition that Janie herself receives for it, must remain open to revision.

Finally, what makes Tea Cake's illness such a powerful metaphor in the novel is that it points not only to the persistent incompleteness of the middle-class self as it pursues psychic repair, but again, as in the story of John Pearson, to the insufficiency of that same self as a remedy for the social injury inflicted on the folk. Once sick, Tea Cake will not be restored to health by Janie, just as he will not reveal himself in the form of a solution for Janie's deprivation. His resistance to healing has its cause, it would seem, in the mad dog, a figure that belongs to the natural world and to the divine judgment that Hurston associates with it. But on close inspection, the unpredictable judgment that leads to Tea Cake's illness operates through other agents as well. Tea Cake himself attributes the disease to the presence of a light-skinned, upwardly mobile man, with whom he imagines Janie having an affair. "Mrs. Turner's brother was back on the muck and now he [Tea Cake] had this mysterious sickness" (*TE*, 171). We have, by this point, already witnessed the consequences wrought by Mrs. Turner's worship of white features, her degradation of African anatomies and folk cultural practices, and her desire to lure Janie, as a light-skinned woman, away from Tea Cake. The latter ploy has inspired Tea Cake to go so far as to stage a fight in Mrs. Turner's restaurant and to hit Janie in order to make public his claim to her.

Despite its inaccuracy, then, Tea Cake's perception concerning the cause of his illness raises questions about the sequence of injuries he has suffered. Which came first—the madness brought on by the dog or the pain triggered by Mrs. Turner?[54] Did the dog bite aggravate a wound that was already present, or does the rabid jealousy have its source in the bite and the ensuing fever? In conflating the two causes, Hurston suggests that the fatal injury suffered by Tea Cake stems, at least partly, from Mrs. Turner's diminishment of him on the basis of his skin color, anatomy, and cultural practices. What Hurston struggles with in the end is the failure of a psychic injury, traceable to the dominant racial hierarchy, to be corrected by any union between the black middle class and the folk—by the formation, that is, of a cultural tradition linking the one to the other. Nothing that Janie can provide, not her love nor her lyrical voice, will fully recover—cure and possess—Tea Cake. This too is information that Pheoby must pass along to Eatonville residents. Whether these residents represented other folk populations like the one on the Everglades or, on the contrary, were represented by northern intelligentsia, the unavoidable reality was the same for Hurston: a racial tradition designed to offset cultural abuse and secure adequate recognition for a folk community would always have its limits, always leave its residues.

Local Community and the "Whole Round World"

Jonah's Gourd Vine and *Their Eyes* suggest that Hurston became more conscious of these residues as she committed herself to the method of knowledge acquisition embraced by the Eatonville porch talkers. In the world according to Hurston and her porch talkers, only God had access to absolute justice. Human authority was never total because the validity of judgments remained mortal and unconfirmed, always in need of revision, always part of a discursive process leading to greater experience and improved forms of knowledge. Judging the world around one was an essential obligation, particularly in contexts that were characterized by disproportionate injury. Hurston could be intensely critical of figures like John Pearson who ignored the obligation to judge and thus compounded the injuries of those who suffered most. But if judgments intended to offset the effects of racism were necessary, they were also necessarily incomplete. While southern African Americans shared a common situation, they could not afford—as members of communities and as individuals—to convince themselves of a single exhaustive solution for it.[55] "I too yearn for universal justice," she wrote in *Dust Tracks*. "[B]ut how to bring it about is another thing. It is such a complicated thing, for justice, like beauty is in the eye of the beholder. There is universal agreement of the principle, but the application brings on the fight." Hurston's discomfort with 1930s-style Communism, and revolutionary politics more generally, clearly coincides with this approach toward justice.[56] Those, like herself, who proposed correctives to American racism, needed to keep in mind that people experienced their social situation in manifold ways. To pursue a single program in an overly zealous way was to risk reducing the experience of the people and defining their needs and desires much too narrowly.

If excessive faith in any form of justice came to seem injurious and self-defeating for Hurston, the problem was not simply that such faith eliminated differences within a population. By limiting the sphere of legitimate speech and action, it also cut off the ongoing quest for new forms of recognition so crucial to an individual's freedom and a community's growth. To a writer thus invested in provisional judgment as the basis of both freedom and communal formation, the notion that a cultural tradition could make the self whole again posed, at the least, a difficult problem. Any such idea rested on a belief that certain minds knew the order of the social world and could, with authority and finality, delimit themselves and their fellow human beings. Tea Cake expresses Hurston's ridicule of this kind of authority after the hurricane, as he is forced to divide bodies too mutilated to be assigned a race and to bury them in the appropriate hierarchical fashion (blacks in a ditch, whites in a coffin): "Look at they hair, when you cain't tell no other way," says a guard, leading Tea Cake to remark that "[t]hey's mighty particular how dese dead folks goes tuh judgment. . . . Look lak dey think God don't know nothin' 'bout de Jim Crow law" (*TE*, 163). In their anxiety to segregate even the illegible dead, the guards betray their own sense of how precarious, how hasty and artificial, the work of racial classification is.

The above passage reads not only as a critique of racial hierarchy, but of racial difference as well, for clearly the inability to decipher bodies reflects the underlying mystery of human essence. The guards of these bodies transgress upon God's authority, as they seek to situate bodies once and for all according to a social order of their own creation. If Hurston herself had sought to make injured selves whole through the formation of a self-reparative racial tradition, *Their Eyes* offers evidence that she was already rethinking this pursuit of wholeness at the time that she wrote the novel. At stake was the sense of her own life as an unfinished, unforeseeable quest narrative: "I do not wish to close the frontiers of life upon my own self," she wrote in an expurgated section of

Dust Tracks. "I do not wish to deny myself the expansion of seeking into individual capabilities and depths by living in a space whose boundaries are race and nation. Lord, give my poor stammering tongue at least one taste of the whole round world, if you please, Sir."[57] In Hurston's novels, the recognition of the poor and stammering tongue helps to free the subject from the restrictiveness of the "big voice" (*TE,* 27), too sure in its designation of the self's own limits. It is no wonder, then, that many of her writings after *Their Eyes*—from *Moses, Man of the Mountain* to articles like "What White Publishers Won't Print," "Crazy for This Democracy," and "High John De Conquer"—place emphasis on imaginative mobility in the world, while attacking entrenched parochialism and assertions of cultural purity.[58]

This belief that all selves are entitled to mobility (or "distance," as John Pearson puts it) is at the heart of Hurston's conception of local community. Those characters in her work who set out from a local community in order to gather experience and achieve a wider recognition usually make their way back to the place where they started, before leaving once again. The traveler feels the pull of a given place, as she or he realizes that both a sense of kinship and the adequate representation of a community require a degree of proximity. This is the case for the character of Zola herself in *Mules and Men;* following Hurston's own career trajectory, Zola returns to Eatonville, Florida, in order to collect folklore. But it is equally true of nomadic characters like John Pearson and Janie Crawford, who confront the challenges of communal reintegration. Passage into and out of the community, whether literal or imaginative, ensures that community is a process of creation and renewal, not a fact encumbering the individual, reflecting old conditions and closed judgments. As a social entity without any permanent boundaries, Eatonville and communities like it could no longer be responsibly celebrated as the "crib of negroism."[59] Indeed, the source of the racial heritage seemed much more plausibly to lie in the places where it was imagined, namely in the metropolitan centers of American and African American power.

In *Moses, Man of the Mountain* (1939), her final literary effort of the decade, Hurston again addresses the issue of locality, using a biblical community to express her minimal ethics. Once again she takes care to safeguard a fictive community's flexible boundaries and encourage its worldliness. Moses travels out of the metropole in Egypt and into the small village community of Midian, home of Jethro, his soon-to-be father-in-law. What marks the village is in part its proximity to the infinite divine presence, which hovers around the mountain in the village's backdrop. But this proximity has at least something to do with Jethro's approach to intellectual travelers, like Moses, from outside the village. Jethro realizes a rare tribelessness in adopting Moses as a surrogate son and absorbing his knowledge: "Moses told [Jethro] about what he had learned among the priests in Egypt . . . and Jethro was eager to hear all he had to say." In taking this approach to the newcomer, Jethro helps to give new life to Midian, for as he acknowledges to Moses, "You came and found us in a pretty low state. . . . Why, we are eating high on the hog now, and all because you are here with us."[60]

Like Pheoby, Jethro accommodates a traveling subject bearing knowledge and experience that will benefit the community. Moreover, while Jethro is at first intent on keeping Moses within the limits of Midian, he reconsiders after several years, recognizing that Moses must convey the wonders of monotheism to the wider world: "I been sort of thinking we ought to let more people know about what we done found." Rather than cutting off his new son from the persecution taking place in Egypt, he reminds Moses of the need to engage with his old country—to take back the wisdom he has absorbed in Midian and use it as a means of improving the world. In this retelling of the Exodus story, big Egypt, with its emphasis on national purity, is the site of the narrow and parochial: "Pharaoh was not interested in the ways of other peoples. He was not interested in their wars and warfare unless they were enemies of Egypt or Egypt's allies." Visits to Midian, in contrast, "never failed to benefit both Moses and Israel." Back and forth Moses travels, trafficking in the knowledge that he gathers. Despite his own sedentary status, Jethro both thrives on the unfamiliar knowledge that Moses brings to him and passes out of his community imaginatively, advising Moses on how he needs to meet particular challenges of leadership. As Moses explains, "Lying shut-in was no place for you, Jethro. You are a man without bounds."[61] Moses's praise should remind us, however, that the boundlessness of men such as Jethro and localities such as Midian derives not from any claim of absolute knowledge, but from doubt, hesitancy, and revision—from the "stammering tongue," to use a term that suggests Hurston's own identification with the hero of Exodus. In Hurston's work, worldliness hinges on seeing oneself as a judge with an impediment.

7

CONCLUSION

Flem Snopes and the Problem of the Open Border

TWO FREQUENTLY DIMINISHED FEATURES OF MODERN LIFE COME TO-
gether in the preceding chapters, each of them adapting to the other, each of
them becoming more significant, consequential, and enduring as a result of
the encounter. There is, on the one hand, the locally affiliated writer, sus-
pending judgment, revising moral assumptions, and endlessly problematizing
relations with the object world. In her well-known essay "Place in Fiction," Eudora Welty wrote of the danger to this figure of remaining perspectivally in
place: "for the artist to be unwilling to move, mentally or spiritually or physically, out of the familiar is a sign that spiritual timidity or poverty or decay has
come upon him."[1] Welty's approach to the artist is embodied by characters like
Howard McLane, Shaya, Joseph Vaillant, Jean-Marie Latour, and Janie Woods,
all of whom share a nomadic orientation toward the production of knowledge.
In dialogue with the writer, and her surrogates in fiction, is the local, face-to-
face community. Hindered by remoteness, with often compromised access to
modern networks and decision making, these communities emerge as future
players and beneficiaries in an interconnected global world. The promise of
regionalism as an enduring form of writing lies in the encounter between the
artist with literary aspirations and the local community. Embedded in such encounters is the potential for mutual empowerment.

For writers of American regionalism in the 1890s, the simultaneous diminishment of the regionalist artist and the local community was an ever-
present authorial problem. The status of regionalism as a minor literary form
rested on the alleged parochialism and limited scope of the communities it depicted. Regionalism, so the argument went, attended to communities and cultures with only a minor significance. As a result of the partiality of such cultures, this body of literature was ill equipped to address the monstrously
distended and ever-changing world at large. What regionalism did offer, in the
form of tightly knit communities and stable group dynamics, was compensa-

tion for that impermanent, unmanageable modern world. William Dean Howells makes this point clearly when he notes that

> [t]here are few places, few occasions among us in which a novelist can get a large number of polite people together, or at least keep them together. . . . Perhaps it is for this reason that we excel in small pieces with three or four figures, or in studies of rustic communities, where there is propinquity if not society. Our grasp of more urbane life is feeble; most attempts to assemble it in our pictures are failures, possibly because it is too transitory, too intangible in its nature with us, to be truthfully represented as really existent.[2]

Howells suggests that the unreality of American life compels writers to focus on "small [literary] pieces" and, correspondingly, on social groups that lack urbanity and possess "propinquity" rather than "society." Yet for writers like Hamlin Garland and Abraham Cahan, the trade-off that Howells proposes between unreal, modern life and real, but limited, American regional literature leaves the latter in a place of weakness and irrelevance. Portraying tangible social relations seems to require the literature of "propinquity" to accept its own smallness and marginality. The crucial point is that regionalist writers who chafed against such a trade-off were acting not only from noble benevolence for the local communities that they represented but also from their own desire to make things of lasting modern significance. In order for their artwork to mean something important, the towns, villages, and ghettos that they depicted needed to be more than objects of fascination, focused on their own miniature corner of the world. They had to be seen as players in the drama of modern life and participants in its most crucial conversations. Through the lens of the regionalist writer aspiring to be "major," "rustic communities" were not nearly as static and opposed to urbane forms of life as Howells suggested; and likewise, modern life was not necessarily so transitory and unreal.

For both Garland and Cahan, the problem with the regionalism of the 1890s lay not only in its tendency to minoritize the places it represented but in the narrowness of its point of view as well. Regionalism could indeed be parochial, but that parochialism had much less to do with the blinkered localism of regional populations than it did with the interestedness of the American reading public. Attempting to write for the ages entailed confronting this audience with its own impoverishing habits, and with perspectives that were less familiar to it. The interests of American editors and readers threatened simultaneously to remove the local community from modern history *and* to reinforce the monologic character of the conversation on locality. Writing that wished to create a lasting impression as literature had an obligation to challenge the all-too-often untroubled assumptions of this conversation.

In Garland's case, meeting a high enough standard of dialogism meant offering regional subjects a place in the conversation that drew on them as objects and examples. These subjects needed to be imagined as critics of their own representation, capable of judging the methods and allegiances of the artist. A fully realized regional literature would recognize that regional subjects were not only artists but deliberating citizen-critics, with strong opinions about the way in which they were represented in a national public sphere. In Cahan's work, the aspiration for a more complicated, more richly textured regionalism than the kind that was in circulation took a slightly different form. The Jewish artist's obligation was to explore available approaches to the question of how Jewish communities would take shape in America and to expose the insufficiencies of each one. Cahan transported the views of the Russian-Yiddish intelligentsia into the American conversation on local community, before bringing to light the limitations of those views on the Jewish question. For both Cahan and Garland, however, dissatisfaction with the narrowness of the discourse on locality converged with a desire to recognize the modern power and agency of local populations. A regionalist literature of consequence would place its populations definitively in the modern world, while encouraging its readership to view these groups from a variety of conflicting perspectives.

Regionalism's metropolitan point of view in the 1890s was a point of contention not only for Garland and Cahan, but for the "new regionalists" who came of age in the 1920s and 1930s, as well. Yet for Mary Austin and the Santa Fe "yearners," the goal was not to keep afloat multiple conflicting perspectives in order to empower simultaneously the artist and the community, but rather to root the regional representation more rigorously in a unified communal viewpoint, emanating organically from the locality in question. The local color of the 1890s had erred in allowing the tastes of East Coast, metropolitan audiences to determine the character of the regional folk for a mass audience. In order to redress those violations of the past and heal an atomized nation, the regional writer needed to find and preserve the local community's cultural difference. Regionalists were preservationists, obliged to serve up the community in its purest form, prior to any contestation between members and prior to any corruption by the mass market.

A similar approach to folk community informed the writing of many Harlem Renaissance intellectuals of the same period. For leaders like Alain Locke and Arthur Schomburg, establishing the absolute racial difference of the folk community was crucial to building the perception of a self-determining race. Any confusion about that racial difference threatened to compromise the image of the elite classes, who were always vulnerable to the accusation that they were glorified copyists in a tradition not their own. Like the new regionalists, writers like Locke and Schomburg rejected as potentially injurious any form of assimilation that had for its goal the loss of cultural distinctiveness. To be sure, the Harlem Renaissance intellectuals approached folk representation with their own specific concerns. For one thing, Locke and company needed to negotiate much more carefully between the impulse to preserve folk culture in high art on the one hand and to supplement it with the currency of high modernism on the other. Any neglect of the latter currency in black representation could result in an injury to the race as deep and debilitating as the one associated with the exclusive pursuit of Euro-American culture. Yet both movements placed the tight-knit, folk community at the center of their respective projects, foregrounding its survival as the pure, original expression of a cultural tradition. In both cases, disseminating that tradition in print played a vital role in the healing and wholeness of a larger group.

If this emphasis on difference and preservation held out the promise of healing, however, it also threatened to turn the local community into an alien place for a psychic wanderer or a skeptic—to suppress the very practices that made this person feel most at home in the world. According to both the new regionalists and many contributors to the anthology *The New Negro*, the difference of the local community needed to be approached as a matter beyond deliberation, something that had already been decided by geography or blood, and by an automatic process of cultural transmission. Local residents were encumbered by a tradition that was passed along intact and then translated by the modernist. What marks the fiction of Willa Cather and Zora Neale Hurston is the tendency to bring the unencumbered skeptic or wanderer into the community and to explore how that person might be made to feel at home.

While passage out of and back into the community, whether psychic or physical, is crucial to the needs of these wandering characters in both Cather and Hurston, it is not a sufficient condition for his or her feeling at home in the community. This passage must also be given duration in the form of crafted objects (Cather) and circulating stories (Hurston). Aesthetic products, whether material or oral artifacts, ensure that the unencumbered subject has a place in the surrounding community. Correspondingly, they help to ensure that communal formation hinges on discussion between freely choosing individuals, rather than on assumptions of ascribed belonging. Because the ties that bind community members are provisional in Hurston and Cather's work, always subject to discourse, the wanderer's passage can serve as a source of re-newed tradition. Hurston's work places particular emphasis on this process: the porous borders that enable a Janie Starks to pursue knowledge and expe-rience in the Everglades are the same borders that must be tested, through talk, in response to the news of her travels. It is perhaps this opportunity to serve as an impetus for good talk, and for the process of communal reevaluation, that invites Janie to consider Eatonville a home worthy of return. But if Eatonville is worth the artist's return, it is also deserving of her departure once again. As a locality committed to revisiting its judgments and methods, Eatonville in-corporates the artist figure in order to furnish knowledge that might alter and improve the world.

For Hurston, a local community like Eatonville or Midian usually benefits from the figures that pass through its open borders, bearing both wisdom that advances the judgment of the group and news of global problems that need re-solving. Through the artist figure, the community gains both a powerful means of self-improvement and a voice with which to impact the world. But what of the risks of the open border? The process of communal formation may be in-vigorated by an artist figure, with the interests of the community at heart. But borders that are open to the cooperative artist are open to others as well. And what if the figure passing through is not Hurston's Moses or Janie Woods, but Faulkner's Flem Snopes—an anti-artist whose values and behavior seem to threaten the very existence of the community as a community?

Faulkner's treatment of Flem Snopes resonates with the fears that local populations have often expressed about increased integration into global net-works of communication. A recent issue of *Cultural Survival Quarterly*, which describes itself as "a quarterly magazine for policy makers and others inter-ested in indigenous peoples and their rights, cultures, and concerns," takes up this issue in relation to the Internet.[3] As a whole, the issue works to debunk the myth that "[indigenous peoples] . . . wish to isolate themselves from the rest of the world in order to cling to archaic ways of life." Yet the editorial that frames the issue, written by Harvard anthropologist David Maybury-Lewis, makes an interesting distinction between the usefulness of the Internet as a political instrument and its effects on "social struggles." "Is there not a real danger," he asks, "that an intensification of communication with the wider world may actually undermine the distinctive cultures that indigenous peoples cherish and try to protect?"[4]

Maybury-Lewis avoids any judgment about when, where, and how it might be appropriate to regulate the influx of information, raising the question of how he would respond to some of the more radical cautionary notes that appear in the issue's articles. In one piece on the communities of Canada's North-west Territories, writer Barry Zellen reports on an interview with Metis musi-cian, philosopher, and writer Fred Lepine:

> Lepine . . . believes that . . . "once you learn about other cultures and the outside world, the ideas and habits you take on can replace the relation-ships you establish with your own people in your own community." Lepine believes this "weakens . . . interpersonal relations," and as more and more indigenous people connect to the outside world, the more vulnerable northerners will become to "new habits" such as cyberporn and on-line gambling. The assimilating power of the Internet comes from its accessi-bility, according to Lepine[;] "when you live by yourself in an isolated com-munity for so long and suddenly face an outside world that wants you, there's a big risk."[5]

What Lepine calls the Internet's accessibility works two ways, establishing communication channels between marketers at the centers of wealth and power and consumers on the fringes. Communities in the Northwest Territo-ries can access a variety of markets and information sources without traveling to southern Canada. At the same time, because the Internet requires no hu-man mediation at the local level, vendors can suddenly afford market relations with isolated groups who were previously outside their reach.

In Faulkner's Yoknapatawpha County, the weblike agency that transports goods across the town line and organizes a previously isolated community into a competitive market, linked to other regions of the country, is Flem Snopes. The "Spotted Horses" episode of *The Hamlet* (1940), originally published in 1931 and later incorporated into the fourth book of the novel, tells the story of Flem's return to Frenchman's Bend after a year's absence in Texas, at the same moment when a Texan man enters the town with a pack of wild, spotted horses.[6] The horses are driven violently into a lot, a crowd of townsmen gath-ers to watch them, and before the day is over, all but two of the horses have been sold. For the Texan, who presides over the auction, the objective is to turn the community of men into a group of potential consumers, connected to one another only by the promise of owning a horse for little money and the fantasy of individual transformation. The more spectators he can attract, the more gos-sip he can generate about the specific value of a horse to each man, the better his chances that the entire lot of goods will get sold. When no one responds to his initial offer, he gives a horse away, provided that the new owner will "start the bidding on the next one."[7] The Texan knows that he can afford to lose a few dollars if, in the process, each townsman begins to see the auction as an opportunity to possess something that might change his dismal life. Once a townsman begins to gauge the value of a horse against the bids of others, he changes from a neighbor primarily concerned with his good reputation in the community to a competitor, vying with others both to save currency and to acquire property.

The change in the town, however, cannot be reduced merely to competition or acquisitiveness. Competitive relations existed in Frenchman's Bend prior to the appearance of Flem Snopes and the Texan, as Faulkner makes clear in his consistent depiction of the Varners as the area's previous elite family: Will Varner, we are told at the beginning of *The Hamlet,* was "the chief man of the country" and owner of "the store and the cotton gin and the combined grist mill and blacksmith shop" (*H,* 5). What is at stake for Faulkner in the emergence of aggressive marketers from outside the town and competitive consumers within it is, rather, the nature of communication. Will Varner does not import salespeople like the Texan, who have no intention of remaining in town after a sale has been completed. Because the Texan does not live in Frenchman's Bend and cares nothing about the trust of its residents, he can steel himself against feelings and considerations that might curtail his dishonesty. "I want to get this auction started," he announces. "I ain't come here to live, no matter how good a country you folks claim you got" (293–94). The temporariness of his presence in town means that deceptive communication, and the alienated relations that result from it, are no cost to him at all.

We, like the townspeople, never learn what Flem's precise connection is to either the Texan or the horses. By concealing his own role in the sale, Flem ensures that he can maximize his own profit, while minimizing the consequences to himself of dirty salesmanship. While Flem's concealment functions for him as a means of managing his own residence in Frenchman's Bend, it functions for others as a sign of the alien communicative habits that he embraces. At one point, the townsmen speculate on whether Flem's cousin Eck knows who owns the horses: "His own kin will be the last man in the world to find out anything about Flem Snopes's business," says one man. "No," counters another, "The first man Flem would tell his business to would be the man that was left after the last man died. Flem Snopes don't even tell himself what he is up to" (*H,* 284). Unlike Will Varner, whose methods of accumulation may be brutal at times but remain transparent to the community, Flem uses an outsider to falsify the objects he is selling and to obscure his own role in that falsification. Deception is such a habit for him that it can at times appear as the end of his scheming, rather than a means of profit. As the second villager quite rightly notes, in his awkward desire to complicate schemes and fool others, Flem can forget to remind himself of his own motives.

Flem is thus an importer living in Frenchman's Bend but regarding its residents impersonally, as a heretofore unexploited market to be manipulated rather than as partners to be trusted in laughter and understanding. The creatures that he brings into the community from the outside comment on the kind of business he does, its relation to other expansive enterprises, and its particular effects on local communities. What the townsmen first see, just prior to the appearance of Flem, is "a covered wagon drawn by mules and followed by a considerable string of obviously alive objects which in the levelling sun resembled vari-sized and -colored tatters torn at random from large billboards—circus posters, say—attached to the rear of the wagon" (*H,* 275). Associations between the horses and a traveling circus, or a zoo, are repeated throughout the story, so that Flem comes to resemble a trader in exotic animals, capitalizing on the strange spectacle that the goods present. Flem's relative Lump jokes that "[i]f Flem had knowed how quick you fellows was going to snap them horses up, he'd a probably brought some tigers. . . . Monkeys too" (315). Much like adventurers who were claiming wild tigers as property and marketing them to domestic audiences as art or entertainment, Flem, with the Texan's help, turns unmanageable nature from a far-off place into a commodity for visual consumption—or at least he does so long enough to sell the horses.

Part of the dark comedy of the story stems from the awkward, absurdly tenuous manner with which he and the Texan accomplish this feat. This auction involves no animals jumping through flaming hoops, for the violence required by the exhibition of sublime nature appears here in its raw and most exposed form. In order to demonstrate mastery over his quarry, the Texan shoves his fingers into "the animal's nostrils, holding the horse's head wrenched half around while it breathed in hoarse, smothered groans" (*H,* 277). This is the global trade in animals in its most comic, frightening, and illuminating form. The reality of living beasts, defiant of the human will to own property, remains visible at all times, in spite of the Texan's showmanship.

It comes as no surprise, then, that the horses ultimately refuse to be owned. When the townsmen attempt to gain possession of their new property, the horses break out of the lot, decimating an adjacent house and causing injury and havoc in the county. Their capacity for spreading to other places and for destruction leads Ratliff, the salesman who chastises the other townsmen for their gullibility, to compare the animals to a disease: "what Ratliff had called 'that Texas sickness,' that spotted corruption of frantic and uncatchable horses, had spread as far as twenty and thirty miles" (*H*, 327).[8] Those who come into contact with the horses catch the sickness without catching, or containing, the carriers, suggesting that the epidemic will continue to rampage. By identifying the horses as a rapidly spreading sickness, Ratliff implicates the residents of the county in their own devastation. What role they might play in this drama returns us to the nature of the imported creatures. For these are of course not simply wild horses, but spotted ones, resembling "tatters torn at random from large billboards." If they are the things that get misrepresented by circus-like men, they are also the tools of misrepresentation, linked metonymically to the slogans and images that appear on "circus posters" (275). Despite their uselessness as farm animals, they have high value for Snopes as embodied advertisements, naturally equipped to startle potential buyers into ignoring a commodity's limitations. The fact that the villagers know little about these Texan commodities makes them all the more effective as advertisements. What the horses spread, then—through the sensational coats that they wear and their lack of history in Yoknapatawpha—is a contagion of manipulation and mistrust. Those who catch the sickness become accustomed to deceptive communication, both as victims of it and as perpetrators.

In the "Spotted Horses" episode, the mode of communication that the horses explicitly trample on is what one character later calls "neighborliness" (*H*, 334). We get a taste of this mode when Ratliff chastises a townsman for plowing the fields of another family: "This won't be the first time I ever saw you in their field, doing plowing Henry never got around to. How many days have you already given them this year?" (318). Whether or not Ratliff is right in suggesting that Henry Armstid is lazy, his irritation points to a debilitating weakness in Frenchman's Bend. These villagers extend their generosity indiscriminately, without, in this case, even asking whether or not Henry is worth the labor. Neighborliness requires relaxed judgment, and it applies to anyone who makes an appearance in the community. We hear it in Faulkner's account of the townsmen responding to the distorted rhetoric of the Texan: "there was no mirth or humor in his voice and there was neither mirth nor humor in the single guffaw which came from the rear of the group" (289). Beneath that guffaw, it would seem, is both an uncertainty about the Texan's motives and a compulsion to welcome him in a neighborly way. Insofar as the person who utters it has imbibed the ethos and communicative habits of neighborliness, he must suppress whatever impulse he has toward antagonistic speech.

The same goes for the villager named Tull, who is thrown out of his wagon by a rampaging horse and dragged, unconscious, across a bridge. As Tull's wife makes clear in court, he chafes against the idea of a lawsuit, knowing that it will place him in a position of conflict: "Don't you say hush to me! You'll let Eck Snopes or Flem Snopes or that whole Varner tribe snatch you out of the wagon and beat you half to death against a wooden bridge. But when it comes to suing them for your just rights and a punishment, oh no. Because that wouldn't be neighborly. What's neighborly got to do with you lying flat on your back in the middle of planting time while we pick splinters out of your face?" (*H*, 334). Although directed at her husband, Mrs. Tull's speech works to warn the other spectators in the courtroom that they cannot afford to renounce the capacity for suspicion and verbal aggression, not with Flem Snopes and the Texan pushing spotted horses in town. Neighborliness has become a form of masochism in a Snopes-riddled world.[9] If the goal is indeed to preserve this value intact, the only possible method of achieving it is to shut out the carriers of disease and shut in the neighborly community.

But in Frenchman's Bend, neighborliness cannot realistically be preserved. The horses of deception are already loose, and any protection against them requires an alternative ethic of communication. At the same time, protection in this sense does not, for Faulkner, require adoption of Snopesian techniques. It does not, in other words, mean the collapse of the community entirely. The community survives in the contemporary world because it rests on a communicative foundation that far exceeds, first, the spreading deceptiveness of the Snopeses and, second, the habit of doing indiscriminate acts of kindness and being perpetually hospitable. Much like Eatonville, Frenchman's Bend is supported, perhaps primarily, by the practice of pointed and playful talking. As Will Varner puts it, these people have "[g]ot to set around store and talk" (*H*, 312).

Storefront talking has the potential to respond actively to any of Flem's schemes. Faulkner clearly distinguishes the ritual from neighborly practices by placing his most skeptical character, Ratliff, at the center of it and by highlighting Ratliff's ironic judgment of others.

> At nine oclock on the second morning after that, five men were sitting or squatting along the gallery of the store. The sixth was Ratliff. He was standing up, and talking: "Maybe there wasn't but one of them things in Mrs. Littlejohn's house that night, like Eck says. But it was the biggest drove of just one horse I ever seen. It was in my room and it was on the front porch. . . . And still it was missing everybody every time. I reckon that's what that Texas man meant by calling them bargains: that a man would need to be powerful unlucky to ever get close enough to one of them to get hurt." (*H*, 314)

Ratliff exposes the dishonesty of the Texan's speech by suggesting that there really is no reasonable way to conceive of the horses as "bargains." Throughout this episode on the storefront porch, talking hovers around a series of undecided questions: What exactly happened two days before? What role did Flem Snopes play in the sale? Does Henry Armstid's misfortune conceal an underlying laziness? All of these questions are at stake in the discursive exchange, and all of them call on the participants to make active moral distinctions. Moreover, Ratliff directs his skepticism toward other interlocutors if they act in a manner that arouses suspicion. When the store clerk, Lump Snopes, "cackle[s] suddenly" (315) before revealing his own enthusiasm for Flem's schemes, Ratliff turns on him, effectively excluding him from the conversation. Far from automatic, attitudes toward all who appear in Frenchman's Bend are contingent on the behavior that they exhibit. Because Ratliff himself is a sewing-machine agent, peddling new technology to the entire county, he and his machines must also be measured for their usefulness to the community. The ritual of talking thus functions as a method for gauging the motives of others, the nature of unfamiliar objects, and the meaning of a confusing set of events.

By enabling the residents of Frenchman's Bend to adapt themselves to agents of change, both destructive and constructive, the tradition of talking helps to secure the community's strength and survival. Adaptation, however, is not simply a matter of sorting out the good from the bad, cultivating a welcoming attitude toward the one and an adversarial stance toward the other. It consists, in addition, of prolonging the very process of collective judgment, even when the outcome of that process appears fairly certain. The above passage, in which Ratliff interprets the Texan's use of "bargain," is indicative of this dimension of the ritual. Ratliff appropriates the Texan's deceptive speech in order, first of all, to establish an understanding with his listeners. His intention, unlike the Texan's, is not to fool the group, but to imply a meaning that all of them, accustomed as they are to obliquity, can share. Yet Ratliff's method of truth-telling is, paradoxically, rooted in "the lie." If he says what he believes, he does so under cover of a fictional interpretation of "bargain," according to which the Texan is an honest broker who points to the wildness of his beasts as an attractive feature. Ratliff is in this sense a close cousin of the literary writer, who prefers a transparent lie to an outright expression of belief as a method of knowledge production. Why, in Faulkner's world, such a person might prefer this indirect method returns us to the collective value of talking. Ratliff's irony is both a judgment and a prelude to a conversation—a message that there is more to say before any conclusive judgment is made. "Lying," in other words, allows him to suggest that the Texan misrepresents the horses and, at the same time, to refrain from making manifest his claim. His silence speaks, but it does so without making a closing statement. This voice gains its authority by purposely avoiding the terminating claim and, in doing so, inviting more talk within the interval of the ritual.

Herein lies the ambiguous value of Flem Snopes to Frenchman's Bend. He introduces destructive objects into the town, calls them by another name, and spreads his dishonest method of marketing to other areas. Yet despite his worst intentions, Flem furnishes the basis of occasions in which writerly figures like Ratliff orchestrate particularly vibrant, pleasurable, and prolonged talking sessions. Such sessions can lead, in turn, to a heightened sense of understanding between group members and to incisive judgments about the ludicrous, rampaging world of global trade that Flem reproduces both dangerously and comically. Letting in him and his horses will certainly cause damage, particularly to those who relax their capacity for judgment and relinquish the last word to the Texan; but shutting him out deprives the group of an opportunity for playful solidarity and worldly significance.

In "Centaur in Brass," a story published in the early 1930s as Faulkner was developing the Snopes material, Faulkner aptly turns Flem into a monument builder, whose schemes lead unintentionally to the retirement of a hardy water tank. "In our town," we are told, "Flem Snopes now has a monument to himself."[10] The story of how the tank becomes a monument involves Flem this time not as a covert importer, but as an exporter of the town's valuable resources. Having become cozy with the mayor, he gets himself appointed superintendent of the town's energy plant and begins to remove brass fittings, with the intention of marketing them in an undisclosed location. In order to avoid holding these fittings himself, he deceives one African American worker at the plant into taking them home and another into retrieving them. But after the two workers uncover the scheme collaboratively, one of them places the fittings in the tank, permanently out of market, rendering the water in the tank undrinkable. Thus Flem's elaborate scheming for profit culminates in the contamination of the town's water and the replacement of the tank by an underground reservoir.

Once again, Faulkner shows us the dark consequences of Flem's deception, linking it to the social and environmental disasters that the unfettered profit motive has often caused in places like Frenchman's Bend. Yet the town responds by giving new meaning to the brassy water in the tank: "the tank was a stout one and the water was still good to wash the streets with, and so the town let it stand."[11] While Flem's objective may be the production of fungible currency, he leaves behind an enduring legacy in spite of himself, a material object composed of dirty water and worthless brass inside a metal casing. This tank continues to stand, and to stand not only for the end result of Flem's scheming, but for the new, regenerative purposes to which that result is put, in this case washing streets.

In the final sentence of the story, Faulkner describes the monument as a "shaft taller than anything in sight and filled with transient and symbolical liquid that was not even fit to drink, but which, for the very reason of its impermanence, was more enduring through its fluidity and blind renewal than the brass which poisoned it, than columns of basalt or lead."[12] What gives the tank its endurance, and significance as a highly visible landmark in town—"taller than anything in sight"—is the water that has been contaminated. This "symbolical" liquid lasts precisely because it can be redefined and redirected, whenever necessary. As a protean material, it becomes a powerfully renewable substance, continuous in some of its uses but adaptable to any number of unforeseeable ("blind") contingencies that confront the town. There is perhaps no better metaphor for the initial sullying effects of Flem's schemes and their transformation into valuable talk, open-ended town tradition. "Centaur in Brass," in fact, hinges on the verbal collaboration of the two African American laborers, Tom-Tom and Turl. Flem turns them against each other through his manipulation. But after a period of conflict that culminates in physical struggle, Tom-Tom and Turl have their first real discussion of the story in deciding to take collective action against their exploitative superintendent: "[Tom-Tom] and Turl just sat there in the ditch and talked."[13] Thus Flem's exploitation leads, ironically, to discussion and cooperation. The water monument and the verbal intercourse between Tom-Tom and Turl have their clear analogue in the multivocal story itself, which passes, as if exchanged on the store gallery, from Harker, the night engineer at the energy plant, to the anonymous narrator and finally to the reading public.[14] All of these "symbolical" structures point us to the great irony inherent in Flem Snopes: a character who simultaneously infects Frenchman's Bend and enables it to deliver itself from the threat of stasis, attenuation, and irrelevance—the condition of not talking urgently to one another, not renewing communal ties or tradition in relation to a changing world.

Ratliff and the talkers of "Centaur in Brass" depend on Flem Snopes for conversation that matters. Similarly, Faulkner depends on a community that engages with Flem's schemes, adapting to them with a mixture of ironic reprimand and anticipation of his next antic. If in Garland and Cahan, the writer's pursuit of a lasting dialogic voice leads to the local community's empowerment, here, and in Hurston as well, the community's ritual of significant, never-ending talk provides the basis for the writer's enduring voice. As Faulkner seems to know, a community that gives this talking ritual a prominent place needs to produce its judgments with an eye toward making them last, even as it allows for the revision of these judgments. The contaminated water in Flem Snopes's monument, we should remember, has been put to a particular purpose over a length of time. If the community forfeits the aspiration toward duration altogether, none of its judgments can be taken seriously at all. In other words, Faulkner does not construct his community according to the belief that the more the community revises itself, the more it ensures its survival. Rather, Frenchman's Bend is a place that seeks, where possible, continuity in the modern world but that prepares itself, through its foundational principles, for "blind renewal"—the contingencies that will demand a rethinking of tradition.

In this study I have tried to approach the construction of a particular literary tradition in a similar way. I have based my turn to regionalism on the assumption that late-nineteenth- and early-twentieth-century regionalists were participating in a discussion of local community that continues very actively in our time. At the center of my analyses, therefore, is a question of duration: Given the global conditions that obtain for modern communities, which texts are best positioned to impact the conversation on local community over time? My response to this question has been guided by the belief that literature's orientation toward discourse—its tendency to emphasize open-ended critique and the unencumbered subject—equips it to make its own specific contribution to this conversation. Judgments about duration, such as the ones that emerge in this study, have their place in the making of any meaningful tradition, literary or otherwise. Putting such judgments in their proper place, however, means situating them in the midst of a conversation rather than at the end of one. Treated in this way, they are nothing more or less than provisional attempts to give a tradition some footing in the world.

NOTES

1. Introduction

1. David Noble, "The Coming of the Online University," in *Digital Diploma Mills: The Automation of Higher Education* (New York: Monthly Review Press, 2001), 27.

2. Noble, "Lessons from the Pre-Digital Age: The Correspondence Education Movement," in *Digital Diploma Mills,* 3, 2.

3. Correspondence education allowed students to take courses through the mail, without ever stepping foot on campus. The movement was initiated in the 1880s by commercial schools oriented toward vocational training, but by 1919 state and private universities were offering correspondence-based instruction. See Noble, "Lessons from a Pre-Digital Age," 1–24.

4. For comprehensive accounts of the expansion and consolidation of the United States in the nineteenth century, see Robert H. Wiebe, *The Search for Order, 1877–1920* (New York: Hill and Wang, 1967); and Alan Trachtenberg, *The Incorporation of America: Culture and Society in the Gilded Age* (New York: Hill and Wang, 1982). The seminal study of print capitalism as an instrument of nation-building is Benedict Anderson, *Imagined Communities: Reflections on the Origin and Spread of Nationalism,* rev. ed. (London: Verso, 1991). See esp. chapter 3, "The Origins of National Consciousness."

5. Erving Goffman, "Alienation from Interaction," in *Interaction Ritual: Essays on Face-to-Face Behavior,* by Goffman (Garden City, NY: Doubleday, 1967), 114.

6. As architect Michael Sorkin points out in an argument for recognizing bodily interaction in the construction of modern cities, "democratic deliberation is only possible in an environment that conduces both consensus and accident. This continual potential for conflict is vital to deliberation and marks the vigor of difference within culture." Sorkin, "Introduction: Traffic in Democracy," in *Giving Ground: The Politics of Propinquity,* ed. Joan Copjec and Michael Sorkin (London: Verso, 1999), 6.

7. John Dewey, *The Public and Its Problems* (1927; reprint, Chicago: Swallow Press, 1954), 211, 213.

8. In linking this set of significant activities, values, and/or beliefs to the concept of community, I am drawing on Philip Selznick's loose definition of community. Selznick calls attention to the "framework of shared beliefs, interests, and commitments" that join com-

munity members, creating "a common faith or fate, a personal identity, a sense of belonging, and a supportive structure of activities and relationships." Selznick, *The Moral Commonwealth: Social Theory and the Promise of Community* (Berkeley: University of California Press, 1992), 358–59.

9. On the civil society concept as a response to the loss of God and king as primary social authorities, see Adam Seligman, *The Idea of Civil Society* (Princeton, NJ: Princeton University Press, 1992), 15–16.

10. On the centrality of this question, see Seligman's essay "Civil Society as Idea and Ideal," in *Alternative Conceptions of Civil Society and Social Theory*, ed. Simone Chambers and Will Kymlicka (Princeton, NJ: Princeton University Press, 2002), 13–33.

11. This nineteenth-century concept of civil society is often linked to Georg Hegel. As Charles Taylor notes, in Hegel "[c]ivil society exists over against the state, in partial independence from it. It includes those dimensions of social life which cannot be confounded with, or swallowed up in the state." Taylor, "Modes of Civil Society," *Public Culture* 3.1 (Fall 1990): 95. For a more extensive account of Hegel's ideas on civil society, see Andrew Arato and Jean Cohen, *Civil Society and Social Theory* (Cambridge, MA: MIT Press, 1992), 91–116.

12. I am borrowing here from Michael Walzer's description of civil society as an alternative to both the family, "whose members are not volunteers," and the state, "which, even if its legitimacy rests on the consent of its members, wields coercive power over them." Walzer, "Equality and Civil Society," in Chambers and Kymlicka, *Civil Society and Social Theory*, 35.

13. Several texts have been instrumental in reviving interest in the civil society concept. Two important points of origin, which predate the surge in eastern European discourse on civil society, are Peter L. Berger and Richard John Neuhaus, *To Empower People: The Role of Mediating Structures in Public Policy* (Washington, DC: American Enterprise Institute, 1977); and Robert N. Bellah, Richard Madsen, William M. Sullivan, Ann Swidler, and Steven M. Tipton, *The Habits of the Heart: Individualism and Commitment in American Life* (1985; reprint, Berkeley: University of California Press, 1996). The most influential and widely contested empirical study of civil society's weakening during the latter half of the twentieth century is Robert D. Putnam's *Bowling Alone: The Collapse and Revival of American Community* (New York: Simon and Schuster, 2000). For a skeptical response to Putnam's emphasis on decline, with a focus on the contemporary rights-bearing citizen as a source of political engagement, see Michael Schudson, *The Good Citizen: A History of American Civic Life* (New York: Free Press, 1998). A useful collection—which includes Michael Walzer's classic essay "The Idea of Civil Society: A Path to Social Reconstruction," published originally in *Dissent* 38.2 (Spring 1991): 293–302—is E. J. Dionne Jr., ed., *Community Works: The Revival of Civil Society in America* (Washington, DC: Brookings Institution Press, 1998). For a discussion that distinguishes effectively between different versions of civil society, see Benjamin Barber, *A Place for Us: How to Make Society Civil and Democracy Strong* (New York: Farrar, Straus and Giroux, 1998). An oft-cited resource that presents the republican-communitarian perspective lucidly is Michael J. Sandel, *Democracy's Discontent: America in*

Search of a Public Philosophy (Cambridge, MA: Harvard University Press, 1996). For a study that questions any programmatic attempt to bolster civil society and the belief that we can predict the benefits it promises, see Nancy L. Rosenblum, *Membership and Morals: The Personal Uses of Pluralism in America* (Princeton, NJ: Princeton University Press, 1998).

14. To be sure, distinctions need to be made between civil society advocates on the right and those on the left. The former tend to treat the modern welfare state as a threat to civil society, much in the way that eastern Europeans regard the totalitarian state; greater investment in the social groups of civil society, therefore, must coincide with reduced government involvement in and regulation of the market. Those on the left argue that civil society does not relieve government of its responsibility for regulating the market, providing necessary services, and protecting rights. Rather, a healthy civil society requires state involvement and regulation in order to function appropriately. For discussions of the relation between right and left among civil society advocates, see Taylor, "Modes of Civil Society," 98–99; and Barber, *Place for Us*, 4–6, 63–68.

15. My comments here respond to Sandel's exceptionally lucid account in *Democracy's Discontent* of the modern American subject's loss of empowerment and belonging.

16. Interestingly, Sandel does not eliminate reflexivity—or the rational consideration of one's situation—from his theory of the encumbered subject. See, for instance, his discussion of Robert E. Lee's decision to fight for the Confederacy. Ibid., 15–16. Yet we need to ask whether this reflexivity has any teeth at all—that is, any transformative potential—if the subject's relation to his allegiances remains wholly involuntary.

17. The model of selfhood with which I am working builds on Philip Selznick's attempt to reconcile liberalism and the socially implicated self. Selznick notes that "liberal doctrine does not necessarily deny that selves are socially constituted or that deeply held convictions stem from communal involvements and attachments. The concept of a social self is wholly compatible with the recognition that people do make choices." *Moral Commonwealth*, 380.

18. My point is not that the liberal state is morally neutral, but rather that it is invested in constitutional restrictions and obligations that protect the individual's right to choose between versions of the good life. We fight for these restrictions and obligations because they ensure a measure of individual self-determination for all (regardless of their relation to the current government) and, correspondingly, comity among disparate sectors of the polity. Anthony Appiah has remarked, along these lines, that "liberalism must, in the end, be ready to be a fighting creed." "Identity, Authenticity, Survival: Multicultural Societies and Social Reproduction," in *Multiculturalism: Examining the Politics of Recognition*, ed. Amy Gutmann (Princeton, NJ: Princeton University Press, 1994), 159.

19. E. J. Dionne Jr., "Introduction: Why Civil Society? Why Now?" in *Community Works*, 7–8; Lucy Lippard, *The Lure of the Local: Senses of Place in a Multi-Centered Society* (New York: New Press, 1997), 5.

20. See, for instance, Amy Kaplan, "Nation, Region, and Empire," in *The Columbia History of the American Novel*, ed. Emory Elliott (New York: Columbia University Press, 1991), 240–66; Richard Brodhead, "The Reading of Regions," in *Cultures of Letters: Scenes of Read-*

ing and Writing in Nineteenth-Century America (Chicago: University of Chicago Press, 1993), 107–41; and June Howard, ed., *New Essays on "The Country of the Pointed Firs"* (Cambridge: Cambridge University Press, 1990). More recently, scholars have been grappling with the first wave of nation-based critics mentioned above, often focusing on regionalism's counterhegemonic projects. Along these lines, see Carrie Tirado Bramen, "The Uneven Development of American Regionalism," in *The Uses of Variety: Modern Americanism and the Quest for National Distinctiveness,* by Bramen (Cambridge, MA: Harvard University Press, 2000), 115–55; Stephanie Foote, *Regional Fictions: Culture and Identity in Nineteenth-Century American Literature* (Madison: University of Wisconsin Press, 2001); Judith Fetterley and Marjorie Pryse, "Regionalism and the Question of the American," in *Writing Out of Place: Regionalism, Women, and American Literary Culture* (Urbana: University of Illinois Press, 2003), 214–47; Marjorie Pryse, "Sex, Class, and 'Category Crisis': Reading Jewett's Transitivity," *American Literature* 70 (September 1998): 517–49; Nancy Glazener, "Regional Accents: The *Atlantic* Group, the *Arena,* and New England Women's Regionalism," in *Reading for Realism: The History of a U.S. Literary Institution, 1850–1910,* by Glazener (Durham, NC: Duke University Press, 1997), 189–228; June Howard, "Unraveling Regions, Unsettling Periods: Sarah Orne Jewett and American Literary History," *American Literature* 68 (1996): 365–84; Kate McCullough, *Regions of Identity: The Construction of America in Women's Fiction, 1885–1914* (Stanford, CA: Stanford University Press, 1999); Sandra Zagarell, "Crosscurrents: Registers of Nordicism, Community, and Culture in Jewett's *Country of the Pointed Firs,*" *Yale Journal of Criticism* 10.2 (1997): 355–70; and Zagarell, "Troubling Regionalism: Rural Life and the Cosmopolitan Eye in Jewett's *Deephaven,*" *American Literary History* 10.4 (Winter 1998): 639–63.

21. Approaching regionalism through the lens of a feminist analytic, Fetterley and Pryse's recent book, *Writing Out of Place,* is an exception to this emphasis on the contemporary evidentiary function of regionalism. Fetterley and Pryse write, at the beginning of their book, about a literate community spanning generations, with writers speaking to readers who live well after their time. Several other scholars do, at certain moments, prioritize regionalism's interlocutory potential, its capacity to enter actively into cultural worlds other than the one of origin. See, for instance, Stephanie Foote's final chapter, "Representation and Tammany Hall: Locating the Body Politic," in *Regional Fictions,* 154–79; and the final two pages of Carrie Tirado Bramen's account of regionalism in *Uses of Variety,* 154–55. Yet neither Foote nor Bramen treats this interlocutory function as a primary basis for constructing a regionalist tradition. Tom Lutz writes of an American literary field covering 150 years, and of writers of one period appealing to readers from another by way of a common commitment to literariness, to discursive multiplicity. Yet Lutz does not distinguish regionalism's ability to travel temporally from the same ability in other literary forms. *Cosmopolitan Vistas: American Regionalism and Literary Value* (Ithaca, NY: Cornell University Press, 2004), 12. In this book I attempt to offset the distancing effect of historicist analyses, in which readers confront regionalist texts primarily as objects to be situated in a prior dis-

cursive context, as evidence of how people used to think. Arguing for an ongoing conversation on local community in which regionalism participates, I regard regionalist texts as perfectly at home in discursive settings other than the ones that inform their original production and reception.

22. I share with Tom Lutz an emphasis on the "cosmopolitan openness" that can, at certain moments, characterize regional literature. While Lutz sees this ethos informing regionalism's mainstream, however, I view it as always struggling to find a foothold against the fantasies of rootedness and cultural difference that often seem to dominate the tradition. My own emphasis, therefore, is on the selective work that needs to be done in order to make regionalism a durable contributor to modern conversations. See Lutz, *Cosmopolitan Vistas*, 14.

23. Walzer, "Idea of Civil Society," 300.

24. Recent critics have at times reinforced this tendency by treating regionalism's emphasis on a community's cultural difference as its most important attribute. David Jordan, for instance, has argued that the promise of regionalist literature lies in its capacity to resist the unities upon which nationhood and Western humanism depend. According to this logic, claims of universal sameness do violence to populations as they impose on them the hegemonic forms, values, and histories of a particular elite group; regionalism, for its part, exposes that violence by insisting on a region's difference. Jordan ignores, however, that regionalist writers could celebrate both "difference" from the dominant society and purity and stasis at the local level. See David Jordan, introduction to *Regionalism Reconsidered: New Approaches to the Field*, ed. Jordan (New York: Garland, 1994), ix–xxi.

25. Roberto M. Dainotto, *Place in Literature: Regions, Cultures, Communities* (Ithaca, NY: Cornell University Press, 2000), 2. Dainotto is responding, in particular, to postmodern Marxist geographers like Edward Soja, who, in recognizing cultural and economic differentiation as part of the process of globalization, have often embraced "the local" as a privileged site of resistance to global capitalism. See Soja, *Postmodern Geographies: The Reassertion of Space in Critical Social Theory* (London: Verso, 1989). For an essay that argues, from a Marxist perspective, for a "critical localism"—attentive to both the "promise and predicament" (22) of the local as a tool of resistance—see Arif Dirlik, "The Global in the Local," in *Global/Local: Cultural Production and the Transnational Imaginary*, ed. Rob Wilson and Bimal Dissanayake (Durham, NC: Duke University Press, 1996), 21–45. From the civil society perspective that I offer in this chapter, "the local" needs to be considered not only as a potential site for political *movements*—that is, not only as a tool to counteract an unjust global order—but as a political end as well (both promising and problematic), part of any new world that is ultimately brought into being.

26. Quotation in Dainotto, *Place in Literature*, 25. Bruce Robbins, *Feeling Global: Internationalism in Distress* (New York: New York University Press, 1999), raises similar concerns in his attempt to treat cosmopolitanism as "an extension of existing interests, affections, and loyalties" (22). For Robbins, just as international commitments can seem familiar, em-

bodied as "feeling," so too affective attachments at the local level can give rise to international commitments. There may be points of tension between the two claims, but no necessary antagonism that demands choosing one over the other.

27. Philip Fisher, *Still the New World: American Literature in a Culture of Creative Destruction* (Cambridge, MA: Harvard University Press, 1999), 171.

28. On the reciprocal relationship between modernization theory (specifically, its narrative of progress according to which community, or gemeinschaft, has been replaced by increasingly modern and abstract forms of association, or gesellschaft) and the resurgence of nostalgic notions of community, see Thomas Bender, "Epilog: History and Community Today," in his *Community and Social Change in America* (New Brunswick, NJ: Rutgers University Press, 1978), 143–50.

29. Barber, *Place for Us*, 22. Fisher may be unsympathetic to Barber's description of solidarity and identity as fundamental needs, but his account of late-nineteenth-century regionalism actually reinforces Barber's point. Fisher depicts regionalism not as antithetical to the processes of innovation and abstraction that he celebrates, but as contingent on these very processes: "Once again it is the trunk-line rail system that made [regionalism] possible, and the automobile that kept it possible. It was the national magazines and the book culture of Boston and New York that promoted the regional." *Still the New World*, 179. In Fisher's account, this relationship points to regionalism's relative weakness in the United States, its subordination to the logic of creative destruction. But it points also to a reciprocal relation between the two at the specific moment that Fisher describes. The attributes of regionalism to which he objects, in other words, appear as the expected offspring, part and parcel, of the unrestrained processes that he treats as normative. What then are we to think of these unrestrained processes? If the closed cultures of regionalism are the pathological by-products of the ongoing revolution within capitalism, it stands to reason that there is something pathological about that very revolution itself when perceived as unmitigated and left to its own devices.

30. Doris Sommer, "The Places of History: Regionalism Revisited in Latin America," in *The Places of History: Regionalism Revisited in Latin America*, ed. Doris Sommer (Durham, NC: Duke University Press, 1999), 3–4; K. D. M. Snell, "The Regional Novel: Themes for Interdisciplinary Research," in *The Regional Novel in Britain and Ireland, 1800–1990*, ed. K. D. M. Snell (Cambridge: Cambridge University Press, 1998), 18.

31. In American literary studies, Tom Lutz places the question of literary value at the center of his analysis in his recent book *Cosmopolitan Vistas*. Lutz argues that regionalism, like American literature more generally, has always aspired to a standard of cosmopolitanism and to the inclusion of multiple perspectives. The normative definition of literary value that I propose further on in this chapter, with its emphasis on open-ended critique, coincides with the standard that Lutz describes. In my account of regionalism, however, the question of literary value always returns to the topic of local solidarity. My focus is on how literature's approach to knowledge prepares it to contribute to the modern conversation on local community.

32. Barbara Herrnstein Smith, *Contingencies of Value: Alternative Perspectives for Critical Theory* (Cambridge, MA: Harvard University Press, 1988), 30, 31.

33. Ibid., 11–12.

34. In the language that Gilles Deleuze and Félix Guattari have made familiar, readers and writers territorialized regionalism, reinforcing official relations between major and minor in the linguistic, literary, and geopolitical spheres. On the process of territorialization in language and literature—and the resistance (deterritorialization) and return (reterritorialization) to it—see Deleuze and Guattari, "What is a Minor Literature?" in *Kafka: Toward a Minor Literature*, trans. Dana Polan (Minneapolis: University of Minnesota Press, 1986), 16–27. For a study that applies Deleuze and Guattari to the American context, attempting to read a text historically designated as minor without "reproduc[ing] it in terms of received or revised criteria of 'major literature,'" see Lewis Renza, "*A White Heron*" and the Question of Minor Literature (Madison: University of Wisconsin Press, 1984), xxviii.

35. Brander Matthews, "The Centenary of Fenimore Cooper," *Century* 38.5 (September 1889): 796–98. For a persuasive account of the way in which the emergence of regionalism as a literary category presumes the economic subordination of local populations, see Raymond Williams, "Region and Class in the Novel," in *The Uses of Fiction: Essays on the Modern Novel in Honor of Arnold Kettle*, ed. Douglas Jefferson and Graham Martin (Milton Keynes, Eng.: Open University Press, 1982), 59–68. Williams foregrounds the historical connection between "the region" as an idea and the class-based asymmetry that characterized nineteenth-century nationalization. I would argue, however, that regionalism represents more than a desire either to maintain or to challenge class hierarchy. Judging from the literature I cover, those who benefited from economic disparity sought not only the subordination of regional populations but an antidote to impersonal, abstract communication. Similarly, the populations who suffered the most from the expanding networks of communication sought not simply their equal inclusion in such networks but an inclusion that would allow for the concrete belonging characteristic of local communities.

36. Carey McWilliams, "Young Man Stay West," *Southwest Review* 15 (Spring 1930): 305; Henry Smith, "Localism in Literature," in *Folk-Say: A Regional Miscellany*, ed. Benjamin A. Botkin (Norman: University of Oklahoma Press, 1930), 301. The phrase "the new regionalism" was used by Botkin in his introduction to the 1929 version of *Folk-Say* (Norman: Oklahoma Folk-Lore Society), entitled "The Folk in Literature: An Introduction to the New Regionalism." It was picked up again by McWilliams in *The New Regionalism in American Literature* (Seattle: University of Washington Book Store, 1930).

37. Moreover, if the new regionalists diminished the ongoing textual tradition *descriptively*, by dismissing the work of their predecessors, they also did their damage *prescriptively*, by tending to make regionalism's value contingent on its indigenousness. More often than not, they promoted a regionalism of organic, tradition-bound communities and, in doing so, severely curtailed regionalism's ongoing meditation on local community. By advocating a discourse that would fix these communities over time and thus place them beyond the

reach of further discussion, the "new regionalists" tended toward impoverishing—rendering superfluous—the entire public conversation in which they took part.

38. For examples of criticism that looks to the literary region as an alternative feminist space, see Josephine Donovan, *New England Local Color Literature: A Woman's Tradition* (New York: Frederick K. Ungar, 1983); Fetterley and Pryse, *Writing Out of Place*, as well as their introduction to *American Women Regionalists, 1850–1910: A Norton Anthology*, ed. Fetterley and Pryse (New York: Norton, 1992), xi–xx; Sherrie A. Inness and Diana Royer, introduction to *Breaking Boundaries: New Perspectives on Women's Regional Writing*, ed. Sherrie A. Inness and Diana Royer (Iowa City: University of Iowa Press, 1997), 1–16; Jacqueline Shea Murphy, "Replacing Regionalism: Abenaki Tales and 'Jewett's' Coastal Maine," *American Literary History* 10.4 (Winter 1998): 664–90; and Sarah Way Sherman, *Sarah Orne Jewett, an American Persephone* (Hanover, NH: University Press of New England, 1989). For a contrasting feminist account, treating regionalism as an "impoverished" form, see Ann Douglas Wood, "The Literature of Impoverishment: The Women Local Colorists in America, 1865–1914," *Women's Studies* 1.1 (1972): 3–45. Whereas sentimentalism retained hope in women's political activism and their influence over the public domain, regionalism, Wood argues, represented a fearful retreat into decaying, anachronistic spaces.

39. See Kaplan, "Nation, Region, and Empire"; Richard Brodhead, "The Reading of Regions," in Brodhead, *Cultures of Letters*; and the essays by June Howard, Sandra Zagarell, and Susan Gillman in Howard, *New Essays on "The Country of the Pointed Firs,"* 1–38, 39–60, and 101–18, respectively.

40. Quotation in Fetterley and Pryse, *Writing Out of Place*, 247; Glazener, "Regional Accents." Glazener links New England women's regionalism to a "reading formation" equipped to read these works as populist social protest; Fetterley and Pryse locate the promise of regionalism in its potential to resist or reject corporate globalization and nation-building. In comparison, my study distinguishes between types of "resistance." It privileges the local community's struggle for some measure of control over public decision making at the national and global levels, as opposed to its struggle for autonomy and self-determination. For other examples of this second wave of nation-based criticism on regionalism, see note 20 in this chapter.

41. Fetterley and Pryse are, as previously stated, a welcome exception to the recent new historicist investment in regionalism's evidentiary status. Unlike Fetterley and Pryse, most of the critics who examine regionalism's relation to nation-building focus on the text's active participation in its *original* historical context. In assuming the text's capacity to shape history at a previous time rather than simply reflect it, the nation-based critics respond to older versions of historicist criticism, according to which good writers grasp the truth about conditions and change from transcendent positions on high. For two accounts of regionalism from this reflectionist perspective, see Jay Martin, *Harvests of Change: American Literature, 1865–1914* (Englewood Cliffs, NJ: Prentice Hall, 1967); and Werner Berthoff, *The Ferment of Realism: American Literature, 1884–1919* (New York: Free Press, 1965), 90–103.

42. Such documents would have an interlocutory effect only to the extent that they

caused trial observers to reconsider their standards, values, and commitments. Helping to generate such a relationship between documents and observers, however, is only incidental to a lawyer's aim, which is to expose how the documents functioned in a narrative that has already unfolded and now awaits the crucial interpretation. A lawyer, as opposed to a critic, avoids discussion of how a text might continue to live over time, affecting a new audience of observers who in turn assign it a new meaning.

43. McCullough, *Regions of Identity*, 3.

44. In the same vein, Geoffrey Hartman, in *The Fateful Question of Culture* (New York: Columbia University Press, 1997), writes that we need to avoid "making the arts disappear by instrumentalizing them: seeing them only as 'cultural work,' for example. For this leaves them open to being administered, as well as to the argument that they are expendable: socially, functionally, are there not things of better value? Even art's counter-cultural resistance could then be likened to that of the clown in a royal court: a vaguely restitutive, irrational entertainment" (9).

45. See note 31 above on how I use the discursive value of "open-ended critique," in relation to how Tom Lutz employs the value of cosmopolitan inclusiveness in *Cosmopolitan Vistas*.

46. Friedrich Schiller, *On the Aesthetic Education of Man: In a Series of Letters*, ed. Elizabeth M. Wilkinson and L. A. Willoughby (New York: Oxford University Press, 1982). See, in particular, letters 19–23, pp. 129–69. In Schiller's text, achieving the educative form of determinability means, more specifically, preserving a balance between the drive toward moral form on the one hand and toward the sense world on the other. In other words, the agents that need balancing are, in dualistic fashion, morality and matter, form and sense. Insofar as neither of these agents is dominant, the subject can be described as having realized this determinability.

47. Terry Eagleton, *The Ideology of the Aesthetic* (Oxford: Blackwell, 1990), 19; Wai Chee Dimock, *Residues of Justice: Literature, Law, Philosophy* (Berkeley: University of California Press, 1996), 8, 10.

48. In Mikhail Bakhtin's account of novelistic discourse, the "detour through sensation, experience," as Eagleton puts it, is a detour, on the part of the writer, through a full historical range of speaking modes and perspectives. For Bakhtin, the "internal stratification present in every language at any given moment of its historical existence is the indispensable prerequisite for the novel as a genre." It is, in other words, the speaking world of "heteroglossia" rather than the object world that engenders the text's dialogism. See "Discourse in the Novel," in *The Dialogic Imagination*, ed. Michael Holquist, trans. Caryl Emerson and Michael Holquist (Austin: University of Texas Press, 1981), 263.

49. Derek Attridge, "Innovation, Literature, Ethics: Relating to the Other," *PMLA* 114.1 (January 1999): 21.

50. Ibid., 22–23.

51. Jane Tompkins, *Sensational Designs: The Cultural Work of American Fiction, 1790–1860* (New York: Oxford University Press, 1985), 200.

52. George Levine, "Reclaiming the Aesthetic," introduction to *Aesthetics and Ideology*, ed. Levine (New Brunswick, NJ: Rutgers University Press, 1994), 14. For a response to many of Levine's criticisms of cultural studies, see Michael Bérubé, "Cultural Studies and Cultural Capital," in *The Employment of English: Theory, Jobs, and the Future of Literary Studies*, by Bérubé (New York: New York University Press, 1998), 3–36.

53. Geoffrey Hartman understands the university as a similar kind of space. As Hartman states, "There is a culture of criticism that should precede, in the university, all affirmation. The arts too play a special role in this, for they are a nursery of forms as well as a powerful and complex means of appealing to memory." *Fateful Question of Culture*, 181.

54. Meaghan Morris, "Banality in Cultural Studies," *Discourse* 10.2 (Spring–Summer 1988): 20. Along these lines, see also Ian Hunter, "Aesthetics and Cultural Studies," in *Cultural Studies*, ed. Lawrence Grossberg, Cary Nelson, and Paula Treichler (New York: Routledge, 1992), 347–67. Hunter describes the improper extension of an aesthetic ethos into the realm of politics as a form of "hyper-problematization," an "ethical hyper-critique that leads to no actionable outcomes" (366).

2. The Artist Meets the Rural Community

1. Tom Lutz includes a list of stories from this period that feature "an interloper from outside the local community." *Cosmopolitan Vistas*, 80–81.

2. Hulme and Youngs, introduction to *Cambridge Companion*, 2; Jewett, *Country of the Pointed Firs*, 81, 82 (hereafter cited in the text as *CPF*).

3. Roy Bridges, "Exploration and Travel outside Europe (1720–1914)," in Hulme and Youngs, *Cambridge Companion*, 56–57.

4. Ibid., 60–61.

5. Stephanie Foote also compares Dunnet Landing to the community in Gaffett's story, noting that the former "functions for the narrator as a friendlier version of this polar spirit world that Littlepage talks to her about." *Regional Fictions*, 25.

6. The point here is that writers who, like Jewett, placed their fictional communities on the fringes of the broad communication networks of the nation, thus inviting the designation of regionalist or local colorist, often expressed differing attitudes on the relation between fringe civic community and metropolitan center. In pointing to these differences, I am joining a number of recent critics who seek to complicate the idea that the late-nineteenth-century literary celebration of local culture was only a means of naturalizing the project of bourgeois nationalization. According to the first wave of critics to place regionalism in the context of nation-building, local communities came to function as communal resources for the incorporating nation. They allayed anxieties over sectional conflict and class status by facilitating the construction of a shared national narrative with "rural 'others' as both a nostalgic point of origin and a measure of cosmopolitan development." Kaplan, "Nation, Region, and Empire," 251. While these arguments may be applicable to the

types of texts and the types of readings encouraged by the major monthly magazines, they do not exhaust the genre as a whole. For criticism that understands regionalism as contributing to the national hegemony of a metropolitan elite, see Brodhead, "The Reading of Regions," in his *Culture of Letters*, 107–41; and Kaplan, "Nation, Region, and Empire." For studies that build on Brodhead and Kaplan but point to the limitations of their approach, see the works by Bramen, Foote, Fetterley and Pryse, Glazener, Howard, McCullough, and Zagarell cited in chap. 1, note 20.

7. Stephanie Foote argues convincingly for multiple definitions of foreignness in *Country*. Foote follows the conflicting meanings that attach to "the stranger" and "the native" in both the novel and Jewett's 1900 sequel story "The Foreigner." While my argument is consistent with hers, I attempt to account for the shifts in meaning by focusing on a specific dilemma concerning normative local belonging: Jewett struggles to make such belonging a function simultaneously of ethnic inheritance and the capacity to supersede it through national sentiment. See Foote, "I Feared to Find Myself a Foreigner," in *Regional Fictions*, 17–37.

8. Along these lines, Foote notes that the narrator "include[s] in her descriptions of the region assorted exiles and foreigners who share similarities with her own fears about whether or not she 'belongs.'" *Regional Fictions*, 36–37. When we recognize visitation as, perhaps, the preferred mode of expressing regional identity in *Country*, the entire region seems peopled by exiles. As I have been arguing, however, the kind of exile that the narrator experiences alongside the visiting residents of the region is different in quality from the kind described by Gaffett. See also my discussion of Mrs. Fosdick's description of "painted savages" near note 12 in the text.

9. See, in particular, the essays by Sandra Zagarell, Elizabeth Ammons, and Susan Gillman in Howard's *New Essays on "The Country of the Pointed Firs,"* ed. June Howard, 39–60, 81–99, and 101–18. These essays, like Richard Brodhead's chapter on Jewett in *Culture of Letters* (142–76), revise the celebration of Jewett's matrifocal communities by feminist scholars such as Josephine Donovan, Sarah Way Sherman, Marjorie Pryse, Judith Fetterley, and Elizabeth Ammons herself. Zagarell continues her work on *Country* in "Crosscurrents." Seeking to bridge "apparently antagonistic readings" (355) of *Country* without collapsing them into each other, she reads the Bowden reunion scene as informed by two overlapping but conflicting registers: a nativist nationalist one and an inclusive, maternal one. While I agree with her identification of a discursive tension in the scene, I treat that tension as always equally informed by an ambivalence over national identity. If the discourse of "communitarian inclusiveness" (367) is maternal, it is also as concerned with nation-building as Jewett's Nordicism is. For important feminist criticism on Jewett that preceded the *New Essays* volume, see Elizabeth Ammons, "Going in Circles: The Female Geography of Jewett's *Country of the Pointed Firs*," *Studies in the Literary Imagination* 16 (Fall 1983): 83–92; Josephine Donovan, *New England Local Color Literature*, 99–118; Sarah Way Sherman, *Sarah Orne Jewett*; and Marjorie Pryse's introduction to *Country of the Pointed Firs*, v–xix. In an im-

portant essay that attempts to redeem Jewett from appraisals that highlight her complicity in racism and imperialism, Pryse argues that Jewett's work resists the very categories that critics have been imposing on her. See "Sex, Class, and 'Category Crisis.'"

10. In a now famous essay published twelve years after Jewett's novel, Josiah Royce speaks about the value of local community in similar terms: "Give [a man] the local community that he loves and cherishes . . . and you have given him a power to counteract the levelling tendencies of modern civilization." The residents of Dunnet Landing seem, in part, to answer Royce's call for counteracting modernity in this way. Royce, "Provincialism," in *Race Questions, Provincialism, and Other American Problems,* by Royce (1908; reprint, Freeport, NY: Books for Libraries Press, 1967), 79.

11. This tension in Jewett's work between a communal model that makes genealogy or language the condition of membership and one that privileges the political participation of its members reflects what Eric Hobsbawm, in *Nations and Nationalism since 1780: Programme, Myth, Reality* (Cambridge: Cambridge University Press, 1990), describes as a worldwide "merger of state patriotism with non-state nationalism" (93) at the end of the nineteenth century. This part of my discussion draws also from Werner Sollors's *Beyond Ethnicity: Consent and Descent in American Literature* (New York: Oxford University Press, 1986), which considers the dialectical relation between two types of group formation, or ethnogenesis—one founded on alliances of consent, the other determined by genealogy, or lines of descent. It should be emphasized, however, that consensus-building in Jewett is best understood as a race project in its own right, insofar as the merging of different Anglo populations leads to a community defined, in part, by its inherited whiteness.

12. Tom Lutz argues, for instance, that "the various stories we hear about Dunnet Landing's past, its harbor teeming with ships arriving from every port in the world, . . . suggest that Mrs. Fosdick is probably right as well, that the town has lost some of its particular character." *Cosmopolitan Vistas,* 85. I would agree that the novel compares the worldly community to the contemporary one, depicting some attributes of the former as desirable. But if, as I continue to argue, the novel is about a new kind of *intra*national travel, one that is in accord with an ethics of visitation, it follows that the balance is tipped against the worldly community and toward the version of Dunnet that the narrator encounters.

13. Judith Fetterley and Marjorie Pryse have argued that "[r]ather than viewing the region as a self-contained unit . . . , Jewett perceives region as exchange." *Writing Out of Place,* 371. I would argue that it is crucial to recognize different kinds of region at play in *Country* and different kinds of exchange as well. The new region, situated in a network of local and national visitation, facilitates a more reliable transmission of knowledge than the older one. This kind of knowledge exchange requires, however, that regional residents give themselves over to the narrator as they would to any other guest.

14. See Zagarell, "Country's Portrayal of Community and the Exclusion of Difference"; and Gillman, "Regionalism and Nationalism in Jewett's *Country of the Pointed Firs,*" both in Howard's *New Essays on "The Country of the Pointed Firs,"* 47 and 111, respectively.

15. For more on the cultural awakening that attached to the populist movement, see

Lawrence Goodwyn's authoritative study, *Democratic Promise: The Populist Moment in America* (New York: Oxford University Press, 1976); and Alan Trachtenberg's account in *Incorporation of America*, 173–81.

16. The most nuanced and exhaustive criticism of Garland's fiction remains Donald Pizer's *Hamlin Garland's Early Work and Career* (Berkeley: University of California Press, 1960), which gives an excellent account of the influence that editors such as Richard Watson Gilder of the *Century* and Benjamin O. Flower of the *Arena* had on Garland's publication history. For an account of the reception and critical appraisal of Garland's work, from the time of its publication to the beginning of the 1980s, see James Nagel, introduction to *Critical Essays on Hamlin Garland*, ed. Nagel (Boston: G. K. Hall, 1982), 1–31. An interesting reevaluation of Garland is offered by Bill Brown in "The Popular, the Populist, and the Populace—Locating Hamlin Garland in the Politics of Culture," *Arizona Quarterly* 50.3 (1994): 89–110. Brown argues that Garland's shift to popular Westerns toward the end of the century was not a "fall" from realism, but a reimagining of the "populist possibility" (106).

17. "Recent Fiction," *Critic* 21 (September 3, 1892): 118. The review is of "A Little Norsk," a novelette that first appeared in the *Century* as "Ol' Pap's Flaxen." According to Donald Pizer, this was the only one of Garland's early books that received consistently favorable reviews. See Pizer, *Garland's Early Work and Career*, 109–10.

18. Garland speaks most clearly about the single tax, and its potential to cure the nation's ills, in "A New Declaration of Rights," *Arena* 3 (January 1891): 157–84. It deserves mention that he located "Bellamyist" nationalists and other socialists on the opposite end of the political spectrum. As Garland saw it, the movement to create a single state apparatus to manage production was an egregious extension of the current monopolistic policy (169–70, 184).

19. Garland, *A Spoil of Office* (1892; reprint, New York: Johnson Reprint, 1969), 221; Royce, "Provincialism," 69; for more on the ethics of rootedness and the corresponding pathology of uprootedness in relation to contemporary displacements and homeland movements, see Liisa Malkki, "National Geographic: The Rooting of Peoples and the Territorialization of National Identity among Scholars and Refugees"; as well as Akhil Gupta and James Ferguson, "Beyond 'Culture': Space, Identity, and the Politics of Difference," both in *Cultural Anthropology* 7.1 (1992): 24–44 and 6–23, respectively.

20. Garland, *A Son of the Middle Border* (New York: Macmillan, 1920), 368.

21. Garland, "Up the Coolly," in *Main-Travelled Roads*, by Garland (1891; reprint, New York: Harper and Row, 1899), 64 (hereafter cited in the text as "UC").

22. For a discussion of the arborescent metaphors in Jewett's *Country*, see Zagarell, "Country's Portrayal of Community," 44. Liisa Malkki speaks of these metaphors as crucial to almost all homeland movements. See Malkki, "National Geographic," 27–28.

23. Garland, "Among the Corn Rows," in *Main Travelled Roads*, by Garland, 106.

24. Garland, "Literary Masters," in *Crumbling Idols: Twelve Essays on Art Dealing Chiefly with Literature, Painting, and the Drama*, by Garland (Cambridge, MA: Harvard University Press, 1960), 134.

25. Garland, *Spoil of Office*, 45. Garland's diary entries reveal a growing disgust with Jews and a wish to limit their immigration. As early as 1917, he complains that on a trip to New York, their "nasal voices silenced all other outcry. The few 'Americans' on the train were lost in this flood of alien faces, forms and voices." *Hamlin Garland's Diaries*, ed. Donald Pizer (San Marino, CA: Huntington Library, 1968), 251–56, quotation on 252. If agrarian dissent has suffered frequently from a nativist orientation, Garland's work is no exception. At times, he directs his message of protest not only against speculative landowners and governmental institutions but also against Jews and other urban immigrants who seem to him equally capable of turning naturalized American citizens into foreigners.

26. See Peter S. Onuf, "Federalism, Republicanism, and the Origins of American Sectionalism," in *All over the Map: Rethinking American Regions*, by Edward L. Ayers, Patricia Nelson Limerick, Stephen Nissenbaum, and Peter S. Onuf (Baltimore: Johns Hopkins University Press, 1996), 27.

27. For more on the ties between Confederate nationalism and Scottish separatism, see Drew Gilpin Faust, *The Creation of Confederate Nationalism: Ideology and Identity in the Civil War South* (Baton Rouge: University of Louisiana Press, 1988). Faust comments that Sir Walter Scott's "immensely popular Waverly novels celebrated Scottish struggles against English domination and oppression in a manner southerners found increasingly resonant with their own situation" (10).

28. Garland's correspondence with Gilder extends from 1889 to 1905. In the years 1889 and 1890, Garland wrote to Gilder at least twelve times concerning stories that he had submitted to the *Century*. The correspondence provides an illuminating record of Gilder's variety of realism and its difficulties for an overtly political writer like Garland. See *Selected Letters of Hamlin Garland*, ed. Keith Newlin and Joseph P. McCullough (Lincoln: University of Nebraska Press, 1998), esp. 52–57, 61–68, and 70–71.

29. See Miles Orvell, *The Real Thing: Imitation and Authenticity in American Culture, 1880–1940* (Chapel Hill: University of North Carolina Press, 1989). Orvell distinguishes between this phase of realism, which he links to a "culture of imitation," and a subsequent phase, which belongs to a "culture of authenticity." According to Orvell, the realists of Garland's era participated in a culture-wide celebration of the machine's capacity to produce imitations. In contrast, modernist realists, who opposed themselves to such a sham civilization, sought to collapse the representation into its referent, to make the artwork indistinguishable from "the real thing." See, in particular, Orvell's comments on the Victorian interior (55–60) and on early photography (73–102).

30. Garland, "Local Color in Art," in *Crumbling Idols*, 50; Garland, "A Prairie Heroine," *Arena* 4 (July 1891): 231, 232.

31. "Up the Coolly" was published in *Main-Travelled Roads* in 1891, and the populists had their first national convention in Omaha in 1892. As Alan Trachtenberg points out, by 1896 populism had lost much of its radical force and had been absorbed by the Democratic Party. See Trachtenberg, *Incorporation of America*, 173–81.

32. Garland to Gilder, undated. "There is this saving clause about dialect. . . ." Century Company Records, Manuscripts and Archives Division, New York Public Library, reprinted

in *Selected Letters of Hamlin Garland*, 64–65. Using the letter from Gilder that elicited this reply as a gauge, Keith Newlin and Joseph P. McCullough date Garland's letter *after* April 5, 1890. For more on Garland's ambivalent relationship to dialect, see Gavin Jones, "The Cult of the Vernacular," in *Strange Talk: The Politics of Dialect Literature in Gilded Age America* (Berkeley: University of California Press, 1999), esp. 45, 55.

33. Amy Kaplan, *The Social Construction of American Realism* (Chicago: University of Chicago Press, 1988), 9.

34. Eric Sundquist suggests interesting connections between slum literature and regionalist fiction, both of which reveal "American psychological space . . . being mapped and marketed." "Realism and Regionalism," in *Columbia Literary History of the United States,* ed. Emory Elliott (New York: Columbia University Press, 1988), 503.

35. Miles Orvell understands this practice of posing in Riis as a comment on the premises of photography in the "culture of imitation." Riis posed his subjects in order to make them conform to "a metonymic typology of the urban slums." Orvell, *Real Thing*, 97. I try to extend Orvell's view by focusing not only on the fact of posing but on the textual emphasis that Riis places on it as well. This emphasis reveals the close connection in Riis between the construction of the artwork as transcendent imitation, on the one hand, and the articulation of the social hierarchy, on the other.

36. Jacob Riis, *How the Other Half Lives: Studies among the Tenements of New York* (New York: Dover, 1971), 78.

37. Garland, *Son of the Middle Border*, 363.

38. Garland, "New Declaration," 181–82.

39. Garland, "The Land Question and Its Relation to Art and Literature," *Arena* 9 (January 1894): 167.

40. Garland, *Crumbling Idols*, 43.

41. Garland, *Spoil of Office*, 345. Lamenting the impoverishment of the art consumer, Garland writes in the "Land Question" essay that "there is much talk just now of over production, but the whole trouble is, rather, *under consumption*" (166). The passage is intriguing in light of debates over falling farm prices. As Lawrence Goodwyn explains, the fall in prices was directly attributable to the tightened money supply of the country. While bankers benefited from the increased value of the dollar, farmers found their goods devalued on the national market. In order to protect against any change in monetary policy, the financial establishment frequently blamed the fall in prices on the farmers' "over production." Garland's comment is not only a veiled reference to the injustice of this accusation, but a further attempt to link the plights of the poor farmer and the struggling artist. See Goodwyn, *Democratic Promise*, 17–18, 115, 193.

42. Garland, "Land Question," 167.

3. New World Relations

1. For an account of the Yiddish press in the 1890s and Cahan's repeated disagreements with Yiddish editors and writers, see Ronald Sanders, *The Downtown Jews: Portraits*

of an Immigrant Generation (New York: Harper and Row, 1969), 119–45, 166–70; and Irving Howe, *World of Our Fathers: The Journey of the East European Jews to America and the Life They Found and Made* (New York: Simon and Schuster, 1976), 518–51.

2. For examples of such criticism, see Aviva Taubenfeld, "'Only an "L"': Linguistic Borders and the Immigrant Author in Abraham Cahan's *Yekl* and *Yankel der Yankee*," in *Multilingual America: Transnationalism, Ethnicity, and the Languages of American Literature*, ed. Werner Sollors (New York: New York University Press, 1998), 144–65, in which *Yankel der Yankee* is described as "a bolder, less constrained Yiddish version" of the English story (149); and Susan K. Harris, "Problems of Representation in Turn-of-the-Century Immigrant Fiction," in *American Realism and the Canon*, ed. Tom Quirk and Gary Scharnhorst (Newark: University of Delaware Press, 1994), 127–42. While Jules Chametzky, in *From the Ghetto: The Fiction of Abraham Cahan* (Amherst: University of Massachusetts Press, 1977), emphasizes that English, for Cahan, was a vehicle for reaching a larger audience and the only route to a literary career, he also pays careful and admirable attention to "the problem of the right balance to be struck with a potential American reading public" (54).

3. Hutchins Hapgood, *The Spirit of the Ghetto: Studies of the Jewish Quarter of New York* (1902; reprint, New York: Funk and Wagnalls, 1965), 184. Cahan met Hapgood while the two were writing for the *Commercial Advertiser* and its city editor Lincoln Steffens. When Hapgood set out to write his book on the spiritual and intellectual side of the Jewish quarter, he relied heavily on Cahan as a guide.

4. Of these European groups, the Jewish Labor Bund was undoubtedly the most significant in Europe and the most closely watched among immigrants to the United States. The Bund arose out of the Vilna labor movement in the mid-1890s and became a formalized political party within the Russian Social Democratic Workers' party in 1897. The party encompassed a variety of positions mixing class and national politics, some of which emphasized allegiance to the Russian revolutionary movement and others the need for Jewish self-emancipation and greater autonomy. All Bundists agreed, however, that the national question had to be resolved in the Diaspora. See Jonathan Frankel, *Prophecy and Politics: Socialism, Nationalism, and the Russian Jews, 1862–1917* (Cambridge: Cambridge University Press, 1981), chap. 4, "The Bund: Between Nation and Class," 171–257.

5. For more on the populist response to Jews, see John Higham, *Send These to Me: Immigrants in Urban America* (Baltimore: Johns Hopkins University Press, 1984), 101–3, 110–11, 159–62. Higham qualifies his account of anti-Semitism within the populist movement, arguing that for many among the "discontented," anti-Semitism remained insignificant. For more on the other two social groups prone to overt anti-Semitism in the 1890s (patricians and the non-Jewish urban lower class), see 109–16.

6. Ibid., chap. 6, "The Rise of Social Discrimination," 117–52.

7. Ibid., 101.

8. According to Howe, this last question was at the heart of the debate for many leftists. Internationalists argued that cultural identity consisted entirely of religious practices

and beliefs, and once those had been lost, identity was sure to follow. See Howe, *World of Our Fathers*, 768.

9. Michael Frye Jacobson looks at Cahan's treatment of the Jewish question in *Yekl* and concludes that Cahan was committed to a nationalist position—the separate organization of Jewish labor. I argue that Cahan was highly ambivalent over the question of Jewish essence and that his short fiction from the 1890s reflects this ambivalence. See Jacobson, "'The Quintessence of the Jew': Polemics of Nationalism and Peoplehood in Turn-of-the-Century Yiddish Fiction," in Sollors, *Multilingual America*, 103–11.

10. Cahan, *The Imported Bridegroom* (1898, reprinted in *Yekl and the Imported Bridegroom and Other Stories of the New York Ghetto* [New York: Dover, 1970]), 93 (hereafter cited in the text as *IB*).

11. Cahan, "The Younger Russian Writers," *Forum* 28 (September 1899): 119.

12. Ibid., 120. For a lengthy discussion of the influence of Russian literary criticism on Cahan and his peers, see Steven Cassedy, *To the Other Shore: The Jewish Intellectuals Who Came to America* (Princeton, NJ: Princeton University Press, 1997), 17–32.

13. Cahan, "Younger Russian Writers," 120.

14. Lincoln Steffens, *The Autobiography of Lincoln Steffens* (New York: Harcourt, Brace, 1931), 318.

15. Moses Rischin also designates Cahan as the speaker of these remarks. See Cahan, *Grandma Never Lived in America: The New Journalism of Abraham Cahan*, ed. Moses Rischin (Bloomington: Indiana University Press, 1985), xxii.

16. Hapgood, *Spirit of the Ghetto*, 271, 273–74.

17. Cahan was certainly not alone in his erroneous belief that the limitations and constraints of American literature could be traced to the influence of female readers. For an account of this perception, and of how it led to the displacement of women's local color by adventure fiction and naturalism, see Donna Campbell, *Resisting Regionalism: Gender and Naturalism in American Fiction, 1885–1915* (Athens: Ohio University Press, 1997), 51–55.

18. Cahan, "Rabbi Eliezer's Christmas," *Scribner's Magazine* 26 (December 1899): 661–62.

19. Ibid., 661, 664. For other examples of Cahan's criticism of reform-minded slummers such as Jacob Riis, see *The Rise of David Levinsky* (1917; reprint, New York: Harper and Row, 1960), 284–85; and "The Russian Jew in America," *Atlantic Monthly* 82 (July 1898): 134.

20. Cahan, "Rabbi Eliezer's Christmas," 664.

21. Throughout the 1890s, *Scribner's Magazine* was focusing attention on the slums and the urban poor. An early version of what became Jacob Riis's book *How the Other Half Lives* appeared in volume 6 of *Scribner's* (December 1889): 643–63. Between April 1892 and July 1893, the magazine ran an illustrated series entitled "The Poor in Great Cities," written by a variety of well-known authors including Riis and Joseph Kirkland. In 1898 Walter A. Wyckoff published his series "The Workers," which included what Frank Luther Mott describes

as "a notable discussion of 'The Army of the Unemployed.'" Mott, *A History of American Magazines*, vol. 4 (Cambridge, MA: Harvard University Press, 1957), 721.

22. Cahan, "Rabbi Eliezer's Christmas," 667.

23. Cahan, "The Late Rabbi Joseph, Hebrew Patriarch of New York," *American Monthly Review of Reviews*, September 26, 1902, 313.

24. Kaplan, "Nation, Region, and Empire," 251.

25. One of the best examples of Cahan's insistence on the contemporaneity of his characters' nostalgia is the story "Tzinchadzi of the Catskills," *Atlantic Monthly* 88 (August 1901): 221–26, in which a Circassian horseman seems to emerge on the scene directly out of a narrator's sense of boredom and repetition in the Catskills. Tzinchadzi responds to the desires of vacationers like the narrator as much as he does to the Caucasus. As the title suggests, he is *of* the Catskills, not the Caucasus.

26. Hapgood, *Spirit of the Ghetto*, 223, 228.

27. *Arbayter Tsaytung*, October 10, 1890, quoted in Nora Levin, *When Messiah Tarried: Jewish Socialist Movements, 1871–1917* (New York: Schocken Books, 1977), 98. Cahan was, in fact, elected as organizer of the Hebrew Federation of Labor and more than likely played a significant part in drafting the statement. The organization survived less than a year.

28. Abraham Cahan, *The Education of Abraham Cahan*, 5 vols. (1926–31); translation from the Yiddish of vols. 1 and 2 by Leon Stein, Abraham P. Conan, and Lynn Davison (Philadelphia: Jewish Publication Society of America, 1969), 204.

29. Howe, *World of Our Fathers*, 291.

30. For an analysis of the influence of Russian populism on the Yiddish press, see Cassedy, *To the Other Shore*, 37–48, 77–104. The first major theorist of the Russian revolutionary movement to mix socialism with the recognition of a specifically Jewish segment of the working class was Aaron Lieberman. See Frankel, *Prophecy and Politics*, 28–47, for an account of Lieberman's career.

31. Cahan, "Di tages frage in di yidishe abtaylung fun der sotsyalistisher bavegung," *Di Tsukunft*, July 1896, 50, 354, quoted in Frankel, *Prophecy and Politics*, 466.

32. Cahan, quoted in Eliahu Tscherikover, "Di Ershte Yidishe Delegaten oif di Kongresen fun Sotsialistishen International," *Historishe Shriften* 3:791–92, quoted in Levin, *When Messiah Tarried*, 99–100.

33. Cahan, quoted ibid., 788; and Edmund Silberner, "Anti-Semitism and Philo-Semitism in the Socialist International," *Judaism* 2.2 (1935): 118; both Tscherikover and Silberner quoted in Levin, *When Messiah Tarried*, 100.

34. On the literacy test bill, See Higham, *Send These To Me*, 41–42; Cahan, "Russian Jew in America," 131.

35. Cahan, "Late Rabbi Joseph," 313.

36. Along similar lines, Stephanie Foote, in "Marvels of Memory: Citizenship and Ethnic Identity in Abraham Cahan's 'The Imported Bridegroom,'" *MELUS* 25.1 (Spring 2000): 46, notes that Shaya is missing "what we might call interiority." For Foote, Shaya's emptiness points to his escape from a reified idea of selfhood; unlike Asriel and Flora, Shaya will

treat his public identity as a negotiation, an open-ended process of cosmopolitan definition, rather than a closed product either American or Jewish, New World or Old. I would add that Shaya's empty interior renders him a test case for Jewish American affiliation more generally. As a kind of a cipher, he is a pure expression of the forces that are shaping Jews in the modern world.

37. See György Lukács, *The Historical Novel* (1962; reprint, Lincoln: University of Nebraska Press, 1983), 35. Measured against Lukács's standard of "a total historical picture," however, Cahan falls short. According to Lukács, "a total historical picture depends upon a rich and graded interaction between different levels of response to any major disturbance of life. It must disclose artistically the *connection* between the spontaneous reaction of the masses and the historical consciousness of the leading personalities" (44). As the description of Shaya suggests, Cahan gives us much spontaneous response to history and almost no historical consciousness in his characters. The consciousness of "world-historical individuals" (39) lies outside the narrative, in the mind of the omniscient narrator.

38. Treife is food (or a source of food) that is considered impure and nonkosher.

39. See, for instance, Howe, *World of Our Fathers*, 204–8, who writes that as late as World War I, Zionism "struck most Jews as an exotic fantasy nurtured by littérateurs" (206).

40. Cahan, as the intellectual descendent of Russian populists like Petr Lavrov and Dmitri Pisarev, frequently used the word *popularization* to articulate the relationship between the intelligentsia and the masses. See, in particular, Cassedy, *To the Other Shore*, 83.

41. Cahan, *Education*, 264–66.

42. Sanders, *Downtown Jews*, 185.

43. Doris Sommer, *Foundational Fictions: The National Romances of Latin America* (Berkeley: University of California Press, 1991), 15, 7.

44. For more on the *landsmanshaftn*—the organizations on the Lower East Side where people from the same hometown congregated with one another—see Howe, *World of Our Fathers*, 183–90. Quotation in Cahan, *Education*, 47.

45. Levinsky's first love is an assimilated Russian Jew named Matilda, who flirts with him by encouraging his transformation from a Talmud student to a secularly minded subject. See Cahan, *Rise of David Levinsky*, 65–81.

46. Cahan, *Education*, 146.

47. Cahan, "The Apostate of Chego-Chegg," *Century Magazine* 59 (November 1899): 94 (hereafter cited in the text as "AC").

48. Levin provides an interesting account not only of the conflict that followed the founding of the Bund but also of the influence of Polish Socialist Party criticism on the Jewish labor movement. See Levin, *When Messiah Tarried*, 255, 261–62. For more on the history of this conflict and on the divisions within the Yiddish American press over it, see Frankel, *Prophecy and Politics*, 198–210, 469.

49. On the close relation between American melting-pot rhetoric and Saint Paul's epistles, see Sollors, *Beyond Ethnicity*, 81–84.

50. Sommer, *Foundational Fictions*, 47–48.

51. William Dean Howells, *Literature* (December 31 1898), quoted in Bernard G. Richards, "Introduction: Abraham Cahan Cast in a New Role," in Cahan, *Yekl and the Imported Bridegroom*, vii.

52. For the *Forward's* and *Dos Abend Blatt's* response to the Dreyfus Affair, see Frankel, *Prophecy and Politics*, 467–69. According to Hannah Arendt's version of events, Jean Jaurès needed to be convinced by Georges Clemenceau before he became a defender of Dreyfus. See Arendt, *The Origins of Totalitarianism* (New York: Harcourt Brace, 1951), 105, 112.

53. Frankel, *Prophecy and Politics*, 472, 468–69.

54. See Levin, *When Messiah Tarried*, 166, for an account of the Bund's establishment in the United States. It is worthwhile to note that 1903 was a significant year in Yiddish socialist journalism not only because of the Kishinev pogrom, but also because the Bund left the Russian Social Democratic Workers' Party (RSDWP) in response to that organization's rigid assimilationism. For many Jewish socialists in the United States, the Bund's departure from the RSDWP pointed to the intractable nationalism of Russian workers and the futility of investing in any putatively internationalist alliance. See Frankel, *Prophecy and Politics*, 227–46, for an account of the conflict between the Bund and Lenin's Iskra party leading up to the climactic events at the Second Congress of the RSDWP.

55. Jacob Milch, "New Movements amongst the Jewish Proletariat," *International Socialist Review* 7.6 (1906): 354.

56. Frankel, in *Prophecy and Politics*, clarifies that while the *Forward* may not have become "less nationally oriented" during this period, relative to the range of socialist movements it became "a standard bearer of 'internationalism'" (484). He provides several telling examples of the internationalist rhetoric that appeared in the *Forward*. See 497.

4. An Interlude

1. An account of the Culture Center controversy can be found in Arrell Morgan Gibson, *The Santa Fe and Taos Colonies: Age of the Muses, 1900–1942* (Norman: University of Oklahoma Press, 1983), 255–58. For coverage of the controversy by the *Santa Fe New Mexican*, see Oliver La Farge, *Santa Fe: The Autobiography of a Southwestern Town* (Norman: University of Oklahoma Press, 1959), 287–94.

2. See Gibson, *Santa Fe and Taos*, 40–49, for more on the museum's centrality to the region.

3. Oliver La Farge recalls that "between the mid-1920's and early 1930's, for a little less than a decade, [the art colony] was the most influential group in the city." *Santa Fe*, 287.

4. As I discuss further on, the Santa Fe group was not alone in rejecting forms of regionalism that seemed touristic, detached from their local referents. Benjamin A. Botkin, and later Carey McWilliams, dubbed the nationwide movement of artists and intellectuals who shared many of the views of the Santa Fe group "the new regionalism." See Botkin, "The Folk in Literature: An Introduction to the New Regionalism," in Botkin, *Folk-Say* (1929); and McWilliams, *New Regionalism*. For a comprehensive account of the new re-

gionalism, see Robert Dorman, *Revolt of the Provinces: The Regionalist Movement in America, 1920–1945* (Chapel Hill: University of North Carolina Press, 1993).

5. Gibson, *Santa Fe and Taos*, 256–58.

6. Leah Dilworth, *Imagining Indians in the Southwest: Persistent Visions of a Primitive Past* (Washington, DC: Smithsonian Institution Press, 1996), 80. In chapter 2, "Discovering Indians in Fred Harvey's Southwest," Dilworth provides a fascinating description of these domesticated Indian displays organized by the Harvey Company.

7. Gibson, *Santa Fe and Taos*, 57.

8. On the Indian Detour, see ibid., 91; and T. C. McLuhan, *Dream Tracks: The Railroad and the American Indian, 1890–1930* (New York: Harry N. Abrams, 1985), 41–45.

9. Mary Austin, "Indian Detour," *Bookman* 68.6 (February 1929): 656.

10. Austin, "The Town That Doesn't Want a Chautauqua," *New Republic*, July 7, 1926, 196; "Assets," *Santa Fe New Mexican*, April 19, 1926, quoted in La Farge, *Santa Fe*, 292.

11. This cross-section included B. A. Botkin, Lewis Mumford, Howard Odum, Henry Smith, and Carey McWilliams, as well as southern agrarians like John Crowe Ransom and Allen Tate. For more on the common assumptions shared by folklorists, artists, literary critics, and historians who identified themselves as regionalists during the 1920s and 1930s, see Robert Dorman's *Revolt of the Provinces*.

12. Lewis Mumford, *The Golden Day: A Study in American Literature and Culture* (1926; reprint, New York: Dover, 1968), 139; Austin, "The American Form of the Novel," *New Republic* 30 (1922), reprinted in Austin, *Beyond Borders: The Selected Essays of Mary Austin*, ed. Reuben J. Ellis (Carbondale: Southern Illinois University Press, 1996), 87; Henry Smith, "The Feel of the Purposeful Earth: Mary Austin's Prophecy," *New Mexico Quarterly* 1.1 (February 1931): 28.

13. Austin's description of the location that concerns her is intentionally ambiguous: "East away from the Sierras, south from Panamint and Amargosa, east and south many an uncounted mile, is the Country of Lost Borders." In this first sentence of the book, she rejects manmade boundary lines as a way of defining the place. The desert has a way of disregarding such borders. As Austin puts it, "Not the law, but the land sets the limit." Austin, *The Land of Little Rain* (New York: Modern Library, 2003), 3.

14. Ibid., 41, 60, 102.

15. Ibid., 107.

16. Smith, "The Feel of the Purposeful Earth," 29.

17. Austin, *Everyman's Genius* (Indianapolis: Bobbs Merrill, 1923), 46.

18. See Leah Dilworth's discussion of "the interplay between racial and environmental sources in the construction of Austin's notion of American and in the figuration of the Indian as pure." *Imagining Indians*, 184.

19. Austin, *Everyman's Genius*, 44. Examples of Austin's anti-Semitism—and more particularly her insistence that Jews were genetically incapable of producing and interpreting American culture—are abundant. See, for instance, her "New York: Dictator of American Criticism," *Nation*, July 31, 1920, 129–30; Ludwig Lewisohn to Mary Austin, March 11, 1921,

in Austin, *Literary America, 1903–1934: The Mary Austin Letters,* ed. T. M. Pearce (Westport, CT: Greenwood Press, 1979), 147–48; and Austin's "Social Survey of Taos County, New Mexico," 10–11, quoted in Henry J. Tobias, *A History of the Jews in New Mexico* (Albuquerque: University of New Mexico Press, 1990), 158.

20. Austin, *The American Rhythm: Studies and Reëxpressions of Amerindian Songs* (Boston: Houghton Mifflin, 1930), 9.

21. Austin, *Everyman's Genius,* 38–39. Austin juxtaposes Indians with Jews, "in whom the blood stream is more mixed" (38).

22. Austin, *Land of Journey's Ending* (New York: Century, 1924), 89. For more on Austin's refiguring of the land as an active feminine agent, see Vera Norwood, "The Photographer and the Naturalist: Laura Gilpin and Mary Austin in the Southwest," *Journal of American Culture* 5.2 (Summer 1982): 1–28; Lois Rudnick, "Re-Naming the Land: Anglo Expatriate Women in the Southwest," in *The Desert Is No Lady: Southwestern Landscapes in Women's Writing and Art,* ed. Vera Norwood and Janice Monk (New Haven, CT: Yale University Press, 1987), 16–19, 21; and, in a book chapter that challenges Rudnick's argument that Austin envisioned the natural world as an enlarged domestic sphere, Stacy Alaimo, "The Undomesticated Nature of Feminism: Mary Austin and the Progressive Women Conservationists," in *Undomesticated Ground: Recasting Nature as Feminist Space,* by Stacy Alaimo (Ithaca, NY: Cornell University Press, 2000), 63–84.

23. Elaine Showalter has written of a "feminist crash of the twenties," a period of backlash during which the New Woman took stock of her relatively paltry gains. Showalter calls 1925 the decisive turning point "when suffragists, activists, and radicals were having to acknowledge the awkward reality of a declining American feminism." Showalter, introduction to *These Modern Women: Autobiographical Essays from the Twenties,* ed. Showalter (Westbury, NY: Feminist Press, 1978), 9.

24. Austin, "Greatness in Women," *North American Review* 217 (1923), reprinted in Austin, *Beyond Borders,* 93, 90.

25. Austin, "Sex Emancipation through War," *Forum* 59 (1918), reprinted in Austin, *Beyond Borders,* 53.

26. Austin, "Greatness in Women," 91.

27. Austin, *Earth Horizon* (Albuquerque: University of New Mexico Press, 1932), 73.

28. Whether or not this portion of the autobiography is a direct reference to Charlotte Perkins Gilman's story "The Yellow Wallpaper," Austin knew Gilman personally and was influenced by the ideas on communal living arrangements in Gilman's widely recognized book *Women and Economics* (1898). See Austin's *Earth Horizon,* 325–26. Clearly, the figure of wallpaper suggested a range of inhibiting conventions to the New Woman.

29. Austin, *Earth Horizon,* 164, 319.

30. Austin, "Women as Audience," *Bookman* 55 (1922), reprinted in *Beyond Borders,* 77.

31. Ibid., 82.

32. Ibid., 79.

33. See John F. Huckel, ed. *American Indians: First Families of the Southwest,* 2nd ed.

(Kansas City, MO: Fred Harvey, 1920). This source and the George Wharton James source in note 34 were suggested to me by Leah Dilworth's *Imagining Indians*.

34. George Wharton James, *Indian Basketry*, 2nd ed. (New York: Frank M. Covert, 1902), 231.

35. Austin, *Land of Little Rain*, 67.

36. Austin, "Town That Doesn't Want a Chautauqua," 195, 197.

5. Art Objects and the Open Community in Willa Cather's Southwest

1. In a letter from this visit, Cather thanked Austin for the use of the house and praised its spaciousness and comfort. See Cather to Austin, June 26, 1926, in the Mary Austin Collection, Huntington Library, San Marino, CA. Because Cather's correspondence may not be reproduced, T. M. Pearce paraphrases this and other somewhat formal letters from Cather to Austin in Austin, *Literary America*, 202–5. According to Elizabeth Sergeant, *Willa Cather: A Memoir* (Lincoln: University of Nebraska Press, 1953), Cather denied writing the novel at Austin's house, insisting that she had left her manuscript in a vault in New York and had used the house only to write letters (225–26). But Austin's copy of *Death Comes for the Archbishop*, now in the Huntington Library's Austin Collection, contains an inscription from Cather indicating that she wrote part of *Archbishop* at Austin's house.

2. Austin, *Earth Horizon*, 359. As Austin knew quite well, Cather's novel was based roughly on the lives of Archbishop Jean Baptiste Lamy and Father Joseph Machebeuf. Lamy's cathedral stands in the middle of Santa Fe in stark contrast to "the Santa-Fe style" of adobe and Spanish missionary architecture. In order to familiarize herself with her models, Cather drew on Rev. W. J. Howlett, *Life of the Right Reverend Joseph P. Machebeuf*, a history that was itself based on Father Machebeuf's letters.

3. Mary Austin, "Regionalism in American Fiction," *English Journal* 21.2 (February 1932): 106. For other examples of Austin's questioning of Cather's status as a regional "insider" and the influence of this critique, see Austin, "Indian Detour," 657; and an article by Austin's niece, Mary Hunter, "Two Southwestern Novels," *Laughing Horse* 14 (Autumn 1927): 25–26. Several critics have pointed to textual correspondences between Cather's work and Austin's and have suggested in turn that Cather was familiar with Austin's writing. See, in particular, Janis P. Stout, "Willa Cather and Mary Austin: Intersections and Influences," *Southwestern American Literature* 21.2 (1996): 39–59; and Mary Chinery, "Willa Cather and the Santos Tradition," in *Willa Cather and the American Southwest*, ed. John N. Swift and Joseph R. Urgo (Lincoln: University of Nebraska Press, 2002), 97–107. For a comparison of *Archbishop* to Austin's *Starry Adventure*, see Mark Schlenz, "Rhetorics of Region in *Starry Adventure* and *Death Comes for the Archbishop*," in Jordan, *Regionalism Reconsidered*, 65–85. I engage with Schlenz more directly in note 24 of this chapter.

4. Cather herself claimed to be "amused that so many of the reviews of this book begin with the statement: 'This book is hard to classify.'" Such comments suggest not only the formal irregularities of *Archbishop* but also its peculiar place as a regional American novel.

See Cather, "On *Death Comes for the Archbishop*," a letter to *Commonweal*, November 23, 1927, reprinted in Cather, *On Writing: Critical Studies on Writing as an Art* (1927; reprint, New York: Alfred A. Knopf, 1949), 12.

5. Mabel Dodge Luhan to Austin, December 1922, in Austin, *Literary America*, 172–73 (emphasis in original).

6. On the subject of this "ordained" agreement, it is interesting to note that Austin used similar terms to describe the protest of southwestern artists against the Culture Center. This protest was not the result of debate, discussion, and contract. Rather it was a "profound inarticulate agreement of the creative group of New Mexico." Austin, "Indian Detour," 654.

7. Austin, *American Rhythm*, 71–72.

8. Cather, "Light on Adobe Walls," in Cather, *On Writing*, 125.

9. Cather, "Escapism: A Letter to *The Commonweal*" (1936), reprinted in Cather, *On Writing*, 18. The letter was a response to Granville Hicks's essay "The Case against Willa Cather," *English Journal*, November 1933, reprinted in *Willa Cather and Her Critics*, ed. James Schroeter (Ithaca, NY: Cornell University Press, 1967), 139–47. Hicks charged Cather with evading the harsh realities of "our industrial civilization" and pursuing instead the "safe and romantic past" (147).

10. Cather, "Escapism," 19. While this passage was written in 1936, Cather expresses the same interpretation of Pueblo women's pottery in *Song of the Lark* (1915; reprint, Boston: Houghton Mifflin, 1988), when she describes Thea Kronborg's interest in "vessels that could not hold food or water any better for the additional labour put upon them." What is most characteristic about Cather's description is that the vessels resist cultural classification and cannot be reduced to a group consciousness. "There were jars done in a delicate overlay, like pine cones; and there were many patterns in a low relief, like basket work. Some of the pottery was decorated in colour" (274).

11. Cather, "Escapism," 26.

12. Ibid., 20, 26–27.

13. Louise Bogan, "Profiles: American Classic," *New Yorker*, August 8, 1931, in *Willa Cather in Person: Interviews, Speeches, and Letters*, ed. L. Brent Bohlke (Lincoln: University of Nebraska Press, 1986), 118.

14. Hochstein was a violinist who became the model for David Gerhardt in *One of Ours*; Menuhin was a child prodigy on the violin, one of the three Menuhin children whom Cather came to adore in the early 1930s. In *Willa Cather: A Literary Life* (Lincoln: University of Nebraska Press, 1987), 283–84, James Woodress attempts to vindicate Cather by attributing her anti-Semitism to her midwestern upbringing and her short-lived resentment of Jan Hambourg, the man who upset Cather's world by marrying her cherished friend Isabelle McLung. The most condemning recent account of Cather's anti-Semitism and its connection in *The Professor's House* to discourses of nativism is Walter Benn Michaels, *Our America: Nativism, Modernism, and Pluralism* (Durham, NC: Duke University Press, 1995), 29–52. For a fascinating reaction to Michaels that foregrounds Cather's relationship with Yehudi

Menuhin, treating it as indicative of her opposition to biological families as the basis of so-cial bonding, see Christopher Nealon, "Affect-Genealogy: Feeling and Affiliation in Willa Cather," *American Literature* 69.1 (March 1997): 5–37. Other accounts that place Cather's treatment of Jews in the context of early-twentieth-century anti-Semitism are Loretta Wasserman, "Cather's Semitism," in *Cather Studies*, ed. Susan J. Rosowski (Lincoln: University of Nebraska Press, 1993), 2:1–22; and Lisa Marcus, "Willa Cather and the Geography of Jewishness," in *The Cambridge Companion to Willa Cather*, ed. Marilee Lindemann (New York: Cambridge University Press, 2005), 66–85. Both Wasserman and Marcus note that Cather sometimes made distinctions between so-called good Jews of high culture and more threatening types.

15. As Susan Hegeman argues, culture was increasingly being used during this period to connote "the 'spirit' of a group of people, or the 'national genius.'" Hegeman, *Patterns for America: Modernism and the Concept of Culture* (Princeton, NJ: Princeton University Press, 1999), 6.

16. Cather, *Death Comes for the Archbishop* (1927; reprint, New York: Alfred A. Knopf, 1988), 38, 42–45, quotations on 38 (hereafter cited in the text as *DCA*).

17. Walter Benn Michaels takes Bishop Latour's observation that the "Mexicans were always Mexicans, the Indians were always Indians" (Cather, *Archbishop*, 286) as a key to the entire novel. I will argue that this reading overlooks Cather's deep ambivalence over the cul-ture concept. See Michaels, *Our America*, 78–82.

18. This treatment of aesthetic experience as nonutilitarian does not imply that Arendt understands it as autotelic (defined wholly by the art object in question). Rather she means, as Barbara Herrnstein Smith glosses the effort to distinguish artistic practice from utility, that the ends of aesthetic experience "a) are not predictable or quantifiable; b) are likely to be heterogeneous and ongoing rather than specific and terminal; and . . . c) are produced more or less uniquely by that object as distinct from any other of its kind." While Herrn-stein Smith rightly points out that such criteria "cannot be confined to 'works of art,'" I would suggest also that art objects have historically been measured according to these cri-teria and that, as a consequence, their makers have often shown a defining aspiration to measure up to them. See Herrnstein Smith, *Contingencies of Value*, 34. The quotations in the text are from Arendt, *Human Condition*, 168, 170.

19. Arendt, *Human Condition*, 157, 156.

20. This subject is the focus of Joseph Urgo's excellent study *Willa Cather and the Myth of American Migration* (Urbana: University of Illinois Press, 1995), which argues that Cather's work, rather than pathologizing migration, makes it a central fact in modern American life. His reading of *Archbishop* centers on the role that Latour plays as an emissary of American empire, bringing a mind accustomed to migration and an ethic of cultural transaction into a region characterized previously by immobility.

21. As Audrey Goodman explains, "the process of comprehending Southwestern spaces as landscape in *Death Comes for the Archbishop* [becomes] increasingly dissociated from its physical sources" and tied instead to "the representation of the usually intangible air." Good-

man, *Translating Southwestern Landscapes: The Making of an Anglo Literary Region* (Tucson: University of Arizona Press, 2002), 160. For a reading of Cather's Southwest novels that draws on Gaston Bachelard's *Poetics of Space* in order to highlight the correspondences between physical spaces and imaginative liberation, see Judith Fryer, "Desert, Rock, Shelter, Legend: Willa Cather's Novels of the Southwest," in Norwood and Monk, *Desert Is No Lady*, 27–46.

22. Marilee Lindemann makes an important connection between Latour's love for Vaillant and the cultural boundary crossing at the heart of the novel. Cather's novel queers America, in Lindemann's view, because it repeatedly challenges distinctions between natural and unnatural forms of love and affiliation. As Lindemann notes, these distinctions do not hold in *Archbishop*, whether they are rooted in heterosexism or in a pluralist vision of America. See Marilee Lindemann, "Comrades and Countrymen: Queer Love and a Dream of 'America,'" in *Willa Cather: Queering America*, by Lindemann (New York: Columbia University Press, 1999), 115–32.

23. As Jean Schwind points out, the time period in which *Death Comes for the Archbishop* takes place encompasses the 1854 papal conference, where Pius IX essentially deified Mary by making the Immaculate Conception—the belief that Mary was conceived free of the taint of original sin—official church doctrine. See Schwind, "Latour's Schismatic Church: The Radical Meaning in the Pictorial Methods of *Death Comes for the Archbishop*," *Studies in American Fiction* 13.1 (1985): 71–88.

24. For a contemporary critique of the colonialist rhetoric that informs *Archbishop*, see Schlenz, "Rhetorics of Region," esp. 69–70 and 75–76. Schlenz's argument that Cather promotes the inscription of a Euro-American destiny onto the southwestern landscape needs some qualification. What she cherishes about the Southwest is its vastness and possibility—attributes, as I argue further on, that Cather feels are implicitly threatened by American control of the region. She mistakenly envisions the French as ideal administrators, self-restrained authorities who maintain an equilibrium between natural forces, human subjects, and the array of objects produced by them.

25. Cather uses the name of the actual historical priest at Taos, Antonio José Martinez. For another account of her colonialist depiction of Martinez and of the controversy it has generated, see Janis Stout, "Whose America Is This?" in *Willa Cather: The Writer and Her World*, by Stout (Charlottesville: University Press of Virginia, 2000), esp. 236–46.

26. Joseph Urgo makes a similar point in comparing Father Latour and Ike McCaslin (Faulkner's *Go Down, Moses*) to Lucas Beauchamp, one of Faulkner's African American characters. Urgo notes that "multiculturalism creates two classes: those who may perform their lineage and their affinity and those who may not." Urgo, "Multiculturalism as Nostalgia," in Swift and Urgo, *Cather and the American Southwest*, 145.

27. The fourth and fifth major characters are Father Vaillant and Eusabio, a Navajo leader. While Eusabio's wife is also Navajo, according to Edith Lewis, in *Willa Cather Living* (Lincoln: University of Nebraska Press, 1953), 142, the character "was essentially drawn from Tony Luhan," a Taos Indian married to the Anglo writer and patroness Mabel Dodge

Luhan. Cather and Lewis stayed with the Luhans twice while Cather was writing *Archbishop*, and the first time Tony provided the two visitors a guided tour of the outlying areas. For an account of Cather's own brief romantic relationship with a young Mexican man in the Southwest, see Sharon O'Brien, *Willa Cather: The Emerging Voice* (1987; reprint, Cambridge, MA: Harvard University Press, 1997), 403–18. For more on cultural crossings in *Archbishop*, see Guy Reynolds, *Willa Cather in Context* (New York: St. Martin's Press, 1996), 155–64.

28. According to Hermione Lee, Father Vaillant's name most probably has its origins in the character of Valiant-for-Truth in *The Pilgrim's Progress*, who "opposes his family in order to set out on his pilgrimage." Lee, *Willa Cather: Double Lives* (New York: Pantheon Books, 1989), 391n. See also Christopher Schedler, "Writing Culture," in Swift and Urgo, *Cather and the American Southwest*. Schedler identifies Vaillant as a "crosser of cultural boundaries" (120), someone who typifies Cather's emphasis in *Archbishop* on dialogic interaction between cultures.

29. See Susan Rosowski, *The Voyage Perilous: Willa Cather's Romanticism* (Lincoln: University of Nebraska Press, 1986), 164.

30. Marina Warner, *Alone of All Her Sex: The Myth and the Cult of the Virgin Mary* (New York: Alfred A. Knopf, 1976), xx.

31. Marina Warner writes that "Mary's colour is blue. Her starry mantle is a figure of the sky. . . . Blue is the colour of space and light and eternity, of the sea and the sky. The reason for the symbolism is also economic, however, for blue was an expensive pigment, . . . and, after gold, it thus became the medieval painter's most fitting and fervent tribute to the Queen of Heaven." Ibid., 266.

32. John Chapin Mosher, "Willa Cather," interview in *Writer*, November 1926, reprinted in Bohlke, *Willa Cather in Person*, 96.

33. Austin, "Regionalism in American Fiction," 106.

34. Geoffrey Hartman notes the danger of "making the arts disappear by instrumentalizing them: seeing them only as 'cultural work,' for example. For this leaves them open to being administered, as well as to the argument that they are expendable: socially, functionally, are there not things of better value?" Hartman, *Fateful Question of Culture*, 9. For an argument that defends the aesthetic category along similar lines, while at the same time recognizing its entanglements with ideology, see Levine, "Reclaiming the Aesthetic," 1–28.

6. Justice and the Global Folk Community in Zora Neale Hurston

1. Zora Neale Hurston, "John Redding Goes to Sea," in Hurston, *The Complete Stories* (New York: HarperCollins, 1995), 1, 7, 10.

2. Hurston, *Dust Tracks on a Road* (1942; reprint, New York: HarperPerennial, 1996), 65.

3. Hurston, "The Gilded Six-Bits," in Hurston, *Complete Stories*, 98.

4. I borrow here from Nancy Fraser, who argues that in a "postsocialist age," with cultural domination perceived to be as unjust as economic exploitation, justice "requires *both*

redistribution *and* recognition." "From Redistribution to Recognition? Dilemmas of Justice in a 'Postsocialist' Age," in *Justice Interruptus: Critical Reflections on the "Postsocialist" Condition*, by Fraser (New York: Routledge, 1997), 12. On the damage to identity caused by misrecognition or outright invisibility, see Charles Taylor, "The Politics of Recognition," in Gutmann, *Multiculturalism*, 25–73. On the limits of distributive justice, see Iris Marion Young, "Displacing the Distributive Paradigm," *Justice and the Politics of Difference* (Princeton, NJ: Princeton University Press, 1990), 15–38. In a previous version of this chapter on Hurston, I focus on Hurston's relevance to the contemporary debate on slave reparations. See Philip Joseph, "The Verdict from the Porch: Zora Neale Hurston and Reparative Justice," *American Literature* 74 (September 2002): 455–83.

5. "Sweat" appeared in the first and only issue of *Fire!!* published in November 1926. It is reprinted in Hurston, *Complete Stories*, 73–85.

6. Hurston, *Their Eyes Were Watching God* (1937; New York: Perennial Library, 1990), 60 (hereafter cited in the text and the notes as *TE*).

7. In *Mules and Men*, Hurston asserts that she needed to have "the spy-glass of Anthropology" in order to gain perspective on her own culture. My claim here is that Hurston was equally capable of turning the spy-glass of Eatonville on the methods of acquiring knowledge that she had learned in the North. Hurston, *Mules and Men* (1935; New York: Perennial Library, 1990), 1.

8. Dimock, *Residues of Justice*, 10, 6.

9. Critiques of the Harlem Renaissance often hover around this emphasis on art as the central vehicle of improved communication between the races and ultimately of social transformation; see, for instance, Wallace Thurman, *Infants of Spring* (1932; Boston: Northeastern Press, 1992); Nathan Irvin Huggins, *Harlem Renaissance* (New York: Oxford University Press, 1971); and David Levering Lewis, *When Harlem Was in Vogue* (New York: Alfred A. Knopf, 1991). For a contrasting point of view, which confirms the Renaissance assumption that art is crucial in the building of a modern national movement, see Houston A. Baker Jr., *Modernism and the Harlem Renaissance* (Chicago: University of Chicago Press, 1987).

10. William Braithwaite, "The Negro in American Literature," in *The New Negro: Voices of the Harlem Renaissance*, ed. Alain Locke (1925; reprint, New York: Simon and Schuster, 1992), 29.

11. For an extensive account of Braithwaite's attitudes toward writing by African Americans and of his career as both critic and publisher, see George Hutchinson, *The Harlem Renaissance in Black and White* (Cambridge, MA: Harvard University Press, 1995), 149–52, 350–60. Quotation in Braithwaite, "Negro in American Literature," 30.

12. Braithwaite, "Negro in American Literature," 37, 44.

13. Alain Locke, "Negro Youth Speaks," in Locke, *New Negro*, 48; Locke, "Sterling Brown: The New Negro Folk-Poet," in *Negro: An Anthology Made by Nancy Cunard, 1931–1933*, ed. Nancy Cunard (London: Wishard, 1934), 114; Braithwaite, "Negro in American Literature," 34.

14. Alain Locke, "The New Negro," in Locke, *New Negro*, 15.

15. Braithwaite, "Negro in American Literature," 38.

16. Robert Hemenway, *Zora Neale Hurston: A Literary Biography* (Urbana: University of Illinois Press, 1977), 63.

17. Franz Boas, "Lo the Poor Nordic," editorial, *New York Times*, April 13, 1924.

18. See Hegeman, *Patterns for America*, 7, 216n13; and Michaels, *Our America*, 173n199.

19. Franz Boas, *Anthropology and Modern Life* (New York: Norton, 1928), 207, 245.

20. For Boas's views on African Americans, see, for example, "The Problem of the American Negro," *Yale Review* 10 (1921): 384–95; and *The Mind of Primitive Man* (New York: Macmillan, 1913). The bizarre justification that Boas offered for this process of biological whitening concerned the sex of the partners engaging in miscegenation. Because historical circumstances permitted only white men to reproduce with black women and not the inverse, and because fewer black mothers would be left to bear "full-blood negroes" as a result, "the number of full-blood negroes must decrease, while there is no decrease in the number of white children born." "Problem of the American Negro," 391. That there was no such thing as a "full-blood negro" according to much of the rest of his theory appears not to have bothered Boas when the question was how to define assimilation as white; diminishing the effect of Negro blood depended on positing and then excluding full-blood Negroes.

21. Melville Herskovits, "The Negro's Americanism," in Locke, *New Negro*, 353.

22. Ibid., 356, 360.

23. Newbell Niles Puckett, *Folk Beliefs of the Southern Negro* (New York: Negro Universities Press, 1926), 1–2.

24. Ibid., 581; Anthony Buttitta, "Negro Folklore in North Carolina," in Cunard, *Negro*, 66.

25. Arthur A. Schomburg, "The Negro Digs Up His Past," in Locke, *New Negro*, 231 (my emphasis).

26. Horace Kallen's seminal essay defining cultural pluralism is "Democracy versus the Melting Pot," in *Culture and Democracy in the United States*, by Kallen (New York: Boni and Liveright, 1924), 67–125. Both Locke and Kallen were strongly influenced by William James and Josiah Royce (among other Harvard philosophers), although they sometimes interpreted James's philosophy in conflicting ways (see note 28 below). For critical accounts that describe the friendship and reciprocal influence between Kallen and Locke, see Hutchinson, *Harlem Renaissance*, 78–93; Sean McCann, "Governable Beasts: Hurston, Roth, and the New Deal," typescript in Philip Joseph's files, 6–10; Louis Menand, *The Metaphysical Club* (New York: Farrar, Strauss and Giroux, 2001), 388–99, 406–7; Ross Posnock, *Color and Culture: Black Writers and the Making of the Modern Intellectual* (Cambridge: Harvard University Press, 1998), 191–200; and Werner Sollors, "A Critique of Pure Pluralism," in *Reconstructing American Literary History*, ed. Sacvan Bercovitch (Cambridge, MA: Harvard University Press, 1986), 250–79. For polemics that lay bare the limitations of pluralism, see especially the Posnock and Sollors works cited above and Michaels, *Our America*.

27. Alain Locke, foreword, xxvii; and Locke, "The New Negro," 10, both in Locke, *New Negro*.

28. What I have sketched here is only one conception of justice at play in the rhetoric of Harlem Renaissance intellectuals such as Hurston. As Ross Posnock has argued in *Color and Culture,* there is also a tradition of Jamesian "pragmatist [as opposed to cultural] pluralism," evident in W. E. B. Du Bois and in Locke (at certain moments), for instance, which concerns itself with "what escapes the grid of identity and difference" (23). This tradition would conflict with a conception of justice that treats racial identity as the means of achieving full psychological repair (see, in particular, Posnock's chapters "After Identity Politics" and "The Unclassified Residuum," 21–86). For more on the pragmatist character of the Renaissance, see Hutchinson, *Harlem Renaissance,* 29–93. David Kadlec traces Hurston's radical antifoundationalism to Du Bois and Locke, both of whom were critical interpreters of James, as well as to Josiah Royce; see Kadlec, "Zora Neale Hurston and 'The Races of Europe,'" in *Mosaic Modernism: Anarchism, Pragmatism, Culture,* by Kadlec (Baltimore: Johns Hopkins University Press, 2000), 184–222. On Locke's "critical pragmatism," see *The Critical Pragmatism of Alain Locke: A Reader on Value Theory, Aesthetics, Community, Culture, Race, and Education,* ed. Leonard Harris (Lanham, MD: Rowman and Littlefield, 1999), in particular the preface by Leonard Harris and the essay by Nancy Fraser, xi–xxv and 3–20, respectively. On Du Bois's appropriation of pragmatism, see Cornel West, *The American Evasion of Philosophy* (Madison: University of Wisconsin Press, 1989), 138–50.

29. Hurston, "Spirituals and Neo-Spirituals," in Cunard, *Negro,* reprinted in *The Sanctified Church* (New York: Marlowe, 1981), 80; for an account of Hurston's extended involvement with *The Great Day,* see Hemenway, *Zora Neale Hurston,* 177–85.

30. In a 1932 letter to Walter White, she justified her own presentation of folklore in *Mules and Men* by distinguishing it from the work of a "ham like Cohen or Roark Bradford." The letter is quoted in Hemenway, *Zora Neale Hurston,* 163. Bradford's *Ol' Man Adam and His Chillun,* a minstrel-like retelling of Bible stories from a black folk perspective, was published in 1928 and, soon after, made into the hugely successful Broadway production, *Green Pastures,* which subsequently became a film.

31. Hurston, *Mules and Men,* 1, 2.

32. Ibid., 218.

33. Ibid., 223.

34. Ibid., 225; for a discussion of justice in *Their Eyes* and *Dust Tracks* from a postcolonial perspective, see Samira Kawash, "Community and Contagion: Zora Neale Hurston's Risky Practice," in *Dislocating the Color Line: Identity, Hybridity, and Singularity in African-American Literature,* by Kawash (Stanford, CA: Stanford University Press, 1997), 167–209. Kawash avoids the theological dimension of justice, focusing instead on the metaphor of contagion as indicative of Hurston's challenge to notions of the bounded subject, the constituted community, and the purely just response to oppression. For a critical account that briefly addresses the "tension" in Hurston's work between "divine or supernatural and legal retribution," see Henry Louis Gates Jr. and Sieglinde Lemke, "Zora Neale Hurston: Establishing the Canon," introduction to *Complete Stories,* by Zora Neale Hurston, xxii.

35. For other accounts of Hurston's work from an explicitly post-identity perspective,

see Michael Elliott, "Beyond Boas: The Realism of Zora Neale Hurston," in *The Culture Concept: Writing and Difference in the Age of Realism*, by Elliott (Minneapolis: University of Minnesota Press, 2002), 161–88; Barbara Johnson, "Thresholds of Difference: Structures of Address in Zora Neale Hurston," *Critical Inquiry* 12 (Autumn 1985): 278–89; Kadlec, "Hurston and 'The Races of Europe'"; Kawash, "Community and Contagion"; McCann, "Governable Beasts"; Deborah McDowell, "Lines of *Descent* / Dissenting Lines," introduction to Zora Neale Hurston, *Moses, Man of the Mountain* (1939; New York: HarperCollins, 1991), vii–xxii; and Posnock, "Motley Mixtures: Locke, Ellison, Hurston," in *Color and Culture*, 184–219.

36. Hurston, *Dust Tracks*, 248.

37. For instance, Posnock provides an account of the intersection between Boasian anthropology and Jamesian pragmatism as it impacts Hurston's writings of the 1940s. See "Motley Mixtures," in *Color and Culture*, 208–19. McCann, "Governable Beasts," links Hurston's skepticism toward ethnic autonomy and paternalistic authority to a widespread cultural shift ushered in by the New Deal. For a discussion of Hurston's response to World War II in *Moses, Man of the Mountain*, see McDowell, "Lines of Descent."

38. Hurston, *Jonah's Gourd Vine* (New York: Perennial Library, 1990), 184 (hereafter cited in the text as *JGV*).

39. I am agreeing with William J. Maxwell's assertion that Hurston's work, rather than depicting the folk as innocent and isolated from the modern metropolis, addresses the ongoing exchange between city and country. Maxwell's argument responds to Hazel Carby's representation of Hurston as the writer of the ahistorical folk, who replaces "intense urban crisis and conflict" with an "assurance that, really, the black folk are healthy and happy." Carby, "The Politics of Fiction, Anthropology, and the Folk: Zora Neale Hurston," in *New Essays on Their Eyes Were Watching God*, ed. Michael Awkward (New York: Cambridge University Press, 1990), 89, 90. Given Maxwell's focus on the Great Migration, it is surprising that he does not mention *Jonah's Gourd Vine*, a novel that deals explicitly with that subject. See Maxwell, "Is It True What They Say about Dixie? Richard Wright, Zora Neale Hurston, and Rural/Urban Exchange in Modern African-American Literature," in *Knowing Your Place: Rural Identity and Cultural Hierarchy*, ed. Barbara Ching and Gerald W. Creed (New York: Routledge, 1997), 71–104. For an analysis of narrative form in *Their Eyes* using Carby's perspective, see Emily Dalgarno, "'Words Walking without Masters': Ethnography and the Creative Process in *Their Eyes Were Watching God*," *American Literature* 64.3 (September 1992): 519–41.

40. Eric Sundquist notes that "John Pearson is the bard of his people, his ability to 'talk' encompassing the biblical history of enslavement and delivery in the voice of the black ancestors." Sundquist's comment suggests that John acts on behalf of his people not simply by succeeding, but by making the voices of his people more valuable through his own verbal expression. Sundquist, "'The Drum with the Man Skin': *Jonah's Gourd Vine*," in *The Hammers of Creation: Folk Culture in Modern African-American Fiction*, by Sundquist (Athens: University of Georgia Press, 1992), 76.

41. Michael Elliott understands this tension as a comment by Hurston on the inade-

quacies of the Boasian culture concept. Elliott writes that John both "masters culture and resists its constricting force" and, in doing so, challenges the "cultural determinism fashioned by [Hurston's] fellow Boasians." I would only add to this that John's resistance to the constraints of culture stems, paradoxically, from a role that he is asked to play by cultural insiders like Sally, i.e., the role of representative. Elliott, "Beyond Boas," 181.

42. John's sermon is based on an actual sermon that Hurston heard in Eau Gallie, Florida, on May 3, 1929, given by C. C. Lovelace. She published a transcription of the sermon in Cunard, *Negro*, 50–54; it has since been reprinted in *Sanctified Church*, 95–102.

43. Hurston, *Dust Tracks*, 225–26.

44. John's refusal to speak at his own trial (and the implicit message, directed at the reader, to read cautiously, without passing hasty judgment) helps to illuminate Janie's refusal to tell her story to the wider community. In both cases, talented speakers stop speaking for want of good listeners. For an excellent account of Hurston's skepticism toward narration in *Their Eyes*—a skepticism that points to the lack of good listeners for women talkers in Hurston's own historical context—see Carla Kaplan, "The Erotics of Talk: 'That Oldest Human Longing' in *Their Eyes Were Watching God*," *American Literature* 67.1 (March 1995): 115–42. On Janie's silences as part of a quest for the potency of shared narration, see Michael Awkward, "'The Inaudible Voice of It All': Silence, Voice, and Action in *Their Eyes Were Watching God*," in *Inspiriting Influences: Tradition, Revision, and Afro-American Women's Novels*, by Awkward (New York: Columbia University Press, 1989), 15–56.

45. For a reading of *Their Eyes* as a "retrial"—a series of inadequate trials of Janie, leading up to the fair hearing she gets with Pheoby—see Rachel Blau DuPlessis, "Power, Judgment, and Narrative in a Work of Zora Neale Hurston: Feminist Cultural Studies," in Awkward, *New Essays on "Their Eyes Were Watching God*," 95–123. Alternatively, Jon Christian Suggs points out that despite its deficiencies, the legal narrative of the court has an undeniable power insofar as it ensures Janie's innocence. See Suggs, *Whispered Consolations: Law and Narrative in African American Life* (Ann Arbor: University of Michigan Press, 2000), 227–34.

46. John Lowe notes that the porch talkers' "discussion . . . frequently takes on the quality of a legal proceeding," but one where proverbs, as opposed to verdicts, "provide a center for the discourse." Lowe, *Jump at the Sun: Zora Neale Hurston's Cosmic Comedy* (Urbana: University of Illinois Press, 1994), 15.

47. In David Kadlec's ingenious reading of this scene, the talkers leave the question unresolved because both nature and nurture—race and culture—are potentially damaging categories from a black folk perspective. What truly matters, in Kadlec's reading, is "de red-hot stove," a figure for the ideological power of white folks. See Kadlec, "Hurston and 'The Races of Europe,'" 184–85.

48. Because *Their Eyes* deals so explicitly with the pursuit of knowledge and the increase of experience, I make room in my reading for such concepts as "good judgment" or privileged knowledge. This approach distinguishes my reading from that of Sharon Davie,

who points to the way in which Hurston's novel unsettles any "complacent belief in the 'mastery' . . . of a rational and hierarchical ordering of the world." While Hurston certainly challenges *fixed* hierarchies and claims of absolute truth, she allows for asymmetrical relations between people like Janie and Pheoby. Such relations, though never permanent, have a legitimate basis in the degree to which a subject applies the process of knowing that I have outlined. Davie, "Free Mules, Talking Buzzards, and Cracked Plates: The Politics of Dislocation in *Their Eyes Were Watching God*," *PMLA* 108.3 (May 1993): 446.

49. On the ethical emphasis on play in *Their Eyes*, see John Lowe's study of humor in Hurston's writing, *Jump at the Sun*, esp. 31 and 180–82.

50. Houston A. Baker Jr. understands the novel as living out Nanny's "sermon about colored women sitting on high" (*TE*, 15). Nanny, according to Baker, correctly sees that "only property enables expression," although it also places ideological limits on that expression. While Hurston acknowledges such limits, I would argue that she also applauds the challenging and questioning of them. Baker, *Blues, Ideology, and Afro-American Literature: A Vernacular Theory* (Chicago: University of Chicago Press, 1984), 56–60, quotation on 57.

51. Hazel Carby, for instance, argues that Hurston sends her character south because she wishes to displace the historical northward migration of African Americans and to recover an image of "a folk who are outside of history" and of "'Negroness' as an unchanging essential entity." Carby, "Politics of Fiction," 77. What I wish to reveal is the incompleteness of Janie's journey in relation to changing, unrecoverable folk characters.

52. In making this statement, I am both agreeing with Henry Louis Gates Jr.'s description of *Their Eyes* as a "speakerly text" and qualifying that description in an important way. For Gates, Hurston's importance lies in her development of a literary language fully informed by African American oral communication. "Hurston, in this innovation, is asserting that an entire narration could be rendered, if not in dialect, then in a dialect informed discourse." Gates, "Zora Neale Hurston and the Speakerly Text," in *The Signifying Monkey: A Theory of African-American Literary Criticism*, by Gates (New York: Oxford University Press, 1988), 214. While Hurston no doubt wishes to give a rich representation to oral forms, she also problematizes this representation, and its cultural location, by calling attention to the nomadic, unpredictable nature of the forms. As one character puts it in *Moses, Man of the Mountain*, some stories were "unexpected visitors" who "departed about their own business once they had been given outside life by his lips." Hurston, *Moses, Man of the Mountain* (1939; reprint, New York: HarperCollins, 1991), 38.

53. Leigh Anne Duck has recently argued that because the Eatonville of *Their Eyes* is saturated by bourgeois values, Janie can have her pure recovery of the folk only in isolation, through private experience on the margins of the community. See "'Go There Tuh *Know* There': Zora Neale Hurston and the Chronotope of the Folk," *American Literary History* 13 (Summer 2001): 265–94. What this reading misses, for me, is the prevailing sense of loss that characterizes Janie's subjective experience as she struggles to know and remember the folkloric elements of her journey.

54. As Rachel Blau DuPlessis notes, Hurston further implicates Mrs. Turner in Tea Cake's infection by having Tea Cake remark that he has been "listenin' to dat heifer run me down tuh de dawgs" (*TE*, 137). See Du Plessis, "Power, Judgment, and Narrative," 94.

55. Deborah Plant writes of Hurston's anger toward politicians and union organizers who acted as if "Blacks were some monolith." For Plant, Hurston's philosophy is rooted in an uncompromising individualism, traceable to such philosophers as Nietzsche and Spinoza. Plant, *Every Tub Must Sit on Its Own Bottom: The Philosophy and Politics of Zora Neale Hurston* (Urbana: University of Illinois Press, 1995), 121–22; also see 33–35, 53–56, and 175–77.

56. Hurston, *Dust Tracks*, 228; for Hurston's views on the Communist Party in the early 1940s, see 262–63; for her later views on the same subject, see "Mourner's Bench, Communist Line: Why the Negro Won't Buy Communism," *American Legion Magazine*, June 1951, 14–15, 55–60. Her conflict with Richard Wright, as a literary representative of the party and of social realist fiction, has been well documented. See Hurston's review of *Uncle Tom's Children*, "Stories of Conflict," *Saturday Review of Literature*, April 2, 1938, 32; and Wright's review of *Their Eyes*, "Between Laughter and Tears," *New Masses*, October 5, 1937, reprinted in *Zora Neale Hurston: Critical Perspectives Past and Present*, ed. Henry Louis Gates Jr. and K. A. Appiah (New York: Amistad Press, 1993), 16–17. For a recent appraisal that lessens the distance between the two writers, see Maxwell, "Is It True What They Say about Dixie?" Maxwell's article appears in slightly different form as "Black Belt / Black Folk: The End(s) of the Richard Wright–Zora Neale Hurston Debate," in *New Negro, Old Left: African-American Writing and Communism between the Wars*, by Maxwell (New York: Columbia University Press, 1999), 153–78.

57. Hurston, *Dust Tracks*, 253.

58. An excellent account of the "internationalist" Hurston, as exemplified by *Moses, Man of the Mountain* and the essays that follow it, is Deborah McDowell's introduction to *Moses*, "Lines of Descent." McDowell cautions that "however important Eatonville is as the site that birthed and nurtured Hurston's creative genius, much is lost in so circumscribing her work and her world" (xxii).

59. Hurston, *Mules and Men*, 1.

60. Hurston, *Moses*, 98, 108.

61. Ibid., 121, 55, 247, 266.

7. Conclusion

1. Eudora Welty, "Place in Fiction," in *The Eye of the Story: Selected Essays and Reviews*, by Welty (New York: Random House, 1978), 129.

2. William Dean Howells, "Criticism and Fiction," in *Criticism and Fiction and Other Essays*, ed. Clara Marburg Kirk and Rudolf Kirk (1912; reprint, New York: New York University Press, 1959), 63.

3. *Cultural Survival: Promoting the Rights, Voices, and Visions of Indigenous Peoples,* http://209.200.101.189/ (accessed November 18, 2005).

4. David Maybury-Lewis, "The Internet and Indigenous Groups," *Cultural Survival Quarterly* 21.4 (Winter 1998): 3.

5. Barry Zellen, "'Surf's Up!': NWT's Indigenous Communities Await a Tidal Wave of Electronic Information," *Cultural Survival Quarterly* 21.4 (Winter 1998): 52.

6. I am using the version of the story that appeared in *The Hamlet* in 1940 rather than the shorter and less fully elaborated version, first published in *Scribner's* 89 (June 1931): 585–97. The "Spotted Horses" episode has been reprinted several times in more or less the same form as in the original 1940 edition of *The Hamlet*. It has appeared in two subsequent editions of *The Hamlet* (1956 and 1964) and in *Three Famous Short Novels by William Faulkner* (New York: Vintage, 1963).

7. William Faulkner, *The Hamlet* (New York: Random House, 1940), 294 (hereafter cited in the text and the notes as *H*).

8. V. K. Suratt, the sewing-machine agent who appears throughout the early Snopes material, is the prototype for V. K. Ratliff in *The Hamlet*. According to James Meriwether, Suratt is the unnamed narrator of the 1931 version of "Spotted Horses." Faulkner changed the name of the original character when he learned that a man with the name Suratt was living in his town. On Faulkner's decision to change the name, see Joseph Blotner, *Faulkner: A Biography*, Vol. 2 (New York: Random House, 1974), 1010. On Suratt as the unnamed narrator of the 1931 "Spotted Horses," see James Meriwether, *The Literary Career of William Faulkner: A Bibliographic Study* (Columbia, SC: University of South Carolina Press, 1971), 40–41.

9. It is noteworthy that in the "Spotted Horses" episode, female characters, excluded from public activities like the horse auction, provide an outsider perspective on the recklessness and innocence of the men. "You men," says Mrs. Littlejohn, whose lot is the site of the auction. "See if you can't find something else to play with that will kill some more of you" (*H*, 310).

10. William Faulkner, "Centaur in Brass," in *The Collected Stories of William Faulkner* (New York: Vintage, 1995), 149. The story first appeared in the *American Mercury* 25 (February 1932): 200–210.

11. Faulkner, "Centaur in Brass," 168.

12. Ibid.

13. Ibid., 165.

14. In the version of the story that appears in *The Town*, the narrative structure is even more complicated, with more narrators involved in the story's transmission. Charles Mallison takes the place of the unnamed narrator from "Centaur in Brass," relaying the story to the public. Mallison's cousin Gowan, who has a night job at the power plant, first hears of Flem's thefts from Harker. But Harker himself does not know the whole story at first. Tom-Tom Bird, the day worker, tells some of it to Uncle Gavin, who in turn discusses the events

with Harker, Ratliff, and presumably Gowan and Charles Mallison as well. Later, we learn that Cousin Gowan hears part of the story directly from Tomey's Turl Beauchamp, the night worker. Thus, Ratliff gets the story from Uncle Gavin; Gavin from Tom-Tom; Harker from Uncle Gavin and Tom-Tom; Cousin Gowan from Harker, Tom-Tom, Turl, and Gavin; and Charles Mallison from all of the various, multigenerational talkers. See Faulkner, *The Town* (New York: Random House, 1957), 3–29.

WORKS CITED

Alaimo, Stacy. "The Undomesticated Nature of Feminism: Mary Austin and the Progressive Women Conservationists." In *Undomesticated Ground: Recasting Nature as Feminist Space,* by Stacy Alaimo, 63–84. Ithaca, NY: Cornell University Press, 2000.

Ammons, Elizabeth. "Going in Circles: The Female Geography of Jewett's *Country of the Pointed Firs.*" *Studies in the Literary Imagination* 16 (Fall 1983): 83–92.

———. "Material Culture, Empire, and Jewett's *Country of the Pointed Firs.*" In Howard, *New Essays on The Country of the Pointed Firs,* 81–99.

Anderson, Benedict. *Imagined Communities: Reflections on the Origin and Spread of Nationalism.* Rev. ed. London: Verso, 1991.

Appiah, Anthony. "Identity, Authenticity, Survival: Multicultural Societies and Social Reproduction." In Gutmann, *Multiculturalism,* 149–63.

Arato, Andrew, and Jean Cohen. *Civil Society and Social Theory.* Cambridge, MA: MIT Press, 1992.

Arendt, Hannah. *The Human Condition.* Chicago: University of Chicago Press, 1958.

———. *The Origins of Totalitarianism.* New York: Harcourt Brace, 1951.

Attridge, Derek. "Innovation, Literature, Ethics: Relating to the Other." *PMLA* 114.1 (January 1999): 20–31.

Austin, Mary. "The American Form of the Novel." *New Republic* 30 (1922). Reprint in Austin, *Beyond Borders,* 84–88.

———. *The American Rhythm: Studies and Reëxpressions of Amerindian Songs.* Boston: Houghton Mifflin, 1930.

———. *Beyond Borders: The Selected Essays of Mary Austin.* Ed. Reuben J. Ellis. Carbondale: Southern Illinois University Press, 1996.

———. *Earth Horizon.* Albuquerque: University of New Mexico Press, 1932.

———. *Everyman's Genius.* Indianapolis: Bobbs Merrill, 1923.

———. "Greatness in Women." *North American Review* 217 (1923). Reprint in Austin, *Beyond Borders,* 90–94.

———. "Indian Detour." *Bookman* 68.6 (February 1929): 653–58.

———. *Land of Journey's Ending.* New York: Century, 1924.

———. *Land of Little Rain.* 1903. Reprint, New York: Modern Library, 2003.

———. *Literary America: The Mary Austin Letters.* Ed. T. M. Pearce. Westport, CT: Greenwood Press, 1979.

———. "New York: Dictator of American Criticism." *Nation,* July 31, 1920, 129–130.

———. "Regionalism in American Fiction." *English Journal* 21.2 (February 1932): 97–107.

———. "Sex Emancipation through War." *Forum* 59 (1918). Reprint in Austin, *Beyond Borders,* 43–54.

———. *Starry Adventure.* Boston: Houghton Mifflin, 1931.

———. "The Town That Doesn't Want a Chautauqua." *New Republic,* July 7, 1926, 195–97.

———. "Women as Audience." *Bookman* 55 (1922). Reprint in Austin, *Beyond Borders,* 77–82.

Awkward, Michael. "'The Inaudible Voice of It All': Silence, Voice, and Action in *Their Eyes Were Watching God.*" In *Inspiriting Influences: Tradition, Revision, and Afro-American Women's Novels,* by Michael Awkward, 15–56. New York: Columbia University Press, 1989.

———, ed. *New Essays on "Their Eyes Were Watching God."* New York: Cambridge University Press, 1990.

Baker, Houston A., Jr. *Blues, Ideology, and Afro-American Literature: A Vernacular Theory.* Chicago: University of Chicago Press, 1984.

———. *Modernism and the Harlem Renaissance.* Chicago: University of Chicago Press, 1987.

Bakhtin, Mikhail. "Discourse in the Novel." In *The Dialogic Imagination,* edited by Michael Holquist, translated by Caryl Emerson and Michael Holquist, 259–422. Austin: University of Texas Press, 1981.

Barber, Benjamin. *A Place for Us: How to Make Society Civil and Democracy Strong.* New York: Farrar, Straus and Giroux, 1998.

Bellah, Robert N., Richard Madsen, William M. Sullivan, Ann Swidler, and Steven M. Tipton. *The Habits of the Heart: Individualism and Commitment in American Life.* 1985. Reprint, Berkeley: University of California Press, 1996.

Bender, Thomas. "Epilog: History and Community Today." In *Community and Social Change in America,* by Thomas Bender, 143–50. New Brunswick, NJ: Rutgers University Press, 1978.

Berger, Peter L., and Richard John Neuhaus. *To Empower People: The Role of Mediating Structures in Public Policy.* Washington, DC: American Enterprise Institute, 1977.

Berthoff, Werner. *The Ferment of Realism: American Literature, 1884–1919.* New York: Free Press, 1965.

Bérubé, Michael. *The Employment of English: Theory, Jobs, and the Future of Literary Studies.* New York: New York University Press, 1998.

Blotner, Joseph. *Faulkner: A Biography.* Vol. 2. New York: Random House, 1974.

Boas, Franz. *Anthropology and Modern Life.* New York: Norton, 1928.

———. "Lo the Poor Nordic." Editorial. *New York Times,* April 13, 1924.

———. *The Mind of Primitive Man*. New York: Macmillan, 1913.

———. "The Problem of the American Negro." *Yale Review* 10 (1921): 384–95.

Bogan, Louise. "Profiles: American Classic." *New Yorker*, August 8, 1931. Reprint in Bohlke, *Willa Cather in Person*, 112–19.

Bohlke, L. Brent, ed. *Willa Cather in Person: Interviews, Speeches, and Letters*. Lincoln: University of Nebraska Press, 1986.

Botkin, Benjamin A. "The Folk in Literature: An Introduction to the New Regionalism." In Botkin, *Folk-Say* (1929), 9–20.

———, ed. *Folk-Say: A Regional Miscellany*. Norman: Oklahoma Folk-Lore Society, 1929.

———, ed. *Folk-Say: A Regional Miscellany*. Norman: University of Oklahoma Press, 1930.

Bradford, Roark. *Ol' Man Adam an' His Chillun, Being the Tales They Tell about the Time When the Lord Walked the Earth Like a Natural Man*. New York: Harper and Brothers, 1928.

Braithwaite, William. "The Negro in American Literature." In Locke, *New Negro*, 29–44.

Bramen, Carrie Tirado. "The Uneven Development of American Regionalism." In *The Uses of Variety: Modern Americanism and the Quest for National Distinctiveness*, by Carrie Tirado Bramen, 115–55. Cambridge, MA: Harvard University Press, 2000.

Bridges, Roy. "Exploration and Travel outside Europe (1720–1914)." In Hulme and Youngs, *Cambridge Companion*, 53–69.

Brodhead, Richard. *Cultures of Letters: Scenes of Reading and Writing in Nineteenth-Century America*. Chicago: University of Chicago Press, 1993.

Brown, Bill. "The Popular, the Populist, and the Populace—Locating Hamlin Garland in the Politics of Culture." *Arizona Quarterly* 50.3 (1994): 89–110.

Buttitta, Anthony. "Negro Folklore in North Carolina." In Cunard, *Negro*, 62–66.

Cahan, Abraham. "The Apostate of Chego-Chegg." *Century Magazine* 59 (November 1899): 94–105.

———. "Di tages frage in di yidishe abtaylung fun der sotsyalistisher bavegung." *Di Tsukunft*, July 1896, 50, 354.

———. *The Education of Abraham Cahan*. 5 vols. 1926–31. Translation from the Yiddish of original vols. 1 and 2 by Abraham P. Conan, Lynn Davison, and Leon Stein. Philadelphia: Jewish Publication Society of America, 1969.

———. *Grandma Never Lived in America: The New Journalism of Abraham Cahan*. Edited by Moses Rischin. Bloomington: Indiana University Press, 1985.

———. *The Imported Bridegroom*. 1898. Reprint in *Yekl and the Imported Bridegroom and Other Stories of the New York Ghetto*, by Abraham Cahan, 93–162. New York: Dover, 1970.

———. "The Late Rabbi Joseph, Hebrew Patriarch of New York." *American Monthly Review of Reviews*, September 26, 1902, 311–14.

———. "Rabbi Eliezer's Christmas." *Scribner's Magazine* 26 (December 1899): 661–68.

———. *The Rise of David Levinsky*. 1917. Reprint, New York: Harper and Row, 1960.

———. "The Russian Jew in America." *Atlantic Monthly* 82 (July 1898): 128–39.

———. "Tzinchadzi of the Catskills." *Atlantic Monthly* 88 (August 1901): 221–26.

———. "The Younger Russian Writers." *Forum* 28 (September 1899): 119–28.

Campbell, Donna. *Resisting Regionalism: Gender and Naturalism in American Fiction, 1885–1915.* Athens: Ohio University Press, 1997.

Carby, Hazel. "The Politics of Fiction, Anthropology, and the Folk: Zora Neale Hurston." In Awkward, *New Essays on "Their Eyes Were Watching God,"* 71–93.

Cassedy, Steven. *To the Other Shore: The Jewish Intellectuals Who Came to America.* Princeton, NJ: Princeton University Press, 1997.

Cather, Willa. *Death Comes for the Archbishop.* 1927. Reprint, New York: Alfred A. Knopf, 1988.

———. "Escapism." Letter to *The Commonweal,* 1936. Reprint in Cather, *On Writing,* 18–29.

———. "Light on Adobe Walls." In Cather, *On Writing,* 123–26.

———. "On *Death Comes for the Archbishop.*" Letter to *The Commonweal,* November 23, 1927. Reprint in Cather, *On Writing,* 3–13.

———. *One of Ours.* 1922. Reprint, New York: Vintage Books, 1971.

———. *On Writing: Critical Studies on Writing as an Art.* 1927. Reprint, New York: Alfred A. Knopf, 1949.

———. *Song of the Lark.* 1915. Reprint, Boston: Houghton Mifflin, 1988.

Chambers, Simone, and Will Kymlicka, eds. *Alternative Conceptions of Civil Society and Social Theory.* Princeton, NJ: Princeton University Press, 2002.

Chametzky, Jules. *From the Ghetto: The Fiction of Abraham Cahan.* Amherst: University of Massachusetts Press, 1977.

Chinery, Mary. "Willa Cather and the Santos Tradition." In Swift and Urgo, *Cather and the American Southwest,* 97–107.

Cultural Survival: Promoting the Rights, Voices, and Visions of Indigenous Peoples. http://209.200.101.189/ (accessed November 18, 2005).

Cunard, Nancy, ed. *Negro: Anthology Made by Nancy Cunard, 1931–1933.* London: Wishart, 1934.

Dainotto, Roberto M. *Place in Literature: Regions, Cultures, Communities.* Ithaca, NY: Cornell University Press, 2000.

Dalgarno, Emily. "'Words Walking without Masters': Ethnography and the Creative Process in *Their Eyes Were Watching God.*" *American Literature* 64.3 (September 1992): 519–41.

Davie, Sharon. "Free Mules, Talking Buzzards, and Cracked Plates: The Politics of Dislocation in *Their Eyes Were Watching God.*" *PMLA* 108.3 (May 1993): 446–59.

Deleuze, Gilles, and Félix Guattari. "What Is a Minor Literature?" In *Kafka: Toward a Minor Literature,* by Gilles Deleuze and Félix Guattari, translated by Dana Polan, 16–27. Minneapolis: University of Minnesota Press, 1986.

Dewey, John. *The Public and Its Problems.* 1927. Reprint, Chicago: Swallow Press, 1954.

Dilworth, Leah. *Imagining Indians in the Southwest: Persistent Visions of a Primitive Past.* Washington, DC: Smithsonian Institution Press, 1996.

Dimock, Wai Chee. *Residues of Justice: Literature, Law, Philosophy.* Berkeley: University of California Press, 1996.

Dionne, E. J., Jr. *Community Works: The Revival of Civil Society in America.* Washington, DC: Brookings Institution Press, 1998.

Dirlik, Arif. "The Global in the Local." In *Global/Local: Cultural Production and the Transnational Imaginary,* edited by Rob Wilson and Bimal Dissanayake, 21–45. Durham, NC: Duke University Press, 1996.

Donovan, Josephine. *New England Local Color Literature: A Woman's Tradition.* New York: Frederick K. Ungar, 1983.

Dorman, Robert. *Revolt of the Provinces: The Regionalist Movement in America, 1920–1945.* Chapel Hill: University of North Carolina Press, 1993.

Duck, Leigh Anne. "'Go There Tuh *Know* There': Zora Neale Hurston and the Chronotope of the Folk." *American Literary History* 13 (Summer 2001): 265–94.

DuPlessis, Rachel Blau. "Power, Judgment, and Narrative in a Work of Zora Neale Hurston: Feminist Cultural Studies." In Awkward, *New Essays on "Their Eyes Were Watching God,"* 95–123.

Eagleton, Terry. *The Ideology of the Aesthetic.* Oxford: Blackwell, 1990.

Elliott, Michael. "Beyond Boas: The Realism of Zora Neale Hurston." In *The Culture Concept: Writing and Difference in the Age of Realism,* by Michael Elliott, 161–88. Minneapolis: University of Minnesota Press, 2002.

Faulkner, William. "Centaur in Brass." 1932. Reprint in *The Collected Stories of William Faulkner,* 149–68 (New York: Vintage, 1995).

———. *The Hamlet.* New York: Random House, 1940.

———. *The Town.* New York: Random House, 1957.

Faust, Drew Gilpin. *The Creation of Confederate Nationalism: Ideology and Identity in the Civil War South.* Baton Rouge: Louisiana State University Press, 1988.

Fetterley, Judith, and Marjorie Pryse. Introduction to *American Women Regionalists, 1850–1910: A Norton Anthology,* edited by Fetterley and Pryse, xi–xx. New York: Norton, 1992.

———. *Writing Out of Place: Regionalism, Women, and American Literary Culture.* Urbana: University of Illinois Press, 2003.

Fisher, Philip. *Still the New World: American Literature in a Culture of Creative Destruction.* Cambridge, MA: Harvard University Press, 1999.

Foote, Stephanie. "Marvels of Memory: Citizenship and Ethnic Identity in Abraham Cahan's 'The Imported Bridegroom.'" *MELUS* 25.1 (Spring 2000): 33–53.

———. *Regional Fictions: Culture and Identity in Nineteenth-Century American Literature.* Madison: University of Wisconsin Press, 2001.

Frankel, Jonathan. *Prophecy and Politics: Socialism, Nationalism, and the Russian Jews, 1862–1917.* Cambridge: Cambridge University Press, 1981.

Fraser, Nancy. "From Redistribution to Recognition? Dilemmas of Justice in a 'Postsocialist' Age." In *Justice Interruptus: Critical Reflections on the 'Postsocialist' Condition,* by Nancy Fraser, 11–39. New York: Routledge, 1997.

Fryer, Judith. "Desert, Rock, Shelter, Legend: Willa Cather's Novels of the Southwest." In Norwood and Monk, *Desert Is No Lady,* 27–46.

Garland, Hamlin. *Crumbling Idols: Twelve Essays on Art Dealing Chiefly with Literature, Painting, and the Drama.* Cambridge, MA: Harvard University Press, 1960.

———. *Hamlin Garland's Diaries.* Edited by Donald Pizer. San Marino, CA: Huntington Library, 1968.

———. "The Land Question, and Its Relation to Art and Literature." *Arena* 9 (January 1894): 165–75.

———. *Main-Travelled Roads.* 1891. Reprint, New York: Harper and Row, 1899.

———. "A New Declaration of Rights." *Arena* 3 (January 1891): 157–84.

———. "A Prairie Heroine." *Arena* 4 (July 1891): 223–46.

———. *Selected Letters of Hamlin Garland.* Edited by Keith Newlin and Joseph P. McCullough. Lincoln: University of Nebraska Press, 1998.

———. *A Son of the Middle Border.* New York: Macmillan, 1920.

———. *A Spoil of Office.* 1892. Reprint, New York: Johnson Reprint, 1969.

———. "Up the Coolly." 1891. Reprint in Garland, *Main-Travelled Roads,* 45–87.

Gates, Henry Louis, Jr. "Zora Neale Hurston and the Speakerly Text." In *The Signifying Monkey: A Theory of African-American Literary Criticism,* by Henry Louis Gates Jr., 170–216. New York: Oxford University Press, 1988.

Gates, Henry Louis, Jr., and K. A. Appiah, eds. *Zora Neale Hurston: Critical Perspectives Past and Present.* New York: Amistad Press, 1993.

Gates, Henry Louis, Jr., and Sieglinde Lemke. "Zora Neale Hurston: Establishing the Canon." Introduction to *The Complete Stories,* by Zora Neale Hurston, ix–xxiii. New York: HarperCollins, 1995.

Gibson, Arrell Morgan. *The Santa Fe and Taos Colonies: Age of the Muses, 1900–1942.* Norman: University of Oklahoma Press, 1983.

Gillman, Susan. "Regionalism and Nationalism in Jewett's *Country of the Pointed Firs.*" In Howard, *New Essays on "The Country of the Pointed Firs,"* 101–18.

Glazener, Nancy. "Regional Accents: The *Atlantic* Group, the *Arena,* and New England Women's Regionalism." In *Reading for Realism: The History of a U.S. Literary Institution, 1850–1910,* by Nancy Glazener, 189–228. Durham, NC: Duke University Press, 1997.

Goffman, Erving. "Alienation from Interaction." In *Interaction Ritual: Essays on Face-to-Face Behavior,* by Erving Goffman, 113–36. Garden City, NY: Doubleday, 1967.

Goodman, Audrey. *Translating Southwestern Landscapes: The Making of an Anglo Literary Region.* Tucson: University of Arizona Press, 2002.

Goodwyn, Lawrence. *Democratic Promise: The Populist Moment in America.* New York: Oxford University Press, 1976.

Gupta, Akhil, and James Ferguson. "Beyond 'Culture': Space, Identity, and the Politics of Difference." *Cultural Anthropology* 7.1 (1992): 6–23.

Gutmann, Amy. *Multiculturalism: Examining the Politics of Recognition.* Princeton, NJ: Princeton University Press, 1994.

Hapgood, Hutchins. *The Spirit of the Ghetto: Studies of the Jewish Quarter of New York.* 1902. Reprint, New York: Funk and Wagnalls, 1965.

Harris, Leonard, ed. *The Critical Pragmatism of Alain Locke: A Reader on Value Theory, Aesthetics, Community, Culture, Race, and Education.* Lanham, MD: Rowman and Littlefield, 1999.

Harris, Susan K. "Problems of Representation in Turn-of-the-Century Immigrant Fiction." In *American Realism and the Canon,* edited by Tom Quirk and Gary Scharnhorst, 127–42. Newark: University of Delaware Press, 1994.

Hartman, Geoffrey H. *The Fateful Question of Culture.* New York: Columbia University Press, 1997.

"Hebrew Federation of Labor Statement of Aims and Purposes." *Arbayter Tsaytung,* October 10, 1890. Reprint in Levin, *When Messiah Tarried,* 98.

Hegeman, Susan. *Patterns for America: Modernism and the Concept of Culture.* Princeton, NJ: Princeton University Press, 1999.

Hemenway, Robert. *Zora Neale Hurston: A Literary Biography.* Urbana: University of Illinois Press, 1977.

Herrnstein Smith, Barbara. *Contingencies of Value: Alternative Perspectives for Critical Theory.* Cambridge, MA: Harvard University Press, 1988.

Herskovits, Melville. "The Negro's Americanism." In Locke, *New Negro,* 353–60.

Hicks, Granville. "The Case against Willa Cather." *English Journal* (1933). Reprint in *Willa Cather and Her Critics,* edited by James Schroeter, 139–47 (Ithaca, NY: Cornell University Press, 1967).

Higham, John. *Send These to Me: Immigrants in Urban America.* Baltimore: Johns Hopkins University Press, 1984.

Hobsbawm, Eric J. *Nations and Nationalism since 1780: Programme, Myth, Reality.* Cambridge: Cambridge University Press, 1990.

Howard, June. "Introduction: Sarah Orne Jewett and the Traffic in Words." In Howard, *New Essays on "The Country of the Pointed Firs,"* 1–38.

———, ed. *New Essays on "The Country of the Pointed Firs."* Cambridge: Cambridge University Press, 1994.

———. "Unraveling Regions, Unsettling Periods: Sarah Orne Jewett and American Literary History." *American Literature* 68 (1996): 365–84.

Howe, Irving. *World of Our Fathers: The Journey of the East European Jews to America and the Life They Found and Made.* New York: Simon and Schuster, 1976.

Howells, William Dean. "Criticism and Fiction." In *Criticism and Fiction and Other Essays,* edited by Clara Marburg Kirk and Rudolf Kirk, 9–87. 1912. Reprint, New York: New York University Press, 1959.

Huckel, John F., ed. *American Indians: First Families of the Southwest.* 2nd ed. Kansas City, MO: Fred Harvey, 1920.

Huggins, Nathan Irvin. *Harlem Renaissance.* New York: Oxford University Press, 1971.

Hulme, Peter, and Tim Youngs, eds. *The Cambridge Companion to Travel Writing.* Cambridge: Cambridge University Press, 2002.

Hunter, Ian. "Aesthetics and Cultural Studies." In *Cultural Studies,* edited by Lawrence Grossberg, Cary Nelson, and Paula Treichler, 347–67. New York: Routledge, 1992.

Hunter, Mary. "Two Southwestern Novels." *Laughing Horse* 14 (Autumn 1927): 25–26.

Hurston, Zora Neale. *The Complete Stories.* New York: HarperPerennial, 1996.

———. *Dust Tracks on a Road.* 1942. Reprint, New York: HarperPerennial, 1996.

———. "The Gilded Six-Bits." 1933. Reprint in Hurston, *Complete Stories,* 86–98.

———. "John Redding Goes to Sea." 1921. Reprint in Hurston, *Complete Stories,* 1–16.

———. *Jonah's Gourd Vine.* 1934. Reprint, New York: HarperPerennial, 1990.

———. *Moses, Man of the Mountain.* 1939. Reprint, New York: HarperPerennial, 1991.

———. "Mourner's Bench, Communist Line: Why the Negro Won't Buy Communism." *American Legion Magazine,* June 1951, 14–15, 55–60.

———. *Mules and Men.* 1935. Reprint, New York: HarperPerennial, 1990.

———. *The Sanctified Church.* New York: Marlowe, 1981.

———. "A Sermon." In Cunard, *Negro.* Reprinted in Hurston, *Sanctified Church,* 95–102.

———. "Spirituals and Neo-Spirituals." In Cunard, *Negro.* Reprinted in Hurston, *Sanctified Church,* 79–84.

———. "Stories of Conflict." Review of *Uncle Tom's Children,* by Richard Wright. *Saturday Review of Literature,* April 2, 1938, 32.

———. "Sweat." 1926. Reprint in Hurston, *Complete Stories,* 73–85.

———. *Their Eyes Were Watching God.* 1937. Reprint, New York: HarperPerennial, 1990.

Hutchinson, George. *The Harlem Renaissance in Black and White.* Cambridge, MA: Harvard University Press, 1995.

Inness, Sherry A., and Diana Royer. Introduction to *Breaking Boundaries: New Perspectives on Women's Regional Writing,* edited by Sherrie A. Inness and Diana Royer, 1–16. Iowa City: University of Iowa Press, 1997.

Jacobson, Michael Frye. "'The Quintessence of the Jew': Polemics of Nationalism and Peoplehood in Turn-of-the-Century Yiddish Fiction." In Sollors, *Multilingual America,* 103–11.

James, George Wharton. *Indian Basketry.* 2nd ed. New York: Frank M. Covert, 1902.

Jewett, Sarah Orne. *The Country of the Pointed Firs and Other Stories.* Selected by Mary Ellen Chase. 1896. Reprint, New York: Norton, 1982.

Johnson, Barbara. "Thresholds of Difference: Structures of Address in Zora Neale Hurston." *Critical Inquiry* 12 (Autumn 1985). Reprint in Gates and Appiah, *Zora Neale Hurston,* 130–40.

Jones, Gavin. *Strange Talk: The Politics of Dialect Literature in Gilded Age America.* Berkeley: University of California Press, 1999.

Jordan, David, ed. *Regionalism Reconsidered: New Approaches to the Field.* New York: Garland, 1994.

Joseph, Philip. "The Verdict from the Porch: Zora Neale Hurston and Reparative Justice." *American Literature* 74 (September 2002): 455–83.

Kadlec, David. "Zora Neale Hurston and 'The Races of Europe.'" In *Mosaic Modernism: Anarchism, Pragmatism, Culture,* by David Kadlec, 184–222. Baltimore: Johns Hopkins University Press, 2000.

Kallen, Horace. "Democracy versus the Melting Pot." In *Culture and Democracy in the United States,* by Horace Kallen, 67–125. New York: Boni and Liveright, 1924.

Kaplan, Amy. "Nation, Region, and Empire." In *The Columbia History of the American Novel,* edited by Emory Elliott, 240–66. New York: Columbia University Press, 1991.

———. *The Social Construction of American Realism.* Chicago: University of Chicago Press, 1988.

Kaplan, Carla. "The Erotics of Talk: 'That Oldest Human Longing' in *Their Eyes Were Watching God.*" *American Literature* 67.1 (March 1995): 115–42.

Kawash, Samira. "Community and Contagion: Zora Neale Hurston's Risky Practice." In *Dislocating the Color Line: Identity, Hybridity, and Singularity in African-American Literature,* by Samira Kawash, 167–209. Stanford, CA: Stanford University Press, 1997.

La Farge, Oliver. *Santa Fe: The Autobiography of a Southwestern Town.* Norman: University of Oklahoma Press, 1959.

Lee, Hermione. *Willa Cather: Double Lives.* New York: Pantheon Books, 1989.

Levin, Nora. *When Messiah Tarried: Jewish Socialist Movements, 1871–1917.* New York: Schocken Books, 1977.

Levine, George, "Reclaiming the Aesthetic." Introduction to *Aesthetics and Ideology,* edited by George Levine, 1–28. New Brunswick, NJ: Rutgers University Press, 1994.

Lewis, David Levering. *When Harlem Was in Vogue.* New York: Alfred A. Knopf, 1991.

Lewis, Edith. *Willa Cather Living.* Lincoln: University of Nebraska Press, 1953.

Lindemann, Marilee. "Comrades and Countrymen: Queer Love and a Dream of 'America.'" In *Willa Cather: Queering America,* by Marilee Lindemann, 115–32. New York: Columbia University Press, 1999.

Lippard, Lucy. *The Lure of the Local: Senses of Place in a Multi-Centered Society.* New York: New Press, 1997.

Locke, Alain, ed. *The New Negro: Voices of the Harlem Renaissance.* 1925. Reprint, New York: Simon and Schuster, 1992.

———. "Sterling Brown: The New Negro Folk-Poet." In Cunard, *Negro,* 111–15.

Lowe, John. *Jump at the Sun: Zora Neale Hurston's Cosmic Comedy.* Urbana: University of Illinois Press, 1994.

Lukács, György. *The Historical Novel.* 1962. Reprint, Lincoln: University of Nebraska Press, 1983.

Lutz, Tom. *Cosmopolitan Vistas: American Regionalism and Literary Value.* Ithaca, NY: Cornell University Press, 2004.

Malkki, Liisa. "National Geographic: The Rooting of Peoples and the Territorialization of National Identity among Scholars and Refugees." *Cultural Anthropology* 7.1 (1992): 24–44.

Marcus, Lisa. "Willa Cather and the Geography of Jewishness." In *The Cambridge Companion to Willa Cather,* edited by Marilee Lindemann, 66–85. New York: Cambridge University Press, 2005.

Martin, Jay. *Harvests of Change: American Literature, 1865–1914.* Englewood Cliffs, NJ: Prentice Hall, 1967.

Matthews, Brander. "The Centenary of Fenimore Cooper." *Century* 38.5 (September 1889): 796–98.

Maxwell, William J. "Black Belt / Black Folk: The End(s) of the Richard Wright–Zora Neale Hurston Debate." In *New Negro, Old Left: African-American Writing and Communism between the Wars,* by William J. Maxwell, 153–78. New York: Columbia University Press, 1999.

———. "Is It True What They Say about Dixie? Richard Wright, Zora Neale Hurston, and Rural/Urban Exchange in Modern African-American Literature." In *Knowing Your Place: Rural Identity and Cultural Hierarchy,* edited by Barbara Ching and Gerald W. Creed, 71–104. New York: Routledge, 1997.

Maybury-Lewis, David. "The Internet and Indigenous Groups." *Cultural Survival Quarterly* 21.4 (Winter 1998): 3.

McCann, Sean. "Governable Beasts: Hurston, Roth, and the New Deal." 2001. Typescript. In Philip Joseph's files.

McCullough, Kate. *Regions of Identity: The Construction of America in Women's Fiction, 1885–1914.* Stanford, CA: Stanford University Press, 1999.

McDowell, Deborah. "Lines of Descent / Dissenting Lines." Introduction to *Moses, Man of the Mountain,* by Zora Neale Hurston, vii–xxii. New York: HarperCollins, 1990.

McLuhan, T. C. *Dream Tracks: The Railroad and the American Indian, 1890–1930.* New York: Harry N. Abrams, 1985.

McWilliams, Carey. *The New Regionalism in American Literature.* Seattle: University of Washington Book Store, 1930.

———. "Young Man Stay West." *Southwest Review* 15 (Spring 1930): 301–9.

Menand, Louis. *The Metaphysical Club.* New York: Farrar, Strauss and Giroux, 2001.

Meriwether, James. *The Literary Career of William Faulkner: A Bibliographic Study.* Columbia: University of South Carolina Press, 1971.

Michaels, Walter Benn. *Our America: Nativism, Modernism, and Pluralism.* Durham, NC: Duke University Press, 1995.

Milch, Jacob. "New Movements amongst the Jewish Proletariat." Parts 1–4. *International Socialist Review* 7.6 (1906): 354–63; 7.7 (1907): 398–407; 7.8 (1907): 480–88; 7.10 (1907): 599–607.

Morris, Meaghan. "Banality in Cultural Studies." *Discourse* 10.2 (Spring–Summer 1988): 3–29.

Mosher, John Chapin. "Willa Cather." Interview in *Writer*, November 1926. Reprint in Bohlke, *Willa Cather in Person*, 91–95.

Mott, Frank Luther. *A History of American Magazines*. Vol. 4. Cambridge, MA: Harvard University Press, 1957.

Mumford, Lewis. *The Golden Day: A Study in American Literature and Culture*. 1926. Reprint, New York: Dover, 1968.

Murphy, Jacqueline Shea. "Replacing Regionalism: Abenaki Tales and 'Jewett's' Coastal Maine." *American Literary History* 10.4 (Winter 1998): 664–90.

Nagel, James. Introduction to *Critical Essays on Hamlin Garland*, edited by James Nagel, 1–31. Boston: G. K. Hall, 1982.

Nealon, Christopher. "Affect-Genealogy: Feeling and Affiliation in Willa Cather." *American Literature* 69.1 (March 1997): 5–37.

Noble, David. *Digital Diploma Mills: The Automation of Higher Education*. New York: Monthly Review Press, 2001.

Norwood, Vera. "The Photographer and the Naturalist: Laura Gilpin and Mary Austin in the Southwest." *Journal of American Culture* 5.2 (Summer 1982): 1–28.

Norwood, Vera, and Janice Monk, eds. *The Desert Is No Lady: Southwestern Landscapes in Women's Writing and Art*. New Haven, CT: Yale University Press, 1987.

O'Brien, Sharon. *Willa Cather: The Emerging Voice*. 1987. Reprint, Cambridge, MA: Harvard University Press, 1997.

Onuf, Peter S. "Federalism, Republicanism, and the Origins of American Sectionalism." In *All Over the Map: Rethinking American Regions*, by Edward L. Ayers, Patricia Nelson Limerick, Stephen Nissenbaum, and Peter S. Onuf, 11–37. Baltimore: Johns Hopkins University Press, 1996.

Orvell, Miles. *The Real Thing: Imitation and Authenticity in American Culture, 1880–1940*. Chapel Hill: University of North Carolina Press, 1989.

Pizer, Donald. *Hamlin Garland's Early Work and Career*. Berkeley: University of California Press, 1960.

Plant, Deborah. *Every Tub Must Sit on Its Own Bottom: The Philosophy and Politics of Zora Neale Hurston*. Urbana: University of Illinois Press, 1995.

Posnock, Ross. *Color and Culture: Black Writers and the Making of the Modern Intellectual*. Cambridge, MA: Harvard University Press, 1998.

Pryse, Marjorie. Introduction to Jewett, *Country of the Pointed Firs*, v–xxix.

———. "Sex, Class, and 'Category Crisis': Reading Jewett's Transitivity." *American Literature* 70 (September 1998): 517–49.

Puckett, Newbell Niles. *Folk Beliefs of the Southern Negro*. New York: Negro Universities Press, 1926.

Putnam, Robert D. *Bowling Alone: The Collapse and Revival of American Community*. New York: Simon and Schuster, 2000.

"Recent Fiction." *Critic* 21 (September 3, 1892): 118. Review of "A Little Norsk," by Hamlin Garland.

Renza, Louis A. *"A White Heron" and the Question of Minor Literature*. Madison: University of Wisconsin Press, 1984.

Reynolds, Guy. *Willa Cather in Context.* New York: St. Martin's Press, 1996.

Richards, Bernard G. "Introduction: Abraham Cahan Cast in a New Role." In *Yekl and the Imported Bridegroom, and Other Stories of the New York Ghetto,* by Abraham Cahan, with an introduction by Richards, iii–viii. New York: Dover, 1970.

Riis, Jacob. *How the Other Half Lives: Studies among the Tenements of New York.* New York: Dover, 1971.

Robbins, Bruce. *Feeling Global: Internationalism in Distress.* New York: New York University Press, 1999.

Rosenblum, Nancy L. *Membership and Morals: The Personal Uses of Pluralism in America.* Princeton, NJ: Princeton University Press, 1998.

Rosowski, Susan. *The Voyage Perilous: Willa Cather's Romanticism.* Lincoln: University of Nebraska Press, 1986.

Royce, Josiah. "Provincialism." In *Race Questions, Provincialism, and Other American Problems,* by Josiah Royce, 55–108. 1908. Reprint, Freeport, NY: Books for Libraries Press, 1967.

Rudnick, Lois. "Re-Naming the Land: Anglo Expatriate Women in the Southwest." In Norwood and Monk, *Desert Is No Lady,* 10–26.

Sandel, Michael J. *Democracy's Discontent: America in Search of a Public Philosophy.* Cambridge, MA: Harvard University Press, 1996.

Sanders, Ronald. *The Downtown Jews: Portraits of an Immigrant Generation.* New York: Harper and Row, 1969.

Schedler, Christopher. "Writing Culture." In Swift and Urgo, *Cather and the American Southwest,* 108–23.

Schiller, Friedrich. *On the Aesthetic Education of Man: In a Series of Letters.* 1794. Edited by Elizabeth M. Wilkinson and L. A. Willoughby. New York: Oxford University Press, 1982.

Schlenz, Mark. "Rhetorics of Region in *Starry Adventure* and *Death Comes for the Archbishop.*" In Jordan, *Regionalism Reconsidered,* 65–85.

Schomburg, Arthur A. "The Negro Digs Up His Past." In Locke, *New Negro,* 231–37.

Schudson, Michael. *The Good Citizen: A History of American Civic Life.* New York: Free Press, 1998.

Schwind, Jean. "Latour's Schismatic Church: The Radical Meaning in the Pictorial Methods of *Death Comes for the Archbishop.*" *Studies in American Fiction* 13.1 (1985): 71–88.

Seligman, Adam. "Civil Society as Idea and Ideal." In Chambers and Kymlicka, *Civil Society and Social Theory,* 13–33.

———. *The Idea of Civil Society.* Princeton, NJ: Princeton University Press, 1992.

Selznick, Philip. *The Moral Commonwealth: Social Theory and the Promise of Community.* Berkeley: University of California Press, 1992.

Sergeant, Elizabeth Shepley. *Willa Cather: A Memoir.* Lincoln: University of Nebraska Press, 1953.

Sherman, Sarah Way. *Sarah Orne Jewett, an American Persephone.* Hanover, NH: University Press of New England, 1989.

Showalter, Elaine. Introduction to *These Modern Women: Autobiographical Essays from the Twenties*, edited by Elaine Showalter, 3–29. Westbury, NY: Feminist Press, 1978.

Silberner, Edmund. "Anti-Semitism and Philo-Semitism in the Socialist International." *Judaism* 2.2 (1935): 118.

Smith, Henry. "The Feel of the Purposeful Earth: Mary Austin's Prophecy." *New Mexico Quarterly* 1.1 (February 1931): 17–33.

———. "Localism in Literature." In Botkin, *Folk-Say* (1930), 298–301.

———. "A Note on the Southwest." *Southwest Review* 14 (1928): 267–78.

Snell, K. D. M. "The Regional Novel: Themes for Interdisciplinary Research." In *The Regional Novel in Britain and Ireland, 1800–1990*, edited by K. D. M. Snell, 1–53. Cambridge: Cambridge University Press, 1998.

Soja, Edward. *Postmodern Geographies: The Reassertion of Space in Critical Social Theory*. London: Verso, 1989.

Sollors, Werner. *Beyond Ethnicity: Consent and Descent in American Literature*. New York: Oxford University Press, 1986.

———. "A Critique of Pure Pluralism." In *Reconstructing American Literary History*, edited by Sacvan Bercovitch, 250–79. Cambridge, MA: Harvard University Press, 1986.

———, ed. *Multilingual America: Transnationalism, Ethnicity, and the Languages of American Literature*. New York: New York University Press, 1998.

Sommer, Doris. *Foundational Fictions: The National Romances of Latin America*. Berkeley: University of California Press, 1991.

———. "The Places of History: Regionalism Revisited in Latin America." In *The Places of History: Regionalism Revisited in Latin America*, edited by Doris Sommer, 1–10. Durham, NC: Duke University Press, 1999.

Sorkin, Michael. "Introduction: Traffic in Democracy." In *Giving Ground: The Politics of Propinquity*, edited by Joan Copjec and Michael Sorkin, 1–15. London: Verso, 1999.

Steffens, Lincoln. *The Autobiography of Lincoln Steffens*. New York: Harcourt, Brace, 1931.

Stout, Janis P. "Whose America Is This?" In *Willa Cather: The Writer and Her World*, by Janis P. Stout, 220–46. Charlottesville: University Press of Virginia, 2000.

———. "Willa Cather and Mary Austin: Intersections and Influences." *Southwestern American Literature* 21.2 (1996): 39–59.

Suggs, Jon Christian. *Whispered Consolations: Law and Narrative in African American Life*. Ann Arbor: University of Michigan Press, 2000.

Sundquist, Eric. "'The Drum with the Man Skin': *Jonah's Gourd Vine*." In *The Hammers of Creation: Folk Culture in Modern African-American Fiction*, by Eric Sundquist, 49–91. Athens: University of Georgia Press, 1992.

———. "Realism and Regionalism." In *Columbia Literary History of the United States*, edited by Emory Elliott, 501–24. New York: Columbia University Press, 1988.

Swift, John N., and Joseph R. Urgo, eds. *Willa Cather and the American Southwest*. Lincoln: University of Nebraska Press, 2002.

Taubenfeld, Aviva. "'Only an "L"': Linguistic Borders and the Immigrant Author in

Abraham Cahan's *Yekl* and *Yankel der Yankee*." In Sollors, *Multilingual America*, 144–65.

Taylor, Charles. "Modes of Civil Society." *Public Culture* 3.1 (Fall 1990): 95–118.

———. "The Politics of Recognition." In Gutmann, *Multiculturalism*, 25–73.

Thurman, Wallace. *Infants of Spring*. New York: Macaulay, 1932. Reprint, Boston: Northeastern Press, 1992.

Tobias, Henry J. *A History of the Jews in New Mexico*. Albuquerque: University of New Mexico Press, 1990.

Tompkins, Jane. *Sensational Designs: The Cultural Work of American Fiction, 1790–1860*. New York: Oxford University Press, 1985.

Trachtenberg, Alan. *The Incorporation of America: Culture and Society in the Gilded Age*. New York: Hill and Wang, 1982.

Tscherikover, Eliahu. "Di Ershte Yidishe Delegaten oif di Kongresen fun Sotsialistishen International." *Historishe Shriften* 3:791–92.

Urgo, Joseph. "Multiculturalism as Nostalgia." In Swift and Urgo, *Cather and the American Southwest*, 136–49.

———. *Willa Cather and the Myth of American Migration*. Urbana: University of Illinois Press, 1995.

Walzer, Michael. "Equality and Civil Society." In Chambers and Kymlicka, *Civil Society and Social Theory*, 34–49.

———. "The Idea of Civil Society: A Path to Social Reconstruction." *Dissent* 38.2 (Spring 1991): 293–302.

Warner, Marina. *Alone of All Her Sex: The Myth and the Cult of the Virgin Mary*. New York: Alfred A. Knopf, 1976.

Wasserman, Loretta. "Cather's Semitism." In *Cather Studies*, edited by Susan J. Rosowski, 2:1–22. Lincoln: University of Nebraska Press, 1993.

Welty, Eudora. "Place in Fiction." In *The Eye of the Story: Selected Essays and Reviews*, by Eudora Welty, 116–33. New York: Random House, 1978.

West, Cornel. *The American Evasion of Philosophy*. Madison: University of Wisconsin Press, 1989.

Wiebe, Robert H. *The Search for Order, 1877–1920*. New York: Hill and Wang, 1967.

Williams, Raymond. "Region and Class in the Novel." In *The Uses of Fiction: Essays on the Modern Novel in Honor of Arnold Kettle*, edited by Douglas Jefferson and Graham Martin, 59–68. Milton Keynes, Eng.: Open University Press, 1982.

Wood, Ann Douglas. "The Literature of Impoverishment: The Women Local Colorists in America, 1865–1914." *Women's Studies* 1.1 (1972): 3–45.

Woodress, James. *Willa Cather: A Literary Life*. Lincoln: University of Nebraska Press, 1987.

Wright, Richard. "Between Laughter and Tears." *New Masses*, October 5, 1937. Reprint in Gates and Appiah, *Zora Neale Hurston*, 16–17.

Young, Iris Marion. "Displacing the Distributive Paradigm." In *Justice and the Politics of Difference*, by Iris Marion Young. Princeton, NJ: Princeton University Press, 1990.

Zagarell, Sandra. "Country's Portrayal of Community and the Exclusion of Difference." In Howard, *New Essays on "The Country of the Pointed Firs,"* 39–60.

———. "Crosscurrents: Registers of Nordicism, Community, and Culture in Jewett's *Country of the Pointed Firs.*" *Yale Journal of Criticism* 10.2 (1997): 355–70

———. "Troubling Regionalism: Rural Life and the Cosmopolitan Eye in Jewett's *Deephaven.*" *American Literary History* 10.4 (Winter 1998): 639–63.

Zellen, Barry. "'Surf's Up!': NWT's Indigenous Communities Await a Tidal Wave of Electronic Information." *Cultural Survival Quarterly* 21.4 (Winter 1998): 50–55.

INDEX

Austin, Mary (*continued*)

Horizon, 95–96, 100; *Everyman's Genius*, 92–93; "Greatness in Women," 94, 95, 192n24; "The Indian Detour," 90, 191n9; The *Land of Journey's Ending*, 94; *The Land of Little Rain*, 92, 97, 191n13; "Regionalism in American Fiction," 100, 120, 193n3, 197n33; "Sex Emancipation through War," 94–95, 192n25; "The Town That Doesn't Want a Chautauqua," 91, 98, 191n10, 193n36; "Women as Audience," 96–97, 192nn30–32

Automobile, 89

Bachelard, Gaston, 196n21
Baker, Houston A., Jr., 203n50
Bakhtin, Mikhail, 179n48
Barber, Benjamin, 10, 176n29
Bender, Thomas, 176n28
Blacks. *See* African Americans
Boas, Franz, 127–29, 130, 199n20, 201n37, 201–2n41
Bogan, Louise, 104
"The Bone of Contention" (Hurston), 123, 134
Bookman, 90, 96–97
Botkin, Benjamin A., 177n36, 190n3, 191n11
Bradford, Roark, 132, 200n30
Braithwaite, William, 125–27, 128, 130, 131
Bramen, Carrie Tirado, 174nn20–21, 181n6
Bridges, Roy, 23
Brodhead, Richard, 16, 173–74n20, 178n39, 180–81n6, 181n9
Brown, Bill, 183n16
Brown, Sterling, 126
Buttitta, Anthony, 130
Bynner, Witter, 86–87

Cahan, Abraham: English-language versus Yiddish writings by, 51–54, 61–62, 83, 84–85; failed romance plot in fiction by, 72–83; and Hebrew Federation of Labor, 188n27; and historicity of Jewish communities, 21, 54–61, 76–77, 189n37; on immigration policy, 64; and instruction of American readers about American Jewry, 56–61; intellectual community of, 70; marriage of, 73; and mistrust of American reading public, 56; and mistrust of women, 56, 70; on realism ver-

sus romance, 54–55; and regionalism (or local color), 51, 53, 59–61, 88, 157–58; and socialism, 52, 62, 63, 71, 83–85; and Yiddish press, 51, 52, 83–85
—works: "The Apostate from Chego-Chegg," 72, 75–83; "Circumstances," 72, 73; "The Daughter of Reb Avrom Leib," 72; *The Imported Bridegroom*, 54–56, 60, 64–72; "A Providential Match," 72; "Rabbi Eliezer's Christmas," 56–59; *The Rise of David Levinsky*, 72, 75, 189n45; "Tzinchadzi of the Catskills," 188n25; *The White Terror and the Red*, 72; *Yekl*, 72, 187n9
Canterbury Tales (Chaucer), 23
Carby, Hazel, 201n39, 203n51
Cather, Willa: anti-Semitism of, 104, 194–95n14; on artwork, 103–7, 110–16, 120–21; compared with Hurston's view of community, 21–22, 159–60; on national or racial culture, 103–5, 110–21; on Native Americans, 103–4; romantic relationship of, 197n27; in Santa Fe home of Mary Austin, 100, 193n1
—works: *Death Comes for the Archbishop*, 100–101, 104, 105, 107–21; "Escapism," 103–4, 194nn9–12; "Light on Adobe Walls," 103, 194n8; The *Professor's House*, 194n14; *Song of the Lark*, 194n10
"Centaur in Brass" (Faulkner), 167–69, 205n10, 205n14
Century, 40, 183nn16–17, 184n28
Chametzky, Jules, 186n2
Chaucer, Geoffrey, 23
Chinese immigrants, 31, 32, 42
"Circumstances" (Cahan), 72, 73
Civil society: advocates of, on the right and on the left, 173n14; Hegel on, 172n11; nineteenth-century concept of, 3–4; and regionalism, x, 3–6; Walzer on, 172n11
Clemenceau, Georges, 190n52
Cleveland, Grover, 64
Cohen, Octavus Roy, 132, 200n30
Commercial Advertiser, 55, 186n3
Communism, 153, 204n56
Community: all-Jewish community in Cahan's "Apostate of Chego Chegg," 76–82, 85; Austin and cultural pluralism, 93–94; Austin on women's talents for, 88, 94–95,

Gilder, Richard Watson, 40, 41, 183n16, 184n28, 185n32
Gillman, Susan, 31, 181n9
Gilman, Charlotte Perkins, 192n28
Glazener, Nancy, 16, 174n20, 178n40, 181n6
Go Down, Moses (Faulkner), 196n26
Goffman, Erving, 2
The Golden Day (Mumford), 91
Goodman, Audrey, 195n21
Goodwyn, Lawrence, 185n41
Grant, Madison, 127
Great Migration: in Hurston's *Jonah's Gourd Vine*, 136–41, 154, 201n39
"Greatness in Women" (Austin), 94, 95, 192n24
Green Pastures, 200n30
Guattari, Félix, 177n34

Hambourg, Jan, 194n14
The Hamlet (Faulkner), 161–67, 205n6, 205n8
Hapgood, Hutchins, 55, 60, 186n3
Harlem Renaissance, 124–27, 129, 130–33, 158–59, 198n9, 200n28
Harris, Susan, 186n2
Hartman, Geoffrey, 179n44, 180n53, 197n34
Harvey (Fred) Enterprises, 86, 89, 97
Hebrew Federation of Labor, 61–62, 188n27
Hegel, G. W. F, 172n11
Hegeman, Susan, 128, 195n15
Hemenway, Robert, 127
Henderson, Alice Corbin, 86–87
Herrnstein Smith, Barbara, 13–14, 195n18
Herskovits, Melville, 129
Hewett, Edgar, 86, 87–89
Hicks, Granville, 194n9
"High John De Conquer" (Hurston), 154
Higham, John, 53, 186n5, 188n34
Historicity: and Cahan's writings, 21, 54–61, 76–77, 83–85, 189n37; Sommer's definition of, 12
Hobsbawm, Eric J., 182n11
Hochstein, David, 104, 194n14
How the Other Half Lives (Riis), 42–43, 44, 47
Howard, June, 174n20, 181n6
Howe, Irving, 62, 186–87n8, 189n39
Howells, William Dean, 83, 157
Hulme, Peter, 23

Hunter, Ian, 180n54
Hurston, Zora Neale: Boas as influence on, 127–29, 130, 201–2n41; and community generally, 22, 125, 152–55; and Eatonville, Florida, 123, 124–25, 134, 138, 160, 198n7, 203n53; and hoodoo, 132–33; justice as issue for, 122–25, 132–34, 152–53, 200n34; and mother's death, 122; and Negro spirituals concert, 132; philosophy and politics of, 153, 204nn55–56; and pursuit of racial wholeness, 124, 132–33; and racial classification systems, 133, 153
—works: "The Bone of Contention," 123, 134; *The Conscience of the Court*, 123; "Crazy for This Democracy," 154; *Dust Tracks*, 133, 152–54; "The Gilded Six-Bits," 122; "High John De Conquer," 154; "John Redding Goes to Sea," 122; *Jonah's Gourd Vine*, 123, 134–42, 147, 154, 201n39, 202n44; *Moses, Man of the Mountain*, 154–55, 201n37, 203n52, 204n58; *Mules and Men*, 132–33, 134, 154, 198n7, 200n30; "Spunk," 123, 134; "Sweat," 123, 138, 198n5; *Their Eyes Were Watching God*, 123, 124, 134, 135, 142–54; "What White Publishers Won't Print," 154

Identity: in Cahan's "Apostate of Chego-Chegg," 75–83; in Cahan's *Imported Bridegroom*, 64–72; in *Death Comes for the Archbishop* (Cather), 104–5, 115–16; socialist debates on Jewish identity, 84–85
Immigration: in Cahan's "Apostate of Chego-Chegg," 75–83; in Cahan's *Imported Bridegroom*, 54–56, 60, 64–72; and melting-pot rhetoric, 79; Polish versus Jewish immigrants, 75–83; U.S. policy on, 63–64
The Imported Bridegroom (Cahan): Asriel Stroon in, 60, 61, 64–67, 71, 72, 73, 81; cosmopolitanism and identity in, 64–72; ending of, 71–72, 75, 82; feminist perspective on, 56, 70–72; Flora in, 54–56, 61, 64–71, 72, 73; frustrated marriage plot in, 69–73; Howell's review of, 83; multinational community of intellectuals in, 70–72, 73, 75, 85; Old World Jewishness in, 64–67; reading in, 54, 55, 68–69; Shaya in, 65–66,